HEART OF THE CIRCLE

PHOTOGRAPHS BY EDWARD S. CURTIS

OF NATIVE AMERICAN WOMEN

Introduction by Pat Durkin
Captions by Alan Bisbort and Sara Day
Edited by Sara Day
Technical Consultant: Joanna C. Scherer

LIBRARY OF CONGRESS

POMEGRANATE ARTBOOKS
SAN FRANCISCO

Published by Pomegranate Artbooks
Box 6099, Rohnert Park, California 94927

Pomegranate Europe Ltd.
Fullbridge House, Fullbridge
Maldon, Essex CM9 7LE, England

ISBN 0-7649-0006-4
Pomegranate Catalog No. A851

Library of Congress Cataloging-in-Publication Data

Curtis, Edward S., 1868–1952.
Heart of the circle: photographs by Edward S. Curtis/of native American women; introduction by Pat Durkin; captions by Alan Bisbort and Sara Day; edited by Sara Day. —1st ed.
p. cm.
On t.p.: Library of Congress.
ISBN 0-7649-0006-4 (pbk.)
1. Indian women—North America—Portraits. 2. Indians of North America—Portraits. 3. Curtis, Edward S., 1868–1952. I. Bisbort, Alan, 1953– . II. Day, Sara. III. Library of Congress. IV. Title.
E89.C87 1997
920.72.'089'97—dc20 96-28464
CIP

Designed by Rod Wallace/Q Design

Printed in Hong Kong
02 01 00 99 98 97 6 5 4 3 2 1

First Edition

CONTENTS

Introduction

PAT DURKIN

All I hear from my grandparents is how it was.
These photographs prove to me how it was.

—Wanda Frenchman, Oglala Lakota-Delaware

Her lips are just parted. Stray rivulets of hair cling to the ridges of her cheeks. Her narrowed eyes glisten like frozen marshland. Hunkered into a blanket, the rugged Cree beauty glares out of the old photograph, her expression coiling in a jumble of anger, fear, defiance.

You turn away, but you have to look again. Mawinéhikis will not let go.

She is the one you will think of when you read about Indian women who pulled loaded sleds farther with each year to follow a decreasing food supply and who watched their tribes lose ground to new diseases brought in by white intruders. She will come to mind when you hear of families that starved when the buffalo were wiped out and of women desperate enough to suffocate newborn children. The next time you run your thumb over the buffalo on one of those rare old nickels, you will wonder again whether Mawinéhikis lived long enough to tell stories to her grandchildren.

Mawinéhikis's troubled face must have moved Edward Sheriff Curtis when he created her portrait in the 1920s. Ordinarily, he was inclined to romantic poses of feathered chiefs, brawny warriors, or their serene, forebearing women. By the time he reached the homeland of the Western Woods Cree, he had photographed nearly eighty tribes west of the Mississippi River. In the name of "science," he and his small team of assistants had traveled thousands of miles, stopping at settlements from Mexico to Alaska, in an effort to make "a comprehensive and permanent record of all the important tribes . . . that still retain to a considerable degree their primitive customs and traditions." He had taken most of the 40,000 images of Native Americans that would become his monument to a race and their changing way of life. It had taken nearly three decades and all of his money, and it was getting harder and harder on his health. He probably saw in Mawinéhikis's face a reflection of the frustration that had settled in his own soul. He was weary and discouraged but duty-bound to finish what he had started as a cocky young photographer at the turn of the century, sure of his abilities and on fire with romantic notions of a "vanishing race."

America at the turn of the century had changed its view of Indians. They had been hated and feared as well as respected and admired during the long period of colonization. The Wounded Knee massacre in 1890 reinforced the notion of Indians as a vanishing race. White society assumed that Indians were nearly extinct and became fascinated by them. They were thought of as exotic, almost magical, even titillating. Portraits of craggy-faced chiefs began showing up in drawing rooms, interior decorating magazines blossomed with Indian baskets and pots, and railroad companies hawked tours to Indian ceremonies.

Curtis, already in sympathy with the Indian cause, was caught up in the swell of pathos. If the Indians themselves could not survive, at least their culture should be recorded for the ages. The notion of a dying race merged with his own grand ambitions. In the tradition of Karl Bodmer and George Catlin, he would make portraits of Native Americans for a penitent nation. He would compile a series of twenty books, each with an accompanying volume of his lustrous photogravure prints, that would record the myths, music, and ethnological background of tribes that still practiced "the old ways." *The North American Indian* would be a monument to a noble people.

Curtis's masterwork faded into obscurity even before he finished it. But with the revival of interest in Native American life during the 1970s, the Curtis photographs again became popular. His mythic images of chiefs and warriors began appearing on posters, calendars, and notecards. One of his best-known photographs is of Chief Red Hawk astride a white pony under a big prairie sky. *Cañon de Chelly*, which depicts a spare column of southwestern horsemen dwarfed beneath a towering mesa, has become one of the symbols of a disappearing natural Western landscape. Curtis's photographs have been included in virtually every anthology of historical photographs of Native Americans. His work is often used to illustrate books and television documentaries about Native Americans. Collectors pay many thousands of dollars for original prints of their favorite images.

This book is the first devoted exclusively to Curtis's images of Native American women. He photographed the women of every tribe he visited in many stages of life and in many of their activities in the circle of camp life. There are hundreds of images of women making pottery, tending infants in cradleboards, hauling wood, harvesting wild berries, carrying water, grinding corn, stretching hides, and butchering game. His portraits of women are intimate and revealing. Some seem almost alive: faces as nubile and innocent as *Qahátika Girl*, as intellectually cool as the *Klamath Woman*, or as exuberant as *Woman and Child—Nunivak*. The editors found it no easy task to limit the selection to the number of images that could be included in this book.

The photographs in this book are arranged within geographical groups, much as Curtis arranged his series. Within these groups, the greatest possible variation of ages and activities was selected. Tribal names are given following Curtis's notation; where a different name is used today, it has been noted.

One place to see more of Curtis's photographs of Native Americans is at the Library of Congress in Washington, D.C. His photographs are cataloged among thousands of historical photographs of Native Americans on file in the Library's Prints and Photographs Division. Curtis deposited approximately 2,800 images in the process of copyrighting them. The copyright dates noted with each photograph match those given in his published volumes or are taken from the actual copyright prints. It should be noted that Curtis sometimes sent prints to the Library of Congress for copyrighting years after he shot them. His work, along with the work of other world-class photographers such as Alfred Stieglitz, Dorothea Lange, and Lisette Model, also is included in the Prints and Photographs Division's individual photographers filing series.

The Library's collection of Curtis prints is one of the largest assemblages of his work available to the public. The Rare Book and Special Collections Division holds one of the original high-quality, limited editions of Curtis's twenty-volume series, *The North American Indian*, with its accompanying portfolio volumes of photogravure prints.

The Library has indexed the Curtis photographs by tribe so that they are easy to search. Scholars use them in research, collectors order prints of the most famous images, and Native Americans search them for images of their ancestors. Because fewer than 250,000 Native Americans were left in the United States when Curtis set out to document their lifestyles, present-day Indian peoples from tribes west of the Mississippi River have a reasonably good chance of finding ancestors among the prints. Researchers may view the material in the Prints and Photographs and the Rare Book reading rooms. "When someone discovers photographs of a grandmother or great-uncle, it's a great moment," says Jennifer Brathovde, the Library's reference specialist in Native American photographs and a member of the Devil's Lake Sioux tribe of North Dakota. "I look forward to a time when more Indians are drawn to the resources we have here."

◊ ◊ ◊ ◊ ◊

Nico Strange Owl-Hunt holds up one of the photographs Curtis took at the Southern Cheyenne Reservation, for her mother to see. The image is of a woman hanging strips of meat to dry in the sun. "This one reminds me of Grandma," Nico says. "Remember how she used to hang the meat in the laundry room?"

The women begin to giggle, remembering their favorite story about Nico's grandmother. "That time she got stopped in the Billings airport with that big slicing knife in her purse . . . ," Nico says, her eyes twinkling.

"It never occurred to her not to take it along," says Nico's mother, Ann Strange Owl-Raben, smiling.

For a few moments, Ann looks quietly at the photograph, and then she begins to talk about growing up on the reservation, one of eleven children. She remembers her mother hunched over her treadle sewing machine or preparing food. "She worked so hard. So did my father."

Ann's father spent much of his time hunting game for the family table. At age ten, Ann became his hunting partner.

"There were so many of us to feed and no boys the right age," Ann says. "I gutted my first deer when I was eleven."

As a young woman in the 1950s working as a dental hygienist at the reservation school, Ann fell in love with the fifth-grade teacher, Dayton Raben, an Anglo. To get a marriage license, they had to claim that Ann was white. Both sets of parents insisted the couple start their lives together away from people they knew. They moved to a California suburb. Ann cut off her long braids. Dayton says most people assumed she was Italian. After a decade, Ann had had enough. The couple took over an Indian arts gallery/trading post near Estes Park in Colorado, within easy driving distance of the reservation. There, among the red-rocked mountains, the family returned to its Cheyenne roots. Today Ann's braids cascade to her waist. Her smile is peaceful.

Ann and Dayton deliberately raised their only child in both worlds: white schools, Cheyenne home life. After college, Nico worked at an art gallery in Vail, one of Colorado's ski towns. She hoped to marry an Indian, but instead fell in love with an Anglo. They married in the Cheyenne tradition: Nico's father led her to the ceremony on a chestnut horse. She wore a white buckskin wedding dress with long fringe representing the tall prairie grass and intricate bands of beads hand-applied by her mother and aunts.

Nico never felt comfortable in Vail. "I got culturally sick because there were no Indians around," she says. "Indians have something in common. We live for tradition and family."

Today Nico and her husband live in the apartment over the trading post. As a full partner in the business with her mother and father, Nico appraises the fine and antique Indian crafts they sell. The generations mesh in Cheyenne style. Nico keeps up with her network of Native friends on-line.

"We do need to live our lives in a good way, and that means blending the two worlds the best we can," Nico says. Following Cheyenne traditions is a big part of that. "I am determined to learn how to slice meat like Grandma did; I wish she were here to teach me."

◇ ◇ ◇ ◇ ◇

Curtis was one of those rare artists who combine exceptional talent with the necessary other qualities to bring off a great body of work. He had a clearly defined quest, relentless drive, charisma, a monumental ego, and, perhaps the most essential element of a successful visionary, an ability to find funding. He thrived on adventure and risk. Although his formal education stopped at the third grade, Curtis saw himself as a person of great destiny. Adventure called him. He undoubtedly found the process of establishing himself as a studio photographer in turn-of-the-century Seattle tedious and uninspiring. Whenever he could, he wandered about town taking photographs of the dislocated Indians who had collected there, or he set out on camping trips to shoot the wild, rugged landscapes of the Cascade Mountains.

Curtis's signature portrait style, a revealing face with creamy highlights as the centerpiece of a solid, often arresting composition, came through even in his first Indian portraits, as well as in his early society work. He knew how to show people at their best. One of Curtis's first Indian subjects was "Princess" Angeline, the aging, impoverished daughter of Chief Siahl (or Sealth). Curtis paid her a dollar a sitting. His portrait of her shows a radiant but passive face lit up like sunlight on a dew-covered spider web. A photograph of the old woman digging clams in the mudflats outside the city was included in his first group of Indian pictures, which won national prizes and established Curtis in the genre.

In 1892, Curtis married Clara Phillips, a local girl, and little by little became the photographer of Seattle's elite. The society work brought in a comfortable income, and his Indian prints sold well. It was a comfortable life, but not nearly adventurous enough for Curtis—that is, until a chance encounter on the slopes of Mount Rainier. Three scientists who were lost and cold asked Curtis for help. Curtis took them to his camp, warmed them up, and settled them in for the night. The men turned out to be some of the most highly respected and influential men of the time: George Bird Grinnell, well-known author of books about Plains Indians and editor of *Forest and Stream* magazine; Gifford Pinchot, chief of the federal agency that later would become the U.S. Forest Service; and C. Hart Merriam, chief of the U.S. Biological Survey. Curtis guided them to safety and later impressed them with his photographs of wilderness landscapes and Indians.

Through these new connections, Curtis's career took off. The following summer, he was invited to be chief photographer on railroad magnate E. H. Harriman's expedition to Alaska. The team included his three new friends and naturalists John Muir and John Burroughs. On that trip, Curtis earned his reputation as a fearless, unflappable photographer. Muir wrote of the day he assumed Curtis had drowned in an icy fjord. The photographer was shooting from a canoe under the overhang of a glacier. A huge chunk of ice fell near the boat, setting up waves so high that the boat rocked wildly, disappearing from sight of those watching from the expedition ship. Curtis calmly steadied the boat and rowed back, never mentioning the incident.

Curtis found his mission in life during the summer of 1900, when he went with Grinnell to the Blackfeet Reservation in Montana for the annual summer Sun Dance gathering of Plains tribes. From a bluff, the two men watched the tribes gather. Curtis had never seen so many Indians in one place. They arrived by the hundreds, hauling children and possessions on horse-drawn travois. Their tipis fanned out over the plains.

For Curtis, it was a revelation. He had seen impoverished Indians around Seattle and knew about their declining populations on the reservations, where diseases introduced by Euro-Americans were taking their toll. He knew the disastrous effects of fenced ranges, railroad tracks, and the eradiction of the buffalo. The bloody finale of the Indian wars at Wounded Knee had occurred only a decade earlier. Curtis believed, as most people did at the time, that Indian life was doomed. The vitality of this celebration on the Plains took him by surprise. He began to suspect that more Indian culture still existed than was evident. His destiny became clear. He appointed himself the definitive chronicler of Indian culture before it was gone forever. His first trip to photograph the Indians of the Southwest came later that same year.

After that, Curtis virtually abandoned his work as a studio photographer to photograph Indians full time. He hired people to help him in the field, along with darkroom technicians and publicists. He made many of the photographs that were published in his masterwork, *The North American Indian*, during the first two decades of the new century. He supported his work through donations, print sales, and the society photography, which by now he had turned over to his assistants.

It must have seemed to Curtis as if his whole life had been in preparation for this project. He had been introduced to the wilderness and the study of religions by his father, an itinerant preacher who took him on canoe treks into the Minnesota woods each fall to visit parishioners. He had learned how to manage teams in the field as a nineteen-year-old, supervising a track crew of 250 for the Soo Line railroad. He had been teaching himself photography since childhood, when he fashioned his first camera from a wooden box and a stereopticon lens that his father had brought back from the Civil War. His brother, Asahel, would also become a well-known photographer.

If Curtis had stayed focused strictly on photography, he probably would have avoided many of the troubles that later hounded him. But he had competition. Other photographers had taken up the quest to document Indian life. John Alvin Anderson had been photographing the Brulé Sioux on the Rosebud Reservation since 1885. Frank A. Rinehart, Adolph F. Muhr, sisters Mamie and Emma Gerhard, and others photographed Indians at expositions and world fairs. By the late 1890s, George Wharton James, who photographed and wrote about the Indians of the Southwest, was complaining that policemen were required to keep order among all the photographers trying to take pictures of the Hopi Snake Dance.

Curtis moved himself ahead of the pack by promising more. His documentation of Native American life would go far beyond any to date. He would visit eighty tribes—all those, he said, that still retained some of their original culture—and he would not limit himself to photography. His assistants would make wax recordings of tribal music and create a comprehensive written record of each tribe's customs, spiritual beliefs, and survival techniques, all to be compiled in a series of books. The twenty volumes and their supplements of photogravure prints, he promised, would be the most comprehensive ethnological record of Native American culture ever made.

That claim cost him credibility later, but in the beginning, Curtis's grand promises attracted the money he needed to get the project launched. President Theodore Roosevelt, who became a fan, helped Curtis secure a $75,000 loan from millionaire J. P. Morgan. The funding allowed the first books of *The North American Indian* to go to press. Roosevelt's enthusiastic introduction to the series also lent authority to the work.

Suddenly, Curtis was a celebrity. Invitations began to pour in. He lectured at the National Geographic Society in Washington, D.C., and the Century Club in New York City. His lantern-slide shows became the centerpiece of fund-raising efforts that were by now occupying much of his time. He wrote for *Scribner's* magazine and photographed President Roosevelt and his family. He exhibited at the Cosmos Club in Washington and the Waldorf-Astoria in New York. Influence attracted more influence. Before long, he had backers as far away as Europe.

Curtis was charming on the lecture circuit, but he was a bear in the field. He often insisted that the team start work at four in the morning and not quit until after midnight. He allowed mail to arrive only once a week. During the daylight hours, Curtis took pictures and with his assistants conducted ethnological interviews. He processed the film in his tent at night. The next morning, using sunlight, he made work prints on which he scrawled detailed instructions. "Make this look like a chicken," he wrote on one print next to a fuzzy object hanging from a horse. The negatives were sent back to the Seattle studio, where trusted assistants retouched them and did the final printing. Some of the images were printed as "orotones." For these, the print was made on the underside of a glass plate. The back of the image was then coated with a layer of gold to backlight the image with a sunsetlike luster.

The extraordinary level of detail that characterizes Curtis's work is due to very large negatives. The camera he took along on the Harriman Expedition took pictures on huge 14-by-11-inch glass plates. The one he used for most of the 40,000 images he took during his thirty years in the field was a Reversible-Back Premo that used 6½- by- 8½-inch negatives, which are very large even by today's standards. This camera had a number of features that added up to speedier setups. It had a diaphragm shutter, rack-and-pinion focusing, and a double-swing back, which allowed the frame to be switched from horizontal to vertical without removing the camera from the tripod. But its best feature was its light weight. Curtis could use it without a tripod, allowing him to take the more candid shots that characterized his later work.

The equipment Curtis hauled into the field weighed more than a ton. In addition to his camera equipment, he carried an Edison recorder and a trunk filled with reference books about the tribes he was visiting. Overland, the load required a wagon and four horses. But sometimes the only way to get into a place was by water. Boats had to be bought or occasionally built before the team could move on. There was the constant problem of equipment breaking or getting wet. Boats capsized; pack mules fell off the sides of mountains; cameras got jostled into the ocean. Days and sometimes weeks were lost patching up broken cameras or waiting for replacements. Curtis returned from one trip with a camera that was held together with string.

Nothing would stand in the way of getting the unique photograph. To get a reenactment of the massacre at Wounded Knee, Curtis put on a feast for 300 Indians. He danced with snakes, tangled with a giant octopus, and nearly got frozen in for the winter in Alaska when he added extra days to the shooting schedule. He and his assistants thought they were doomed one night on a tiny island off the coast of British Columbia: they had been dropped off earlier to photograph sea lions, unaware that the island became submerged at high tide. They survived, but just barely, by lashing themselves to the rocks so that the waves would not carry them away. On a whaling trip during one of his last expeditions, Curtis insisted that the small boat from which he was shooting be brought dangerously close to a wounded whale. As Curtis stood over the creature snapping pictures, it turned and smashed him with its tail. The camera fell into the ocean, and Curtis's hip was broken. His chief complaint was the loss of the camera.

One of Curtis's detractors was Franz Boas, the former curator of the American Museum of Natural History in New York and Columbia University's first professor of anthropology. Boas complained to President Roosevelt that someone with only a grammar school education could not be trusted with the level of ethnological research Curtis had set out to do. To appease the influential scientist, Roosevelt appointed a board of three top scientists to review Curtis's work. They approved, but Boas was never convinced.

Clara, Curtis's wife, disapproved for other reasons. Curtis came home only once or twice a year. When he was there, he spent nearly all of his hours working. The money dried up with World War I and the nation's new economic troubles. With other issues to concern them, the wealthy people who would have bought his series lost interest in Native Americans. But Curtis's project was far from finished. He continued to work on the series, even though by that time he knew he would never receive any money for completing it. He owed the Morgan family and others full sets of books, so he pressed on, while Clara contended with their creditors. She filed for divorce in 1920.

Seven years later, when she took him back to court for failure to pay alimony, the judge asked Curtis why he continued to work on a project that was costing him money. "Your Honor," Curtis said, breaking into tears, "it was my job. The only thing I could do that was worth doing. . . . I was duty-bound to finish it."

The last book in the series was finished that same year. Many think it is the best of the twenty. Curtis then sank into a depression so deep that he was unable to work or communicate with friends for two years. He probably never completely recovered. Later he dabbled in filmmaking, gold mining, and writing for magazines, but his efforts never amounted to much. By this time, Curtis's health had deteriorated, and his hip injury pained him constantly. He died of a heart attack on his daughter's farm in Whittier, California, at the age of eighty-four. A brief biography that accompanied his obituary in the *New York Times* said simply that he had been a photographer and an authority on the North American Indian.

Curtis was wrong about one thing: Indian people were not dying out. Far from it: today there are eight times as many people who claim to be Native Americans in the United States as when Curtis began his project in 1900. The 1990 census reported a population of nearly two million Indians, Eskimos, and Aleuts—a 38 percent increase in those identifying themselves as Native Americans in one decade alone. The Bureau of the Census projects growth to 4.6 million by 2050. Musing about this, George Horse Capture of the Gros Ventre tribe has been quoted as saying, "We are here now, we have been here for thousands of years, and we will always be here. We have fooled them all."

So much for Curtis's premise that the North American Indian was doomed to extinction. The peoples persist, and so do contemporary deconstructionists who criticize Curtis for wrapping his work in invalid assumptions.

But Curtis could hardly have guessed the tenacity of Native American peoples. Like everyone else of the day, he had heard the news about one tribe after another surrendering to the U.S. Army. He had read the words of once-proud chiefs who were weary of fighting and heartsick over the deaths of so many people in their tribes. The bloody conclusion to the Indian wars at Wounded Knee in

1890 convinced even the skeptics that Manifest Destiny was running its immutable, crushing course. It was. But Indian peoples would survive.

◇ ◇ ◇ ◇ ◇

"Thank God my mother kept us culturally alive," says Val Crews, a White Mountain Apache who has lived all her life in Phoenix, Arizona. "There were only two Native Americans in my elementary school."

Photographs Curtis took of women harvesting mescal remind Val of her childhood days, when her mother brought mescal home to their apartment in the city, wrapped in the folds of her apron.

As a child, Val took her Apache heritage for granted. She hated going to funerals on the reservation, so many miles away. Now, as a single mother, she has come to value the unconditional loyalty of a whole tribe. Dozens of families showed up when her beloved grandfather died.

"My mother's an urban woman," says Val. "But first and foremost, she's an Apache."

When Val is in need of inspiration, she still turns to her mother. "The first thing out of her mouth is something about our culture," she says.

Several years ago, when Val was having trouble juggling the responsibilities of her infant son and a full-time job, her mother insisted that they take a walk to a spring used by Apaches in the nineteenth century. She told Val a story handed down through generations about a band that was nearly waylaid there by U.S. Army troops. The Apaches could not get away in time, so they hid in the rocks. They survived only because the women smothered their noisy infants. The band lost eight children that day.

"Our people have always had it hard," Val's mother told her. "It's up to you to find balance in your life."

Today Val is helping her long-lost brother, who was put up for adoption as an infant and returned looking for his Apache relatives as an adult, find his sense of balance. He, like so many others in contemporary society, was raised without grounding in his own culture.

"He's learning," says Val. "He's on the road to peace."

◇ ◇ ◇ ◇ ◇

Curtis is best known for his photographs of Native American men, but he took thousands of photographs of women in the midst of their daily responsibilities around the camps. Together the photographs show a truth about tribal life that modern Native women recognize: native women are at the heart of their communities. Curtis filmed them gathering berries and seeds, grinding meal, setting up tipis, butchering game, looking after children, and taking part in the unrelenting round of other chores that were vital to the survival of their tribes. In many tribes, women did virtually all the work except slaughtering game and going to war. These usually were men's duties, but occasionally women lent themselves even to those tasks, especially if they were widowed or deserted or grew up in families without boys to help their fathers.

Life for Native women meant endless workdays. They worked from the time they were young girls until they were too old to move. There were no vacations as we know them, although in many tribes women used the days of enforced isolation during monthly menstruation to rest and reflect. As with the men, the most diligent workers earned the highest respect.

Life as a traditional Native woman demanded vigor, determination, and a willingness to sacrifice one's own comforts for the larger cause—qualities a man such as Curtis could appreciate. His empathy comes through in his photograph of a Crow woman trudging back to her tipi through ankle-deep snow with a load of wood on her back. Even from this rear view, we see that the load was heavy but well within her capacities. She was a servant of the fire; her days were counted in loads like these.

Native women spent much of their time gathering up the useful items nature had to offer: water, seeds, berries, clay, reeds. Curtis's photographs of women in the process of harvesting reveal their essential connection to the cycle of natural life. A Kwakiutl woman digs for abalone among the rocks; a Cree woman lugs home a bundle of moss to line baby-bags, a Pomo woman beats seeds into a burden basket; Maricopa women return home with baskets of cactus fruit balanced on their heads; Mandan women carefully strip a branch of its buffalo berries.

These women drew life from the earth and with it created their own. Through this intimate relationship with nature, they came to a deep appreciation of their environment. The tradition of gratitude was handed down through the generations. Native Americans are amused by those Anglos who discovered the environment only in the last quarter century.

⋄ ⋄ ⋄ ⋄ ⋄

The ancient corn kernels should have gone to her mother. That is the Pueblo tradition: grandmother to granddaughter. But Carolyna Smiley-Marquez's mother was an assimilationist, so to ensure the continuity of the tradition, the old woman passed the sacred seeds to her great-granddaughter Carolyna instead.

"I cherish the corn and the pollen and the plants that grow from that corn," she says. "I still plant it today."

The hills that roll through the backgrounds of Curtis's photographs at San Juan Pueblo take Carolyna back to childhood summers spent there, visiting her great-grandmother. They are the same hills the two of them walked on so many afternoons looking for medicinal plants.

"Grandmother didn't call herself a medicine woman, which is the romantic term people use today," Carolyna says. "She was very methodical in the way she gathered medicine and treated the plants as living companions. The earth, trees, water, and sky were part of her, and she was part of them. She had an intimacy with those things, including the plants she grew herself."

The photographs of women gathering piñon nuts bring back memories of happy treks out to harvest the trees, which bear only every few years. "We would travel many miles for the piñon, once the word spread where they were that year," Carolyna remembers. "I can still imagine her shaking the tree and hear the piñon nuts falling onto the tarp she spread under the trees."

Carolyna's job at San Juan was to water the corn, twice a day, one stalk at a time. She carried the water a quarter mile in coffee cans fitted with wire handles. "How can you not know each plant if you water it twice each day?"

Today Carolyna's life as an organizational consultant near Denver leaves little time for the traditions she learned from her great-grandmother, but she still feels the link to her Pueblo heritage.

"One thing that is connected to being Native American is obligation. We take it seriously," she says. "In some ways we are like white women, but in most ways, we are not."

⋄ ⋄ ⋄ ⋄ ⋄

In most tribes, women were revered for wisdom and a sense of balance. They sometimes were the ones who made the decision when to go to war. In agricultural tribes, they usually had the crucial responsibility for choosing the seeds to be saved for the next year's crops. The women of certain tribes nominated their chiefs and could have them removed.

Curtis's photographs suggest the complementary work roles of traditional Native women and men. Almost universally in hunting and fishing tribes, men brought in the game and the women prepared it. Curtis's photographs show the continuity of these traditional tasks: Teton Sioux women, skilled at cutting meat to exactly the right thickness for drying, hang strips of it to dry in the sun; a Crow woman stretches a buffalo hide on the ground in front of her tipi; a Chinookan woman, with freshly caught salmon arranged around her on the ground, guts the fish and prepares them for smoking; a Kotzebue Eskimo woman slices into the fat, bloody carcass of a beluga whale, whose calorie-rich meat will help her family ward off winter's cold.

One could easily mistake this work as thankless drudgery. Indeed, whites considered the "squaw" little more than a burden-bearer and a foil for her husband, who held what they saw as the glamour job: hunter, warrior, or chief. The concept completely overlooks the Native perspective, a tradition of viewing the family as the heart of society and domestic responsibilities as a sacred trust. "The family is not found to be an insignificant domestic side of life in Native North America," write Laura F. Klein and Lillian A. Ackerman in *Women and Power in Native North America* (University of Oklahoma Press, 1995). "By and large, the family is not solely women's domain, nor is it an inferior subordinate institution."

The Native tradition is to view men and women as complementary providers for the group, equal halves of a whole. When a tribe had a puberty ceremony for young men, it usually had a corresponding ritual for women. Among the Plateau tribes, when a boy caught his first fish or a girl gathered her first berries, the child's grandmother organized a feast at which the child's contribution was consumed by the elders with great ceremony. In Eskimo (Inuit) societies, men's reputations are still based on their skill at hunting, women's on their skin work and ability to organize a smooth-running home.

Modern Native women have been criticized for their reluctance to join the feminist movement. Native women counter that they always have been liberated; their traditions allow them to choose their own way. Indeed, there are plenty of examples of Native women holding positions of power. Among the Southern Paiute and many other tribes, women became shamans and curers with the same status as their male counterparts. Curtis's photograph of the self-assured *Hupa Female Shaman* leaves no doubt about this woman's sense of her own importance. Women occasionally also served as warriors and even chiefs. In 1985, Wilma Mankiller became the first female chief of the Cherokee, one of the largest tribes in the United States.

Women often had considerable power because of what they owned by right. Southern Paiute women owned all of the products of their labor and controlled the distribution of the game brought in by the men. Women in Plateau tribes, who owned clothing, tools, horses, the mat lodge, and all of their family's stored food, were thought of as haughty and insubordinate by early European fur traders, settlers, and missionaries, who noted with disapproval that possessions allowed the women sufficient economic independence to drive off a husband who displeased them.

In a few tribes, women had a cultural edge over men. The Iroquois, Navajo, and some other tribes were organized matrilineally. Generally in these societies, the husband moved in with the wife's family and the lineage of the children was traced through the mother's side. Blackfeet women were considered innately more powerful than men because of their ability to create children as well as the material goods of their society. A Blackfeet man had to beg the gods to give him power equal to the creative power a woman had as her birthright.

The women of most tribes expressed their creativity through crafts, especially baskets, pottery, and beadwork. An artist himself, Curtis was impressed with the women's artwork and made many photographs of them creating it. In one photograph, a Navajo woman weaves an intricately striped rug on an outdoor loom the size of a cathedral entrance. In another, a group of Maricopa women sit on the ground in a working circle with their huge, bowl-shaped baskets on their laps. Curtis's photograph of a Santa Clara potter applying a surface design to a large, flare-mouthed jug shows a face so tenderly intent that her expression approaches ecstasy.

It was within crafts especially that a Native woman integrated the practical, cultural, and spiritual aspects of her being. Pottery jars, water baskets, beaded moccasins, and cradleboards—all of these items had obvious practical uses. But they also were vehicles to express cultural identity and testimony to deep religious faith. Unlike white culture, Native societies tend not to isolate artists into a separate class. Art objects were not created for their own sake, but to symbolize the seamlessness of life. A good artisan had the highest respect of everyone in the tribe. Ironically, these same crafts gave Native women access to the capitalistic world that threatened the tribal way of life. For the last hundred years, whites have bought the creative work of Native women for their own collections. Curtis bought their pots, baskets, and other artwork to sell in his Seattle studio.

◇ ◇ ◇ ◇ ◇

"I always wanted to be a photographer," says Lark Real Bird Paz. Looking at Curtis's photographs of her Crow ancestors, she remembers dreaming about her future during her girlhood on the reservation in Montana. "Get an education and you will be able to survive," her grandmother told her.

Lark went to college, became a graphic designer, and settled in Phoenix, Arizona. She struggles to hold on to her Native ways, against the pressures of urban life. The man she married is part Apache; she still speaks Crow fluently.

The high point of Lark's year is the annual Crow Fair, held each summer on the reservation. "This is something I have to go home for. I don't care about holidays and all that, but the Crow Fair, that's my holiday."

Lark studies a portrait Curtis made of one of her ancestors. "She braids her hair just like my grandmother—brings the braid in front of the ear. And she's wearing abalone-shell earrings like my great-grandmother did."

A photograph of a woman in a dress decorated with rows of elk teeth brings to mind her sister, who made this same style dress to wear for the parade at the Crow Fair and the New Year's dances. Lark can tell that the hundreds of teeth adorning the dress in the photograph are real: "The front teeth, only two from each elk. Today we use artificial teeth because you can't kill that many elk." Lark's sister has promised to make Lark an elk-tooth dress.

"I'm glad Edward Curtis took these photographs," Lark says. "They make me think of home. I can look at them for hours and be there."

Lately, Lark has been considering a move back to the reservation, perhaps supporting her family with an on-line graphics business.

"At one time, I felt the need to see what the rest of the world was all about," she says. "All of a sudden, I have realized how important my culture, my family, and my land are. My child is going to speak Crow."

◊ ◊ ◊ ◊ ◊

The question that has hung over Curtis's work from the beginning is accuracy. What does *The North American Indian* tell that is true about Native American life during the first quarter of the twentieth century?

Curtis gave his own immodest assessment of his masterwork in the first paragraph of the introduction. *The North American Indian*, he wrote, is "a comprehensive and permanent record of the important tribes of the United States and Alaska that still retain to a considerable degree their primitive customs and traditions."

Curtis's monumental self-assurance usually served him well. It energized his work and attracted funders and others who could help him. It drove him to ever larger endeavors, eventually to *The North American Indian*, called one of the largest anthropological projects ever undertaken by one man and a small group of assistants. But Curtis's unreserved confidence also stifled realistic self-assessment. His claim of comprehensiveness for an investigation that would take in so many tribes over such a large territory was extravagant. As mentioned, the hyperbole riled Franz Boas. From the time the first book of *The North American Indian* series was published, Boas raised questions about Curtis's competence to produce scientifically valid research.

To be sure, Curtis had undertaken an ambitious data-recording project on top of his commitment to photographically document eighty tribes. He and his assistants interviewed hundreds, perhaps thousands, of Native Americans, recording information about ceremonies, dress, dwellings, art forms, political and social organization, creation myths, religious beliefs, and many other subjects. During the frantically busy weeks with each tribe, the team also made wax recordings of their music, some of which was transcribed into scores, and transliterated lists of commonly used words, such as *rain, mountain, deer, wind,* and *moon*. This information appeared in an organized, succinct format in the appendix of each book.

The scope of the work was unrealistic, even for Curtis. From the start, Boas was convinced Curtis was out of his depth. As it turned out, Curtis underestimated how long it would take to complete *The North American Indian* by twenty-five years and how much it would cost by hundreds of thousands of dollars.

Curtis was shaken by the three-person text review committee appointed to mollify Boas. But he agreed to cooperate with the panel, which consisted of Henry Fairfield Osborn, curator of vertebrate paleontology at the American Museum of Natural History in New York; William Henry Holmes, chief of the Bureau of American Ethnology at the Smithsonian Institution; and Charles Doolittle Walcott, secretary of the Smithsonian. After reviewing suitcases full of the team's field notes, the three scientists concluded that Curtis and his two assistants were in fact meeting scientific standards.

Roosevelt was satisfied. In his glowing foreword to *The North American Indian*, he called Curtis a "trained observer" whose work "has far more than mere accuracy, because it is truthful." However, even the added assurance of final text editing by Frederick Webb Hodge, an ethnologist with the Smithsonian Institution's Bureau of American Ethnology and editor of the Smithsonian's first "handbook" (*Handbook of American Indians North of Mexico*, 1907 and 1910), was not enough for Boas. He and other scientists continued to insist that Curtis's work fell far short of scientific documentation.

From a scientific perspective, there was much about *The North American Indian* to criticize. The sections of the books devoted to Curtis's own observations did little to add to his credibility. He described myths and ceremonies but often neglected to mention the sources of his information. The reader cannot tell whether his accounts of Sun Dances and other rituals were firsthand or retold. He jumped from subject to subject without a unifying format. The discussion of one tribe might emphasize how a lodge was built, another, a creation myth. His style could be sentimental—he wrote of some Indians as "wandering children of Nature." Or he suddenly could turn didactic or cuttingly judgmental. The Cree of Alberta, he wrote, were "decidedly inferior both in physique and in observance of the laws of hygiene." All too often, Curtis gave in to grand generalizations. He wrote of the Walapai that "a more wretched, poverty-stricken tribe of Indians cannot be found within the borders of the United States." Indians in general, he said, "seem to have absorbed all the evil, and to have embodied little of the good, that civilized life teaches."

Still, it is through these more personal accounts that we learn Curtis's view of Native women. Curtis was impressed with their dedication and attitude toward their work. "It is true they did the menial work of the camp, but, strange as it may seem, the task was usually a pleasure rather than a hardship," he wrote of the Teton Sioux women. He observed that these women were at least as strong as their men and that their dispositions were "sunny and full of cheer." He found them devoted wives. "To her husband, she is noticeably affectionate, waiting upon him constantly, seeing that every article of apparel is brought to him as needed, often literally dressing him as she would a child."

He noted that Navajo women achieved satisfaction from their skill as blanket weavers. "It is her recreation, her means of expressing imagination and her skill in execution." He surmised that the women derived a sense of power from ownership. "The independent spirit of the women, instilled by this incontestable property right, manifests itself throughout the tribe, and by reason of it the Navaho [sic] husband is not apt to seek an opportunity to criticize his wife."

Curtis often referred to a coequal relationship between men and women. "As with many tribes, the work of preparing the soil was a task of the women, the men meanwhile performing the sometimes dangerous duty of keeping sharp lookout for Sioux and other Indians of hostile intent," he wrote of Mandan women, who grew corn.

◇ ◇ ◇ ◇ ◇

In 1990, when photojournalist Nancy Ackerman was covering Mohawk resistance to the expansion of a golf course on their sacred burial grounds near Montreal, she noticed that Indian women were calling the shots: "Women were the power, energy, and brains behind the movement."

What Nancy saw kindled an interest in her own ancestry. She is one-quarter Mohawk but was raised as white in suburban Connecticut. Until then, she had not thought much about her Native roots. While on maternity leave from the Montreal Gazette *she began photographing Native women activists of Canada. As she moved from tribe to tribe, her suspicions were confirmed, especially among Inuit communities, where women say they have been persecuted for making a public issue of wife abuse.*

"In Native communities, women are the healers, midwives, teachers, artists. It's the women who start the community centers, alcohol rehabilitation services, and clinics for abused wives," she says. "The women are the real leaders. I don't think it's a new concept."

Nancy's project has much in common with Curtis's. The work has proceeded only as fast as the money has become available. The responsibilities of single-motherhood have interfered. It took five years longer than she expected to assemble enough photographs for her first show, focused on twenty-seven Native Canadian women. Nancy plans to expand the collection to include Native women activists of the United States when funding is available.

Nancy's view of what constitutes documentation is as complex as Curtis's. She says, "I try to be a fly on the wall and let the women show who they are." But she also insists on a creative role in the process. "The duty of the photographer is to draw the personality out to affect the person looking at the photograph."

◇ ◇ ◇ ◇ ◇

Curtis's lively accounts of his field experiences fill volumes of *The North American Indian*. The text sometimes reads like a diary. It makes for interesting reading, but the lack of organization detracts from the more scholarly presentation of data in the appendices. "He was no ethnographer," says David F. Halaas, chief historian of the Colorado State Historical Society.

For nearly a half century, it hardly mattered. By the time Curtis published the last book in his series, it was 1930. The country had plunged into the Depression and had lost its fascination with Indians. Curtis and his work drifted into obscurity. *The North American Indian* was no longer interesting enough to bother criticizing.

Thirty years later, the 1960s brought a backlash against the industrial age. Americans woke up to a poisoned land and the ugly truth of racism. Some found solace in mysticism. Others founded the environmental movement. The American Indian, whose traditional culture had always centered on these ideas, was transformed from know-nothing to prophet. Everything Native American suddenly had renewed value: pottery, jewelry, sculpture, blankets, beadwork, featherwork. People who had tried to hide their Native ancestry began to stand proud. Beginning with the census of 1960, the number of people claiming Native ancestry soared.

Curtis's photographs were rediscovered. By the 1970s, his chiefs, warriors, and horsemen riding into the mist started showing up on posters and T-shirts. The value of the original prints skyrocketed. Curtis, who had been dead for a quarter century, finally was achieving the fame he had pursued all his life. He became arguably the best-known photographer of Indians in America.

The critics returned as well. This time they were not interested in Curtis's research. The American Indian had become one of the most studied fields in American anthropology. Curtis's field techniques had been outdated by more exacting standards; his findings trumped by several generations of ethnologists and folklorists. University libraries had developed whole sections devoted to books and papers on the subject. The text of *The North American Indian* had become irrelevant. The photographs themselves became the new target.

The issue was whether photographs can "lie." In Curtis's day, it was commonly assumed that photographs were objective recorders of the way things are. Photography was another part of the exciting and unchallenged new world of technology. The camera's aperture opened, the film recorded what was in front of the lens, and the "truth" appeared on the print. But by the 1970s, people had lost their blind faith in technology. It was fully understood that cameras, like other machines, are operated by people with flaws and agendas.

Ethnographers, photo historians, and Native American intellectuals began to question the literal content of Curtis's photographs. They discovered manipulations that always had been there to see but had been ignored. Curtis, it turned out, had been much more than a fly on the wall during those years in the field. He staged scenes from the past, costumed people who no longer wore traditional clothes, and edited negatives to remove objects of the modern world in an attempt to show traditional Native life where it no longer existed.

Curtis had made no effort to hide these manipulations. His records show that he routinely paid Natives to pose for him. His writings discuss how he arranged for groups of horsemen in war dress to reenact preparations for battle, although the tribes had not gone to war for decades. He gave his darkroom assistants detailed instructions on how to retouch negatives—where to add highlights, which objects to clarify, and which ones to remove.

Indeed, without the special effects used in studio photography, Curtis could not have produced his signature portrait: a regal face emerging from velvety darkness. His writings describe how he set up his tent as a studio, using an adjustable opening to let in a small patch of daylight that he used as the principal illumination—what today's photographers would call a "key light." Curtis made artful use of this arrangement in *Painting a Hat—Nakoaktok, Old Woman in Mourning—Yuki*, and many other portraits that appear to emerge from the darkness beyond a circle of firelight. Other portraits made in this style tend to downplay reality to make some other point. In *Mohave Potter*, the viewer looks down on a wizened woman sitting in near darkness as she applies glaze to a ceramic pot. A stream of light focuses attention on the contrast between the smooth new pot and the wrinkled old hands.

Still, Curtis wrote the following words about his photographs in his introduction to *The North American Indian*: "Being directly from Nature, the accompanying pictures show what actually exists or has recently existed (for many of the subjects have passed forever), not what the artist in his studio may presume the Indian or his surroundings to be." Later in the introduction, Curtis insisted that the artistic aspects of his work did not compromise reality: "The fact that the Indian and his surroundings lend themselves to artistic treatment has not been lost sight of, for in his country one may treat limitless subjects of an aesthetic character without in any way doing injustice to scientific accuracy or neglecting the homelier phases of aboriginal life."

Christopher M. Lyman's analysis of the Curtis photographs discusses cropping, staging, costuming, soft focusing, retouching, and other methods the photographer used to control his images. In his book, *The Vanishing Race and Other Illusions: Photographs of Indians by Edward S. Curtis* (Smithsonian Institution, 1982), Lyman wrote of possible attempts at deception, such as a distinctive traveling cradleboard that appears in photographs of women of two different tribes. "Either Curtis misidentified the tribes in question, or the cradleboard was one of his props," he wrote. But even Lyman could not unearth a general intention to deceive. He concludes that Curtis failed to document reality but did document an attitude about "Indian-ness" that was important in his day.

We can only speculate why Curtis doggedly insisted that his photographs were scientific documents when they had such obvious aesthetic intentions. It would appear that Curtis did not consider his approach deceptive. Indeed, he was very open in his records and speeches about how he worked. We do know that he was driven by a notion that had prevailed for decades, that Native Americans were doomed to assimilation or extermination. One suspects Curtis had trouble differentiating among masters. His funders called for "scientific truth," the public expected the "noble savage," and his own sensibilities demanded art and a legacy that would perpetuate himself and an exploited people. In his passion, perhaps Curtis failed to see that no single body of work could satisfy them all.

◇ ◇ ◇ ◇ ◇

"I get angry when non-native people say that our women were just burden carriers—meaning 'beasts of burden,'" says Janelle Sixkiller, a Tohono O'odham (Papago)–Pima–Cherokee who works for Native Peoples *magazine. "Our women were tough. They were the ones who kept their families together when things were falling apart. It's still true today."*

Janelle gets frustrated with non-natives who refuse to see Native Americans in a modern context: "Would you believe, the magazine still gets calls from East Coast agencies asking if we still live in tipis?" Or even as human beings: "They will come right up to you (at powwows) and reach out to touch your outfit, the breastplate, or the hair." Or take pictures without asking: "It upsets me, because it demonstrates that some people do not have respect for others."

Indian people who were not raised in their traditions are lost, especially in the cities, or even on their own homelands, says Janelle. "We have had to build our own urban networks, most beginning in city storefronts."

Janelle sees Curtis photographs as a visual "last link with the old ways," one of the things that inspires her to revive the traditions and keep them alive. For her, they are visual proof of her own desert heritage.

"I look at these women who could be my grandmother, my aunts—actually, they are my relatives," she says. "I wonder at the strength that allowed them to survive, to keep it together."

Janelle pauses. Tears are close, but she holds them back. "I look into their eyes and say, 'Oh, yes. I'm here because of you.'"

◇ ◇ ◇ ◇ ◇

In the test of time, Curtis the artist won out. His exhausting attempts at ethnography have all but been forgotten. It is his masterful use of light, texture, and shape to produce an evocative composition and the sheer volume of his work that have made him the best-known photographer of the American Indian. Today his name is virtually synonymous with the genre. Curtis images have such power and are seen so frequently that, for better or worse, they have come to define "Indian-ness." People may not know Curtis's name, but they know his portrait of the pensive but resolute Chief Joseph, who in 1877 helped lead the Nez Perce on a spectacular flight from Idaho to Montana to escape subjugation. They have internalized *The Three Chiefs—Piegan* meeting on horseback out on the wild, unplowed prairie as a symbol of what America once was.

Curtis was one of many photographers working among Native Americans at the time, but he was considered among the best. Other photographers tried to imitate him. Curtis was infuriated to discover that Joseph Kossuth Dixon was openly copying his techniques for the rival Wanamaker Expeditions project. Still, none of Curtis's contemporaries came close to him for impact, comprehensiveness—or his knack for publicity. That is why Curtis's work has been chosen so frequently by publishers and filmmakers to illustrate their works on North American Natives. The National Geographic Society used Curtis images as its source of historic photographs for *The World of the American Indian* (National Geographic Society, 1974). CBS used dozens of his images to illustrate its 1995 television series *500 Nations*.

"People are very moved by the Curtis photographs," says Lois Flury, owner of Flury & Co., a gallery in Seattle, Washington, that has specialized in Curtis photographs since 1981. "Because of increasing demand and diminishing supply, their values have been climbing for years."

In 1996, original photogravures were selling for $200 to $25,000, depending on the size and popularity of the image. *Chief Joseph—Nez Percé* and *Mosa—Mohave*, an elegant portrait of a mysteriously beautiful Mohave maid emerging from the darkness, tied for the top price. The gold-backed orotones on glass were selling for even more—as much as $45,000.

There is an active market for the prints. Sotheby's New York and Christie's New York are among the auction houses that handle them. Collectors tend to be Anglos because "except for tribal organizations, Native Americans don't usually have the money," Flury says. Buyers favor images of men and young, beautiful women. "It's just a fact, more people tend toward the beautiful young girl than the great lined face." In 1996, the book price for *Qahátika Girl* was $12,000. *Lummi Type*, an image of a handsome woman in the prime of life, was selling for $9,000.

Native Americans see Curtis's work less as art and more in terms of what the images project about themselves as a people or tribe. Interpretations vary widely. Some see Curtis's photographs as flattering; others see them as patronizing, even racist. Reactions range from regret to outrage that so much of Native American history before the 1930s was documented by white photographers. Even

Laura Gilpin, a later photographer of Navajos whose work is considered closer to true documentation, is accused of editing out the hard realities of assimilation.

Native American intellectuals tend to be the most critical of Curtis's perspective. Historian Vine Deloria Jr. wrote in his introduction to Lyman's book that Curtis fabricated a romanticized, sanitized Native world that never was: "Since the photographs did not in the slightest degree speak to the reality of the American Indian, either past or present, they became the perfect format for expression of the wistful reservoir of emotions that lay behind the general perception of Indians." Angry essayists, often addressing Curtis directly or indirectly, write of the "trickster photography" and "cultural cannibalism" of early white photographers. "Colonization by camera," inveighed Hopi photographer Victor Masayesva. A common complaint is about pressure to be an Indian stereotype—and the disappointment when one is not.

The nineteenth-century concept of "Indian-ness" was perpetuated first by other Euro-American photographers and later by the film and television industries. As a prominent symbol of the Anglo spin on Native America, Curtis has served as a lightning rod for the anger. But as that symbol, Curtis also has served as a catalyst for a generation of Native American photographers who are deconstructing the sepia-toned, poker-faced images of the nineteenth century with passionate, colorful images of their contemporary life using ironies that are playful as well as bitter. Carm Little Turtle, Hulleah J. Tsinhnahjinnie, and other Native women photographers have brought in the feminist perspective. Some of Little Turtle's best-known work focuses on the effect of modern culture on Native women's sexuality. Tsinhnahjinnie's photocollages address the parallel effects of colonization and oppression on Native Americans and black South Africans.

But Comanche writer Paul Chaat Smith wonders whether Native Americans have become unjustly defensive about white photographers. "From the Curtis stills to our own Kodachrome slides and Polaroid prints and Camcorder tapes, it's obvious we are a people who adore taking pictures and having pictures taken of us. So it should hardly be a surprise that everything about being Indian has been shaped by the camera," he wrote in *Partial Recall* (New Press, 1992), a book of essays about photographs of Native North Americans. "Nothing is quite as American as the American Indian. We've become a patriotic symbol."

Not that all Natives reject the refurbished modern image of Indian-ness. Some find it a welcome, even if somewhat bewildering, improvement over less flattering notions that prevailed earlier in the century. Better to be thought of as the first environmentalists than as losers, as mystics rather than as kooks. Native America has become a marketable idea. Publishers churn out one book after another on Native culture. A mini tourist industry has grown up around providing Native American experiences for culturally undernourished whites. New Agers cannot get enough. Native Americans are amused by their newfound status as sages.

Still, the hoopla has not changed the essential challenge for Native Americans in the modern world, to maintain cultural identity and still thrive. Many Native Americans find they must live away from reservations and trust lands, the centers of their tribal heritage, to make a living. They often find themselves in large urban centers where one's tribal identity is overwhelmed by an identity simply as an Indian or a Native American. Or just another member of a minority group.

Embracing the role of keepers of the culture, contemporary Native women are taking responsibility for maintaining the heart of their traditional cultures against the television age. Many are attempting to maintain circles of their Native communities in the midst of urban sprawl, provide their children with tribal identity to help them resist the assimilating pressures of public school, and even bridge the chasm for Natives who had no Native upbringing. The Internet is peppered with pleas from Native men looking for Native women to help them learn how to be themselves. All this, while holding down full-time jobs.

The tasks may have changed, but the work of being a Native American woman is as challenging as ever. Native women will persevere, as they have for thousands of years, in an imperfect world, shaping life out of what is there. The Native women of today are not fooled by Curtis's manipulations. His trumped-up imagery is discarded like their grandmothers discarded chaff. The valid elements in his photographs serve as reminders of what their elders have told them. They see the day on the horizon when they, like their grandmothers before them, will be the living links to the past. Curtis's legacy will be there to help keep the thread taut.

The Plains and the Subarctic

By the time Curtis visited the Plains Indians, beginning in 1905, the buffalo had been gone for years, the tribes had been living on reservations for decades, and their religion was outlawed; they had been robbed of their traditional means of living and their independence. As for their warrior tradition, although they still possessed the regalia and the memories of war and bravery, it was all in the past. "In gathering the lore of the Indians of the Plains one hears only of yesterday," wrote Curtis. "His thoughts are of the past; today is but a living death, and his very being is permeated with the hopelessness of tomorrow."

By describing this sense of despair as masculine, Curtis may have unwittingly left open the possibility that this point of view was not shared, at least to the same degree, by the women. While Curtis generally photographed the men as warriors or medicine men, he often showed the women occupied with life-sustaining tasks, their faces reflecting the self-confidence arising from their stable roles in society, even in the midst of devastating change, including reliance on government handouts.

In 1905, 1907, and 1908, Curtis studied several of the Plains tribes in Montana and the Dakotas, including the Northern Arapahoe, Blackfeet, Cheyenne, Crow, and Sioux tribes. Returning later to North Dakota, he observed the Arikara, Mandan, and Hidatsa tribes of the Middle Missouri, who had been decimated in the nineteenth century by the introduction of smallpox, liquor, and warfare. Years later, Curtis visited some of the Northern Plains tribes of Canada—the Plains Cree and Sarcee—and also studied the Comanche, Wichita, Southern Cheyenne, and Southern Arapaho, who had been moved to reservations in Oklahoma.

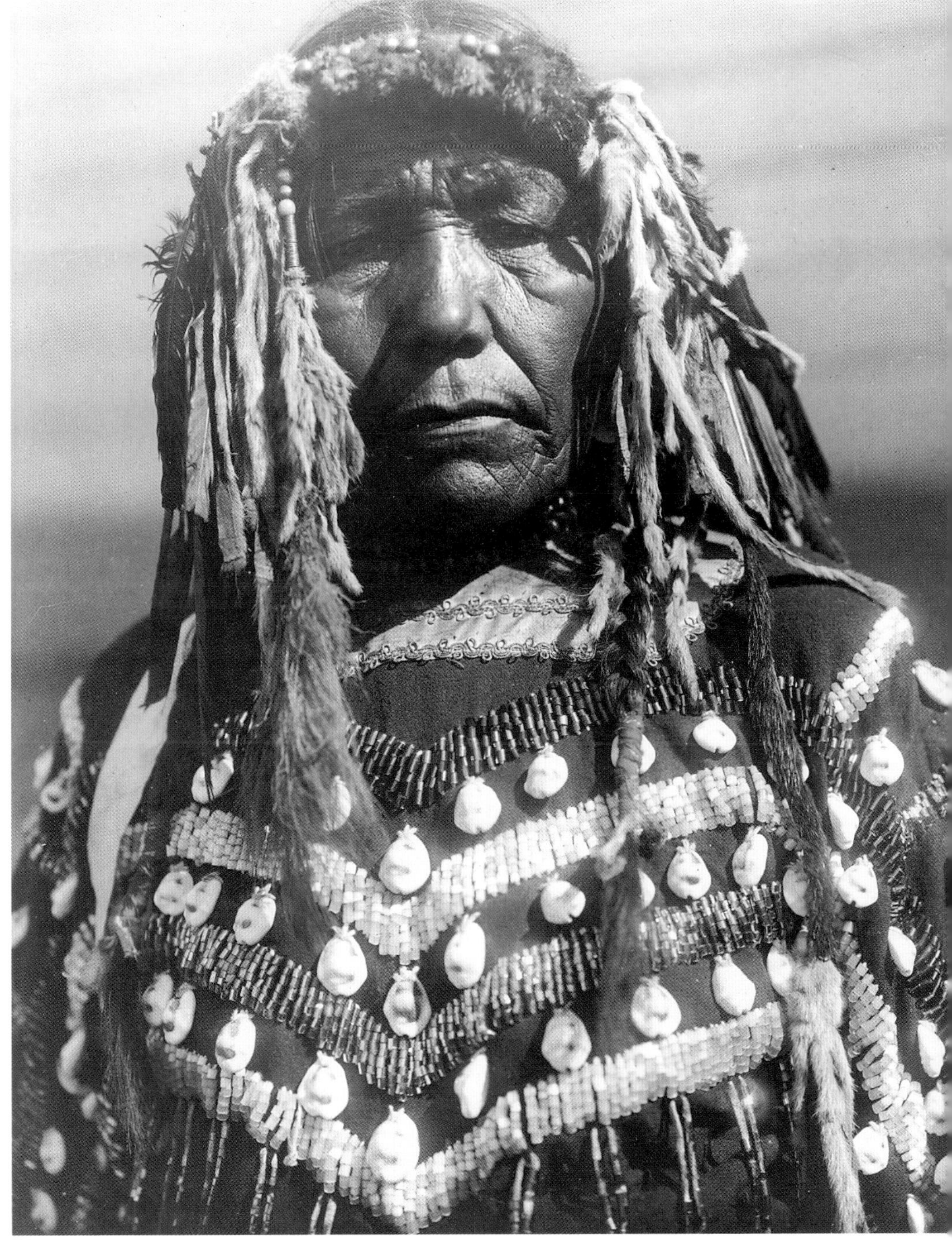

PIEGAN WOMAN, ©1911

This Piegan woman, identified as "Wife of Weasel Head" on another photograph by Curtis, wears a dress decorated with cowrie shells and beadwork and an imposing headdress of strips of fur and feathers. The Piegan (Pikuni) were one of the three divisions of the Algonquian-speaking Blackfeet, the other two being the Blood (Kainah) and Blackfoot (Siksika). While the Blackfeet honored and valued the necessity of male and female division of labor, powerful, or "manly hearted," women were highly regarded in Blackfeet mythology and in public, private, and religious life. The Sun Dance ceremony itself cannot take place unless a woman undertakes an initial vow to sponsor the ceremony.

A Blackfoot Travois, ©1926

In his caption for this photograph of a Blackfeet (called Blackfoot by Curtis) couple with their horse, travois, and dog taken on the Blackfeet Reservation in northwestern Montana, Curtis noted that "the travois is still used for transporting bundles of ceremonial objects." Blackfeet women achieved power and status through personal wealth; they traditionally owned the tipis, the travois, the household implements, and the horses they rode. It was the women who pitched or struck the camps with great rapidity. After collapsing the tipi, they lashed its cover to the packsaddle on the horse's back so that it protruded enough to allow bundles of long tipi poles to be strapped to either side. The poles were attached at their forward tips with long thongs to keep them from spreading as they were dragged along.

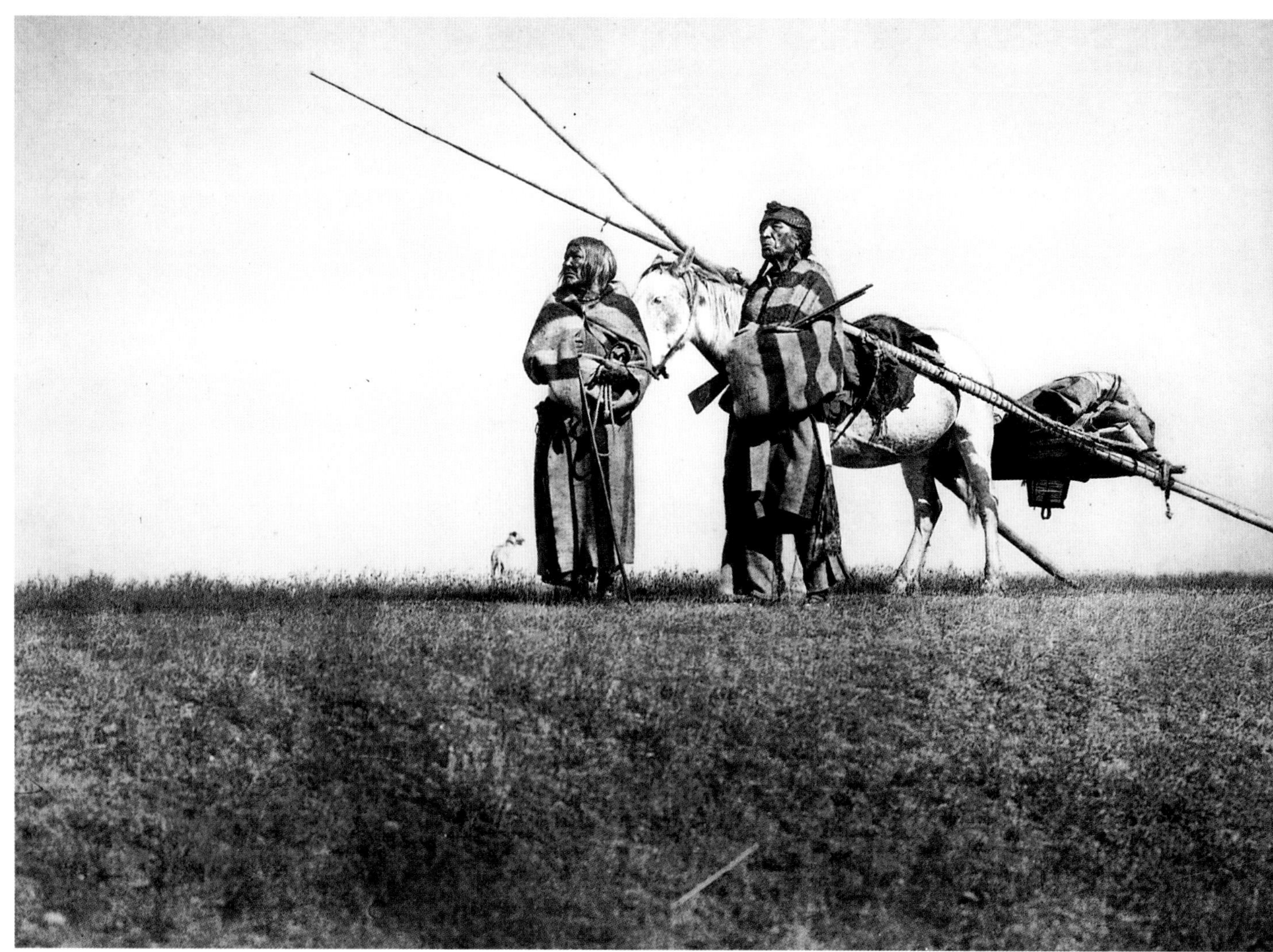

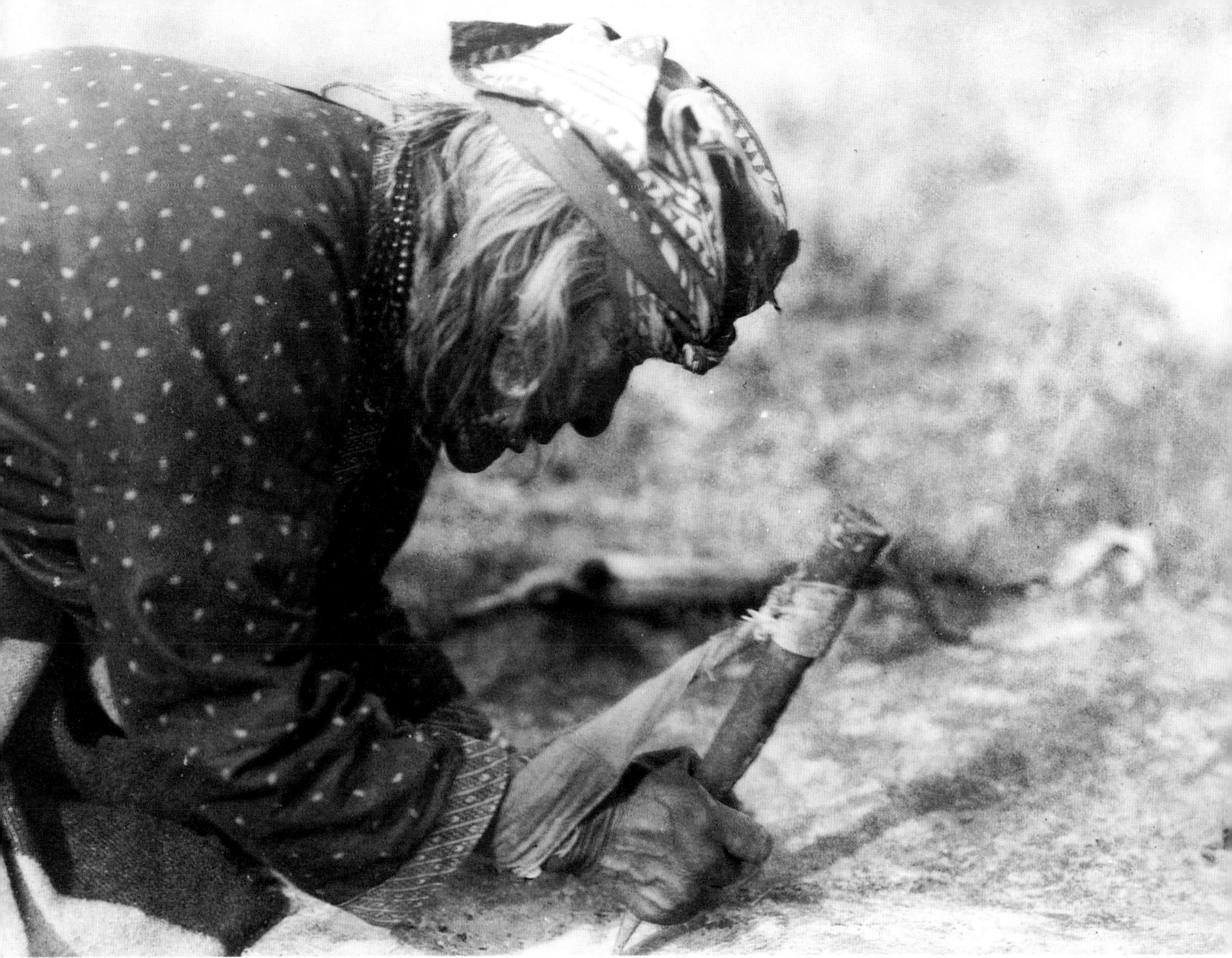

FLESHING A HIDE—BLACKFOOT, ©1926

Women used fleshers, special tools generally made from metal (often from recycled gun barrels, replacing those made from animal leg bones), to scrape a hide, and these were often passed down from generation to generation. Those who were skilled at this task—which could take as long as ten days—were greatly admired. A Blackfeet story set in a world where men and women once lived separately illustrates the value placed on a hardworking and skillfull woman. While the mythological women were all well dressed, lived in handsome lodges, and owned many beautiful possessions, the men were poor and homeless. When each woman invited a man to live with her, most accepted, but the man chosen by the women's leader rejected her because he thought her too plain. In retribution for spurning the loving care of a good woman, he was turned into a precariously rooted pine tree.

THE CHEYENNE

Curtis witnessed a Cheyenne Sun Dance ceremony on the western bank of the Tongue River in southeastern Montana in October 1909. According to Curtis, construction of the sun lodge began after the women erected hundreds of tents in a complete circle. The pledger's wife, her body covered in sacred red paint and wearing a buffalo robe, led the inaugural procession, carrying a red-painted buffalo skull. She and the male leaders, including her husband, then sat in a semicircle while she blessed many women and children, allowing each to sit briefly on her lap. After the principals had sanctioned the completion of the sun lodge, they built an altar within it, upon which the woman placed the buffalo skull.

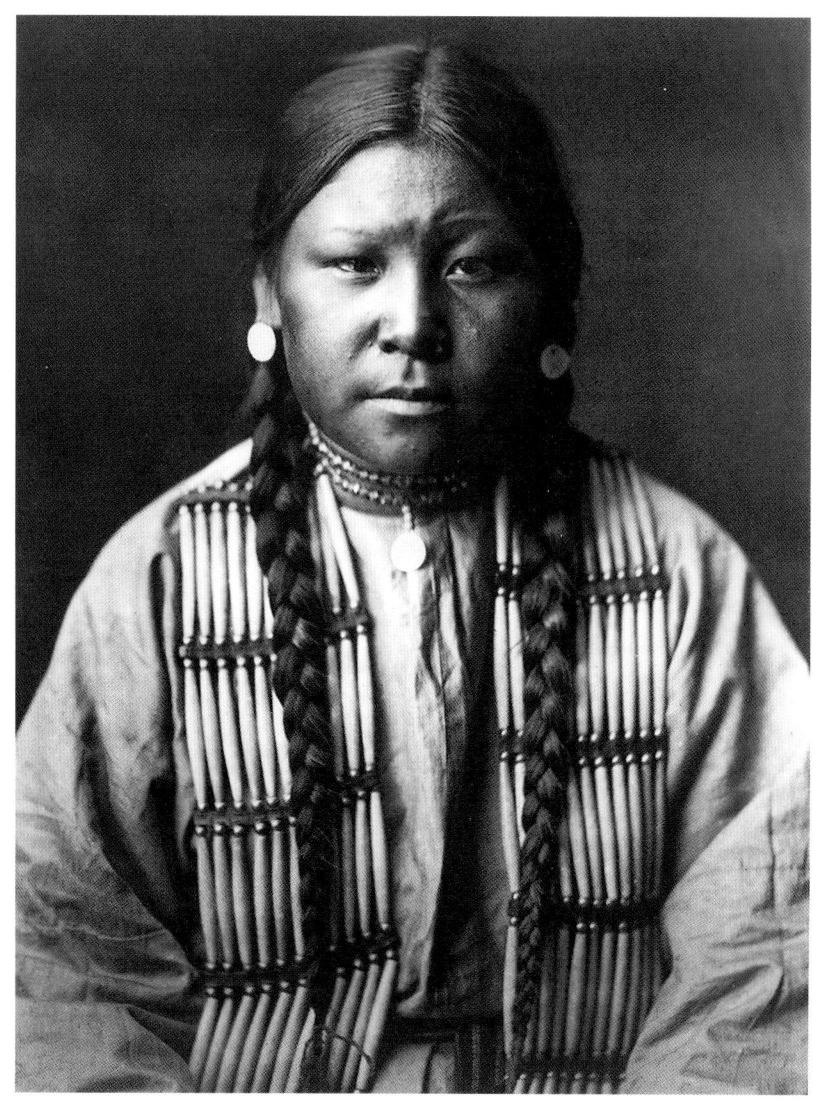

CHEYENNE GIRL, ©1905

This Cheyenne girl with the steady gaze has her hair neatly parted in the middle and braided at the sides in the Sioux fashion worn by men and women of the Cheyenne tribe after about 1855, according to Curtis. She is wearing a cloth dress and a hair-pipe necklace. Plains Indians used shell hair pipes (usually the column of the marine conch) to make breastplates and necklaces until the Ponca chief White Eagle acquired some bone pipestems for corncob pipes from a trader and noticed that they made a sturdier hair pipe than did shell. Bone pipestems were suddenly in unusual demand and, capitalizing on this new demand during the 1880s, traders found manufacturers to produce cheaper hair pipes from the lower leg bones of cattle. Complex necklaces, like the one worn by this Cheyenne girl, were not made until after bone hair pipes were introduced in great quantities. They appear in photographs of other Plains women from about the same date as this photograph.

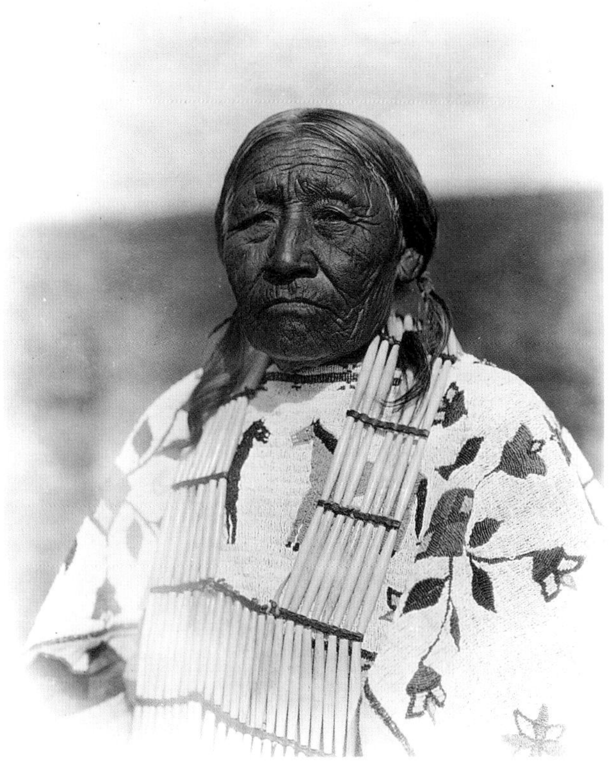

Wife of Old Crow—Cheyenne, ©1927

Old Crow was one of several Southern Cheyenne elders, most of whom were in their nineties, who aided the Curtis project. The Southern Cheyenne were the southern part of the tribe, which lived south of the Arkansas River near Bent's Fort trading post after 1835 while the Northern Cheyenne remained in Montana. The Southern Cheyenne and the Arapaho—still closely associated today—were assigned a reservation together in western Oklahoma by the treaty of 1867. This land was allotted to individual owners in 1891–92. Old Crow's wife's beaded dress shows the great skill of women artisans. Plains Indian bead designs were founded in traditional dyed-porcupine-quill designs. Cheyenne women who were skilled at quillwork belonged to an exclusive quilling society whose members aspired to cover at least thirty full buffalo robes with their craft. When these women met to socialize and teach the art to younger women, they described in detail how they had decorated various robes, baby carriers, and moccasins, much as the men might relate their bravery in war.

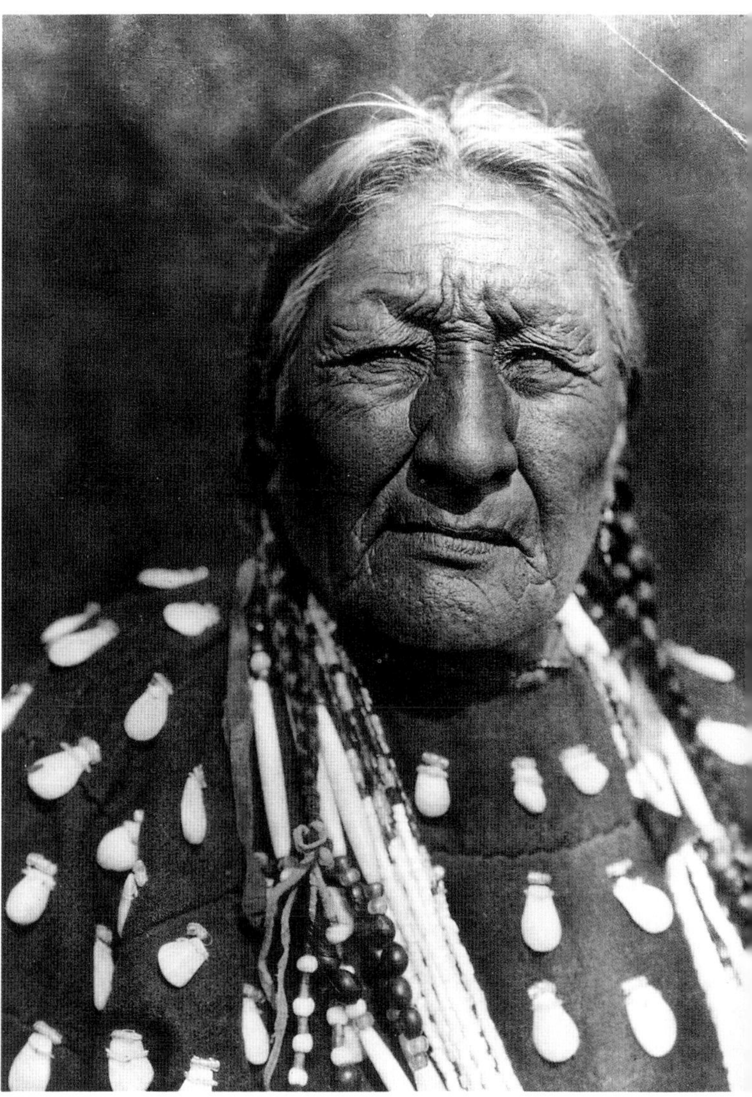

Dog Woman—Cheyenne, ©1927

Dog Woman was clearly a woman of character and stature; her dress is decorated with elk teeth, an indication of wealth. Women played important roles in Cheyenne spiritual ceremonies: medicine men were usually assisted by their wives, and the wife of the pledger of the Sun Dance was central to the ceremony.

CAMP GOSSIPS—ATSINA, ©1908

This peaceful scene of women relaxing and surveying camp life together belies the stereotype of a life of unremitting drudgery for Plains Indian women. An Algonquian-speaking tribe whose population, decimated by smallpox and flu epidemics, fell as low as 576 around the turn of the century, the Gros Ventre were called Atsina, or "big eaters," by their neighbors, the Blackfeet. Curtis visited them on the 600,000-acre Fort Belknap Reservation, where they had been moved with the Assiniboine in 1888. He reported that, according to Gros Ventre legend, they had separated from the Arapaho as the result of a quarrel over the division of a buffalo carcass. It is not known when they settled in their traditional territory. Between 1795 and 1830, the tribe moved south to join the Arapaho—again, tradition has it that when the young wife of the elderly chief ran away with a young brave and took shelter with the Arapaho, the chief persuaded the entire tribe to move south to reclaim her.

This negative was rather crudely retouched, probably in the lab. Note that an object between the middle two tipis, and two more on the hill to the left, have been scratched out, perhaps because they were evidence of modern life.

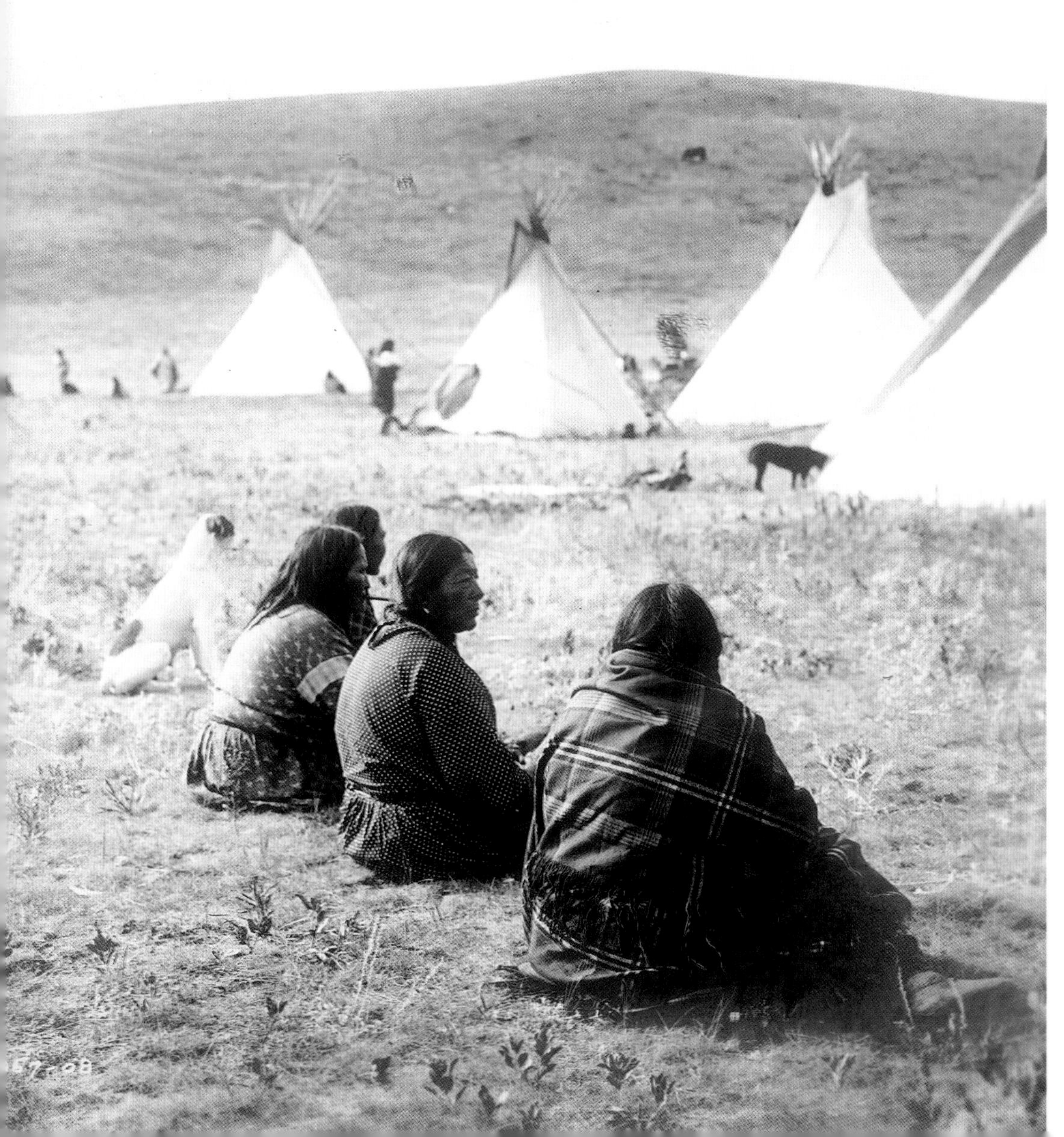

THE CROW

Curtis waxed poetic when imagining the activity around a Crow camp in prereservation days, a description that might apply to any of the buffalo-hunting Plains tribes: "In the camp itself there is an endless panorama of activities and a ceaseless confusion of sounds. Women are everywhere stretching the drying hides, and filling great drying-racks with long thin strips of rich, red buffalo-meat. In the lodges others are tanning skins, and on many sides can be heard the thud of the wooden tray as women gamble with plum-seed dice."

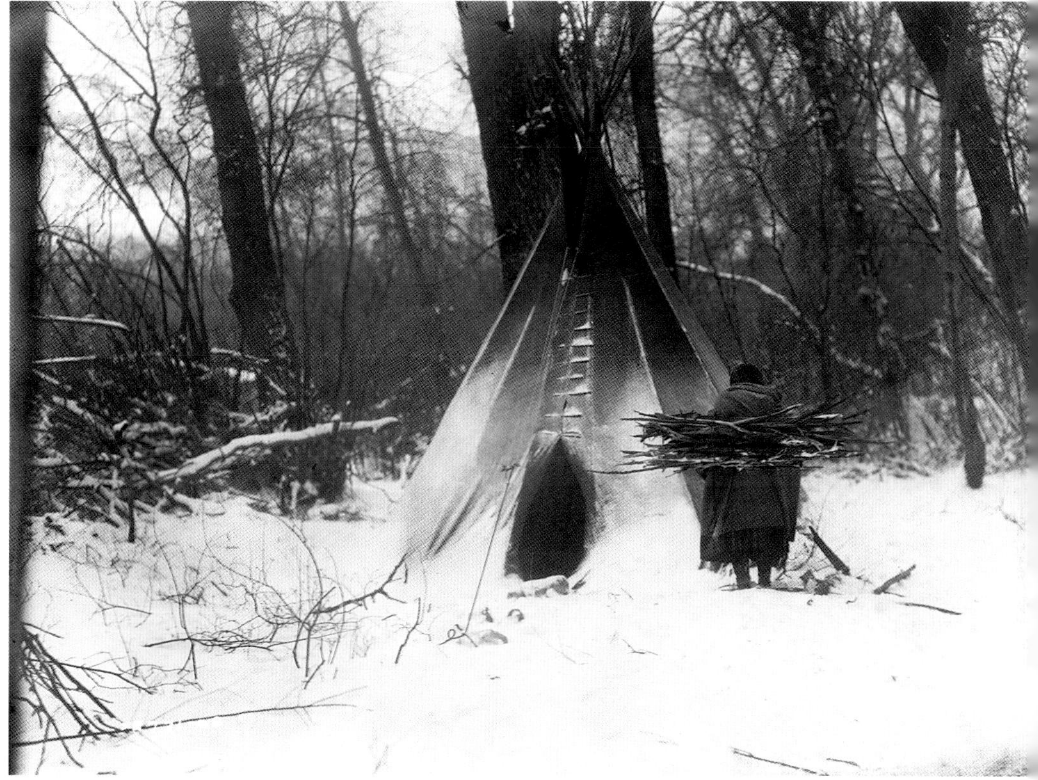

WINTER—APSAROKE, ©1908
Women of the Plains tribes did much of the work around the camp, including—as in the case of this Crow woman—gathering wood to keep the tipi fire burning during the bitter winter months. Mountain Crow bands made their winter camps in thick forests along the banks of mountain streams—at this time, on the Crow Agency on the Little Big Horn River in southeastern Montana. This tipi is noticeably blackened by smoke; when a woman wanted a new tipi, she accumulated sufficient tanned buffalo hides, parceled them out to her friends for softening, and usually commissioned a woman skilled in designing and cutting—the "lodge maker"—to oversee the project. She then prepared a feast and invited the participants for the final assemblage. Large Crow tipis—some were twenty-five feet tall, required as many as fifteen to twenty hides, and could accommodate forty people—were a testament to the diligence and skill of their makers and brought great prestige. The owner of the hides became the owner of the new tipi, which was initially light colored. The old hide, made impermeable by the smoking fires, was turned into moccasins and articles of everyday clothing that might be exposed to rain.

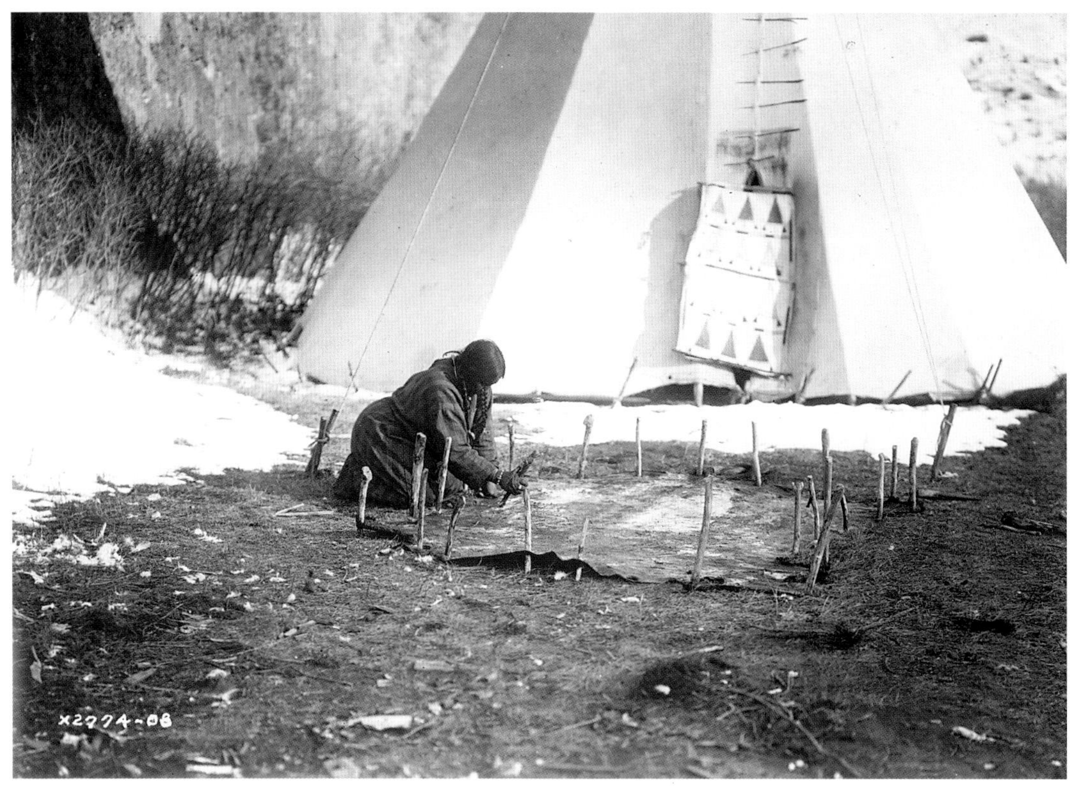

HIDE SCRAPING—APSAROKE, ©1908

Game was processed immediately after it was brought into camp by the hunters. The women would cut the meat into thin strips and drape it over a special rack for drying in the sun. In due course, the skin was processed. The moistened hide was staked out on the ground and scraped of fat and tissue until it was clean and smooth. The next step was to reverse the hide and scrape off the hair with an adze made of elk antler. The skin might be coated with a mixture of buffalo brains, liver, or bird droppings to lighten the hide. After removing the stakes, the hide was laid on a thick mat of old skins, coated with buffalo fat, and alternately wetted, kneaded, dried, and scraped to soften it. The light-colored—and apparently new—tipi in the background, with its handsomely decorated door cover, would have required weeks of arduous work to prepare the requisite number of hides. When the Crow lived on the Missouri River with the Hidatsa, they probably grew corn, but their most important agricultural product after they moved west was the sacred tobacco, which was grown through the 1960s.

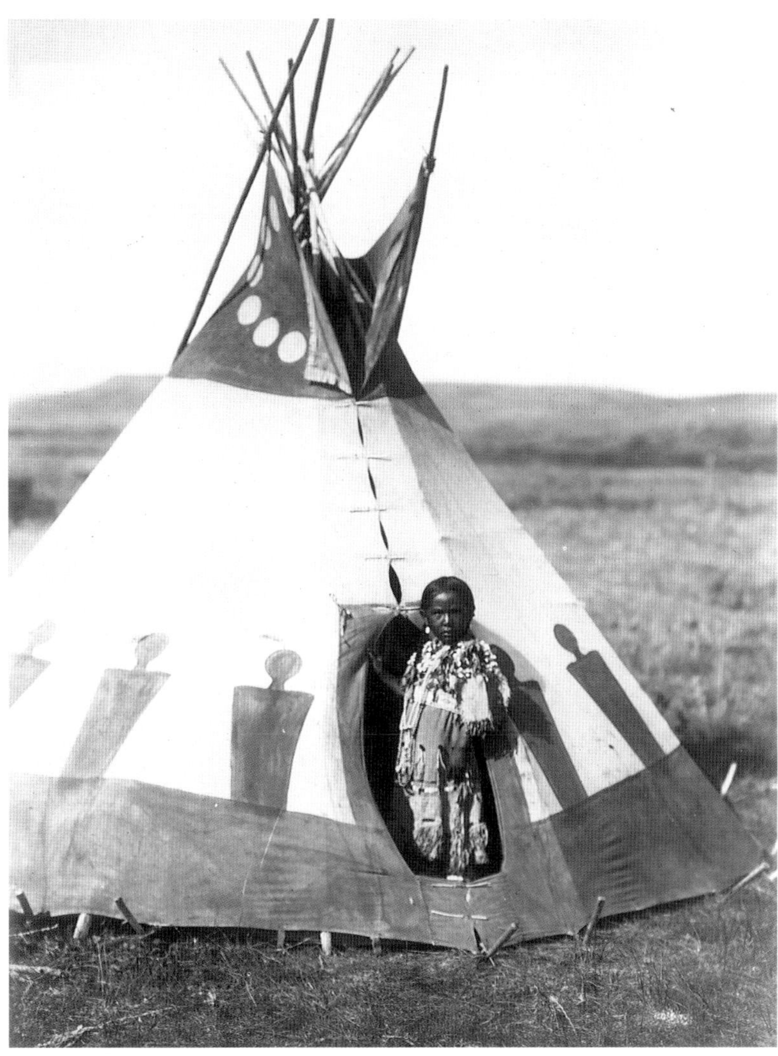

CROW CHIEF'S DAUGHTER, ©1910

Standing in the entrance of her handsomely decorated play tipi, dressed in a fringed dress and wearing long strands of beads, the chief's small daughter was already learning the domestic and artistic skills that brought prestige to Plains women. When describing the Crow tribe, Curtis noted that they were a particularly sensual people with a great love of embellishment: "The women lavished their best thoughts and labor on garments to beautify themselves in the eyes of the men, and still more on the clothing of their husbands in the desire that none should be more splendidly clad. . . . The saddles used by the women were made with a very high horn front and back, ornamented with beads or quills, and from each was suspended a large embroidered pendant. The stirrups, of bent willow, were covered with beaded skin. Just behind the saddle hung large decorated saddle-bags, so long that their fringes almost swept the ground, and an embroidered breast-piece was suspended from the horse's neck."

Slow Bull's Wife, ©1907

This formidable, gimlet-eyed Oglala Sioux woman personifies Curtis's observation that "among the hunting tribes especially the life of the women has been such as to develop the greatest physical strength, resulting in slight differentiation in features or in endurance of the sexes." Judging by the number of dentalium shells adorning her dress and hanging from her ears, she was the wife of a wealthy man. She was an Oglala Sioux warrior's wife and certainly would have derived considerable pride and status from her husband's achievements at war. Before moving to the Pine Ridge Reservation in South Dakota in 1876, Slow Bull had participated in fifty-five battles, with Apsaroke (Crow), Shoshone, Ute, Pawnee, Blackfeet, and Kootenai, and struck seven coups, and had ridden with Chief Red Cloud against the U.S. Army. His wife would have put great effort and artistry into recording these exploits in the decoration of his clothing and regalia. Curtis related that when Slow Bull inherited a sacred pouch that had been in his family for four generations, his father told him to have a beaded hoof added to it for each horse he captured. Slow Bull, born in 1844, captured 170 horses when he was just seventeen years old, and so his young wife's work was already cut out for her.

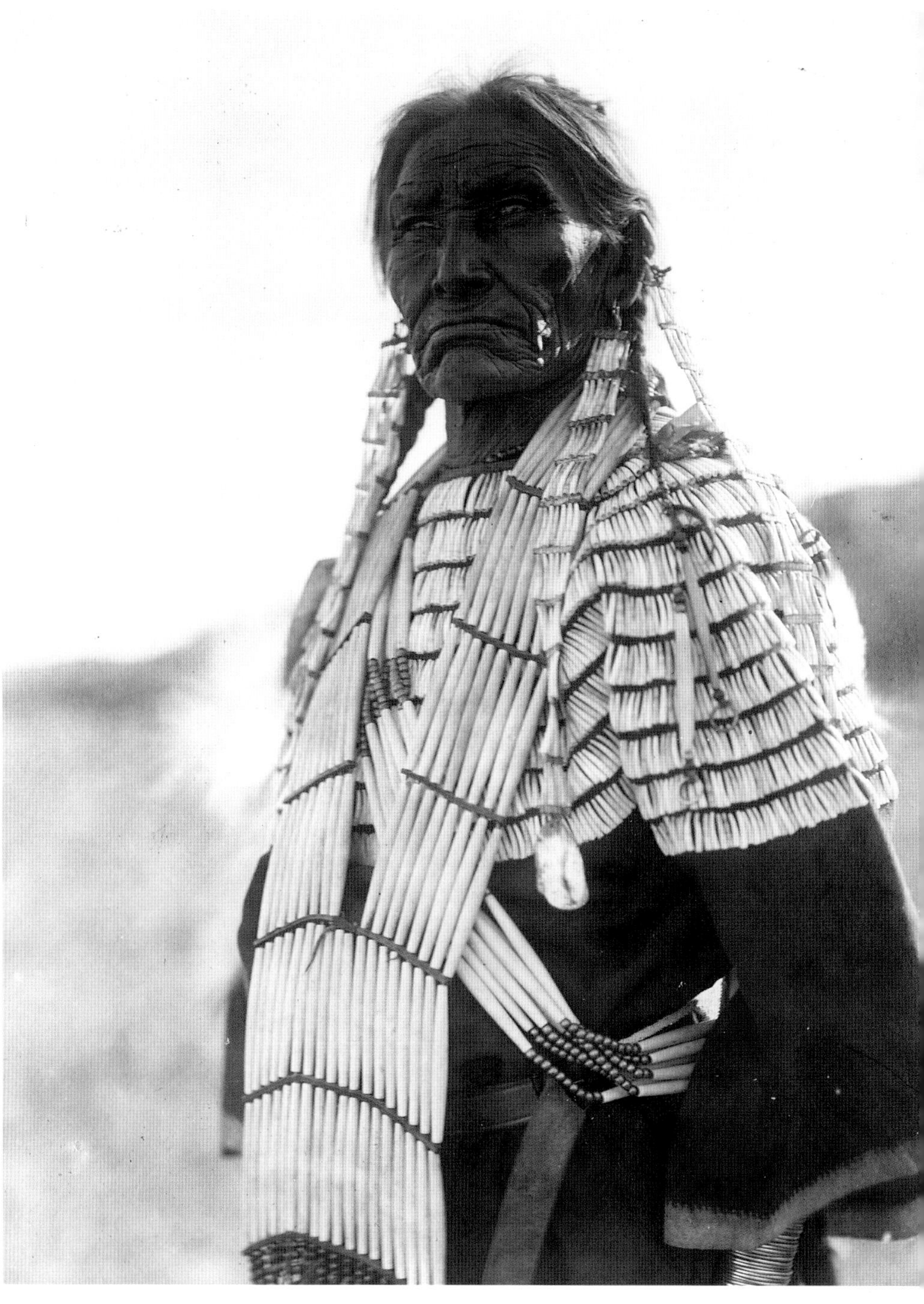

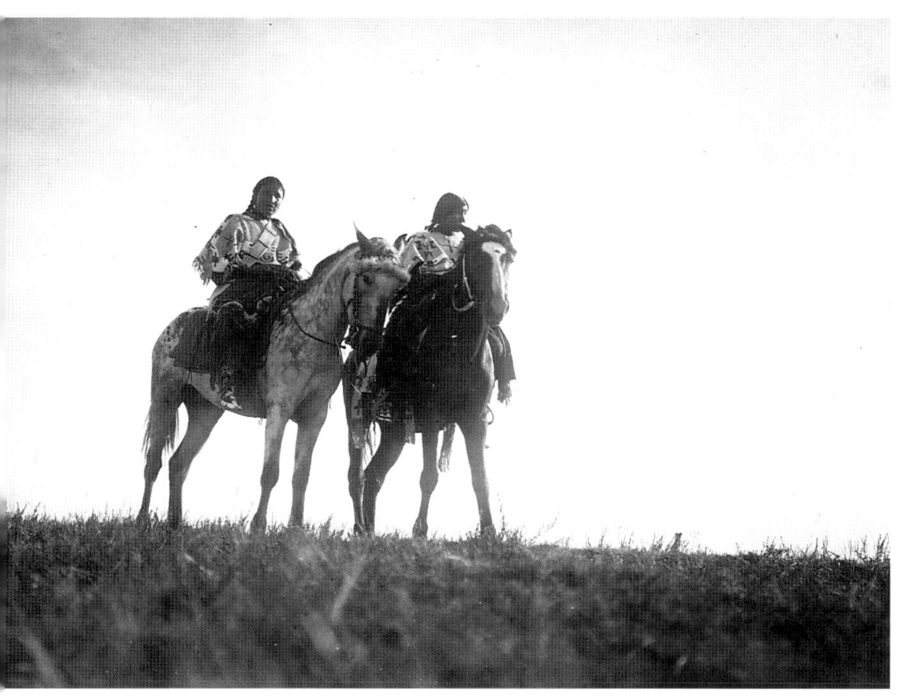

OGALALA GIRLS, ©1907

Horsemanship was as essential for women of the Plains tribes as it was for men. Curtis said that small girls, like small boys, were strapped onto a horse's back until they had mastered equestrian skills. Once horses were introduced to North America by Spanish settlers in the Southwest, they rapidly became a prized commodity among Indian tribes, allowing many that were formerly farmers or local hunters and gatherers to range farther and move onto the Plains in pursuit of larger numbers of buffalo. One of the primary honors that a warrior aspired to was to capture or cut loose an enemy's horses. Oglala (spelled Ogalala by Curtis) Sioux and other Plains Indians living on reservations when Curtis undertook his project were forbidden to sell their horses to another Indian or leave their reservations without permission. These restrictions greatly undermined their traditional lifestyle and contributed to their subsequent poverty.

DRYING MEAT, ©1908

The territory of the Teton, or western Sioux—including the Oglala, Brulé, Hunkpapa, Miniconjou, Sans Arcs, Blackfoot, and Two Kettle—before they were moved to reservations, lay west of the Missouri River and north of the North Platte River, abutting lands dominated by the Siouan-speaking Crow and Algonquian-speaking Cheyenne and Arapaho. By the time Curtis visited them on reservations in the Black Hills region of South Dakota, he found it hard to produce photographs of traditional lifestyles without evidence of Euro-American products and influence. For instance, while these women are preserving meat in the traditional way by hanging strips to dry on frames, the canvas tent in the background is a standard government-issue type. The long, belted dresses worn by the women are cut in the traditional pattern but were now made of cloth instead of deerskin. Several divisions of the Sioux, particularly the western Sioux, had found this loss of culture and freedom so dispiriting that they had joined the Ghost Dance movement that culminated in the massacre of 150 Miniconjou from Cheyenne River at Wounded Knee on the Pine Ridge Reservation, South Dakota, in December 1890.

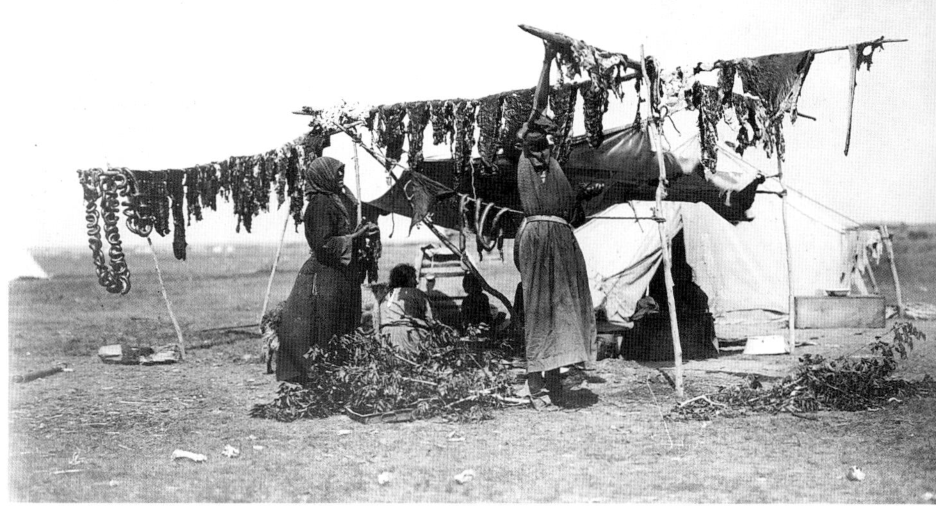

Missouri River Peoples

Yellow Bone Woman, ©1908

The Arikara, Hidatsa, and Mandan are known officially today as the Three Affiliated Tribes, and indeed Curtis noted, when he visited them on the Fort Berthold Reservation in western North Dakota, that already they were losing their separate tribal identities. The man and baby are dressed almost entirely in Euro-American clothing (except for the man's beautifully beaded moccasins) and are seated before a log cabin typical of housing on the reservation. (The tribe formerly lived in semisubterranean earth lodges.) Unlike the Siouan-speaking Hidatsa and Mandan, the Arikara were a Caddoan-speaking tribe, part of a group that included the Pawnee, Wichita, and Caddo. In the late seventeenth century, they had gradually moved north along the Missouri River from Kansas into the Dakotas, separating from the Pawnee in Nebraska.

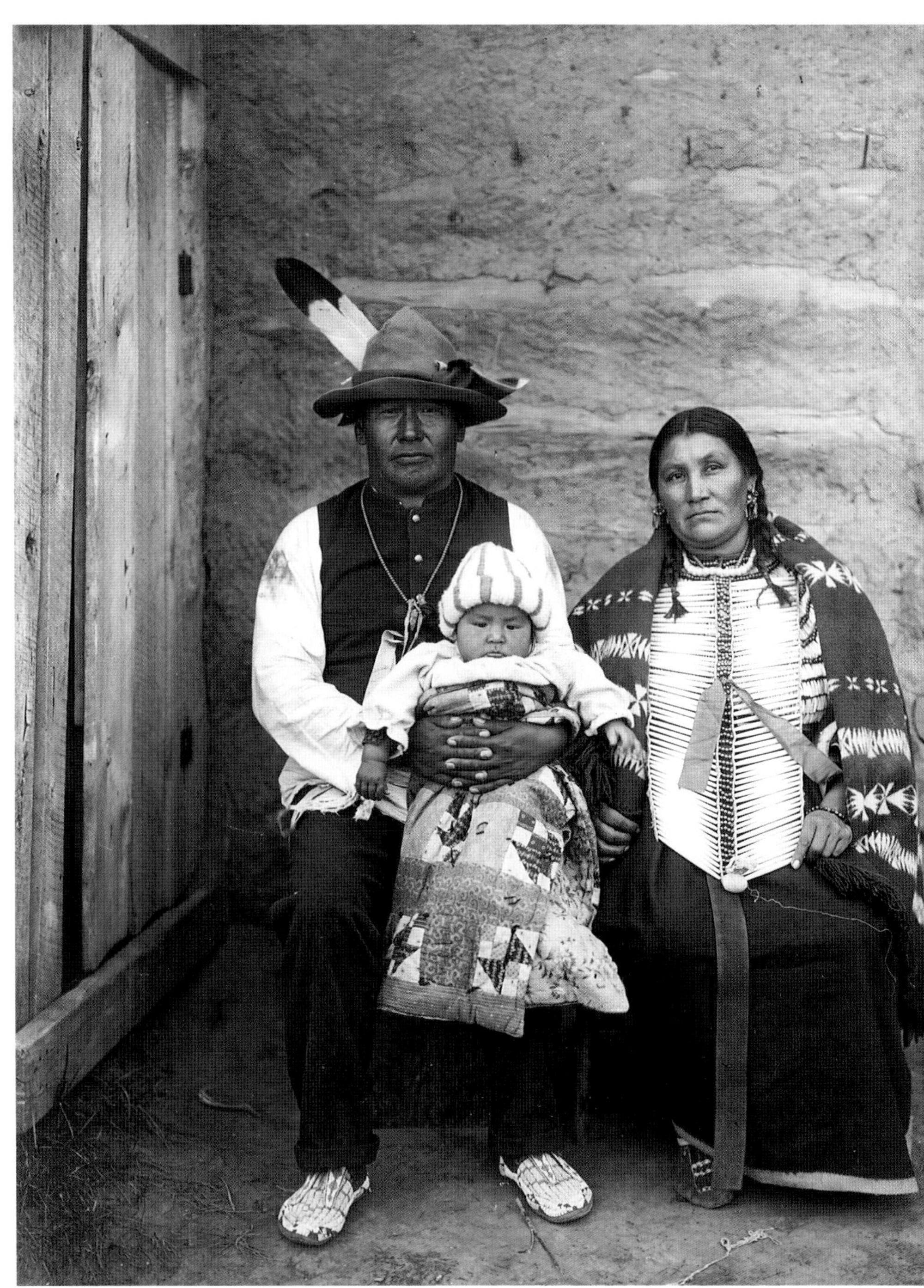

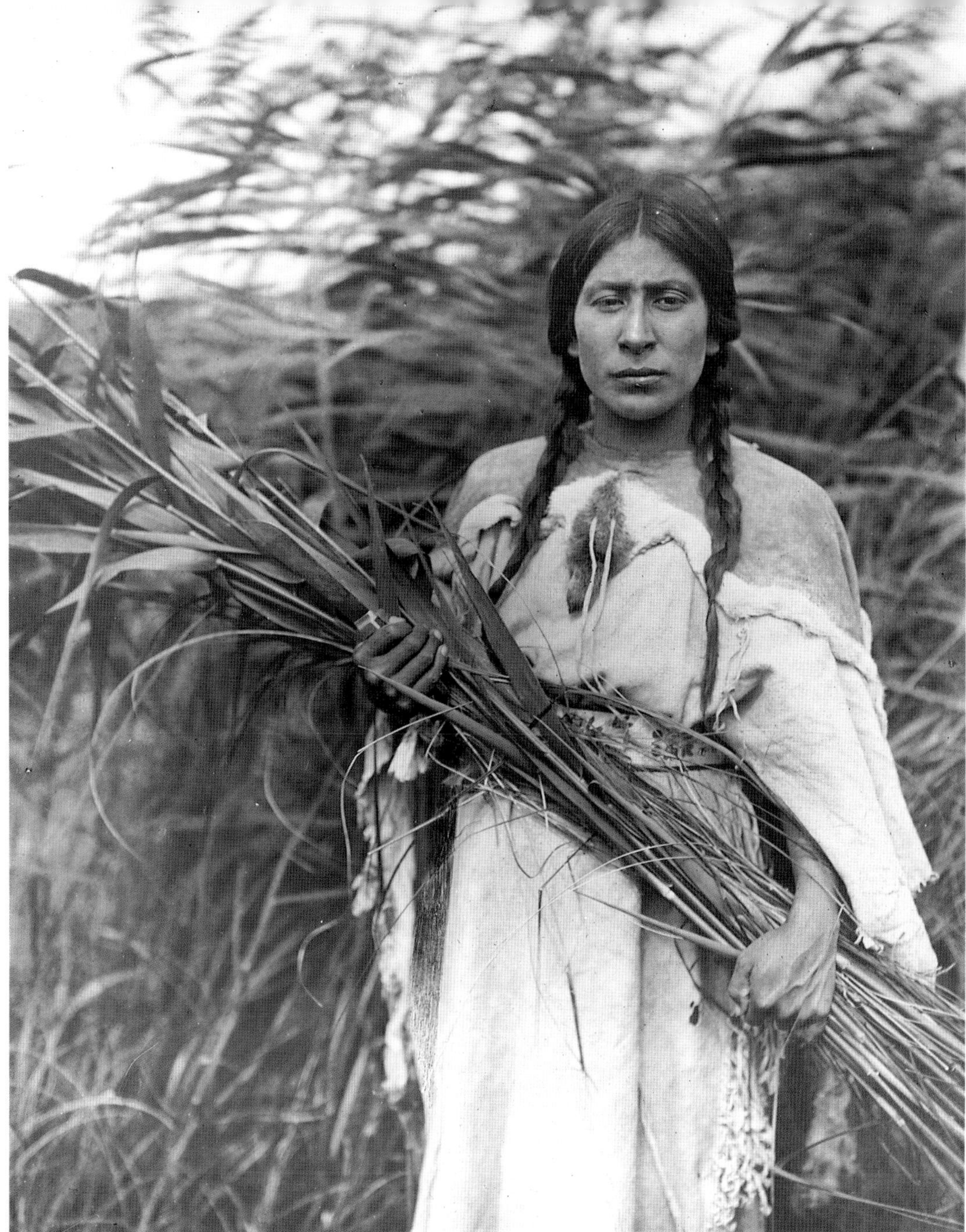

THE RUSH GATHERER—ARIKARA, ©1908

Curtis noted in his caption for this photograph: "The Arikara, as well as their close neighbors, the Mandan and Hidatsa, made many mats of rushes. These were used largely as floor coverings." This woman is wearing a traditional dress made of deer or antelope skins. The sleeves required half a hide each and were left unsewn underneath the arms.

In prereservation days, the three tribes lived in villages along the Missouri River, where the women traditionally grew corn, squash, beans, sunflowers, and tobacco in separate household gardens. The women were in control of the entire agricultural process—planting, maintaining the garden plot, and harvesting. Any surplus was owned by them and might be traded to other tribes for buffalo robes, prepared hides, and dried meat; these in turn might be traded to non-Indian traders in exchange for guns, ammunition, knives, cloth, and other goods. The women kept their profits and used them to acquire trade goods to make their lives more comfortable.

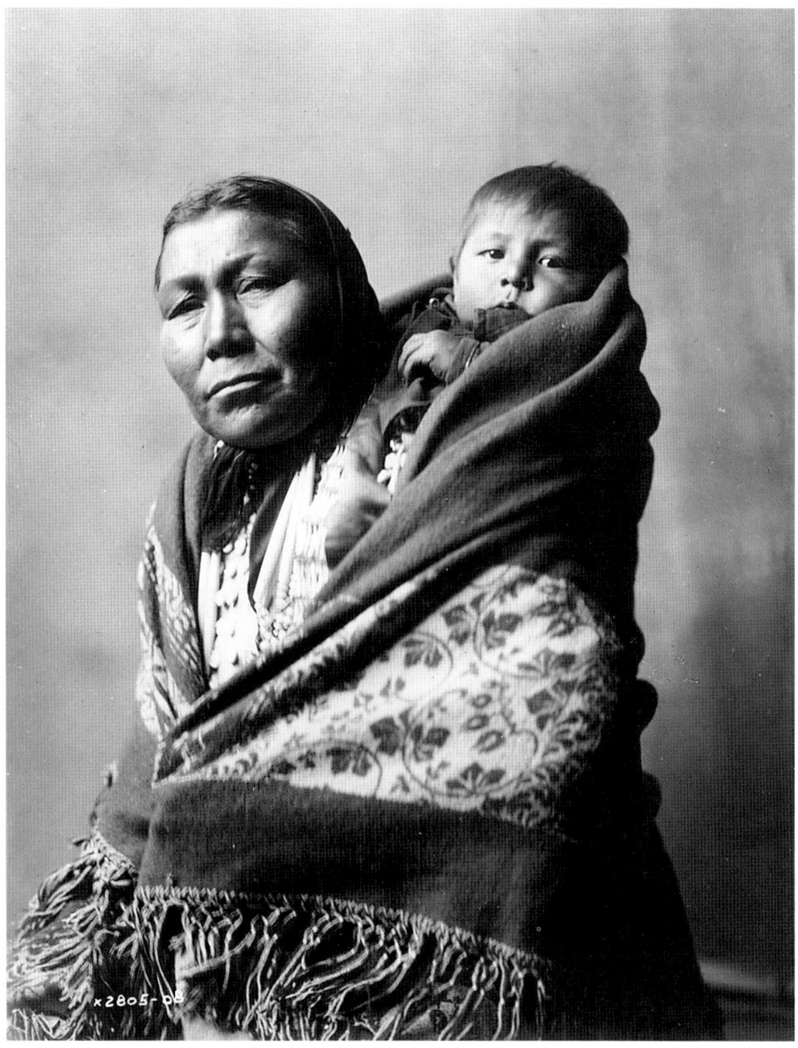

HIDATSA MOTHER, ©1908

This woman is identified as "Mrs. Good Bear" on the back of the copyrighted photograph. When describing the Arikara, whose culture was similar in many respects to the Hidatsa's, Curtis said, "Babies were not strapped to a board but wrapped securely and tied in a calf-skin, then in a heavier piece of buffalo-skin they were stood upright in a deep, narrow sack, which was suspended from a roof-timber." As the babies grew older, they were often carried on their mothers' or grandmothers' or sisters' backs, held in place by a robe or blanket, as in this photograph.

The Hidatsa are very close linguistically to the Crow and tradition says that the two tribes separated in the late seventeenth century, when the Crow moved farther west. One century later, the Hidatsa were greatly reduced by a smallpox epidemic to less than half of their original numbers. When Lewis and Clark visited them in 1804, the Hidatsa were located in several villages near the Mandan villages on the Knife River. Following another smallpox epidemic in 1837, the remnants of the two tribes moved north and established the village of Like-a-Fishhook on a bend of the Missouri River. In 1862, the Hidatsa and Mandan were settled on the Fort Berthold Reservation, where they were joined by the Arikara.

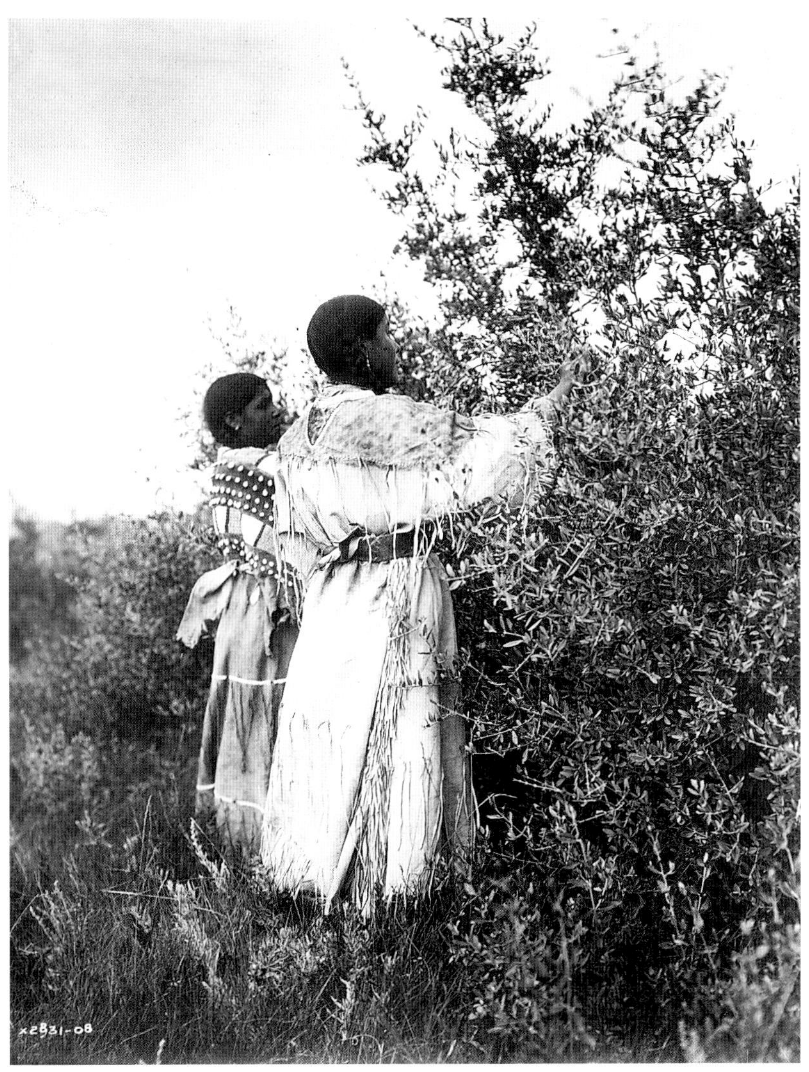

Buffalo-Berry Gatherers—Mandan, ©1908

Beginning in late spring and continuing throughout the summer, picking wild fruits was both an important means of food gathering and a social activity; groups of women picked together, filling work baskets with a variety of fruits. In addition, according to anthropologist Gilbert Wilson, "It was . . . a common thing for a young man to help his sweetheart pick Juneberries. A young man might send word to his sweetheart by some female relative of his own saying, 'That young man says that when you want to go for Juneberries, he wants to go along with you!'" Besides Juneberries, or service berries, other berries collected were gooseberries, raspberries, and buffaloberries. Pemmican, which was a winter staple, was made of dried buffalo meat (deer or antelope in Curtis's day) that had been pounded to a powder and mixed with melted fat, marrow, and crushed berries.

The Mandan were visited and described by the Lewis and Clark Expedition of 1804–1806 and painted by George Catlin and Karl Bodmer in 1832 and 1833, respectively. When Curtis visited the three tribes before 1908, they were still cultivating the rich croplands on either side of the Missouri River. However, the Fort Berthold Reservation was reduced by 25 percent in the 1950s when the Garrison Dam was built; much excellent cropland was lost beneath the waters of the reservoir formed by the dam.

Oklahoma (Indian Territory)

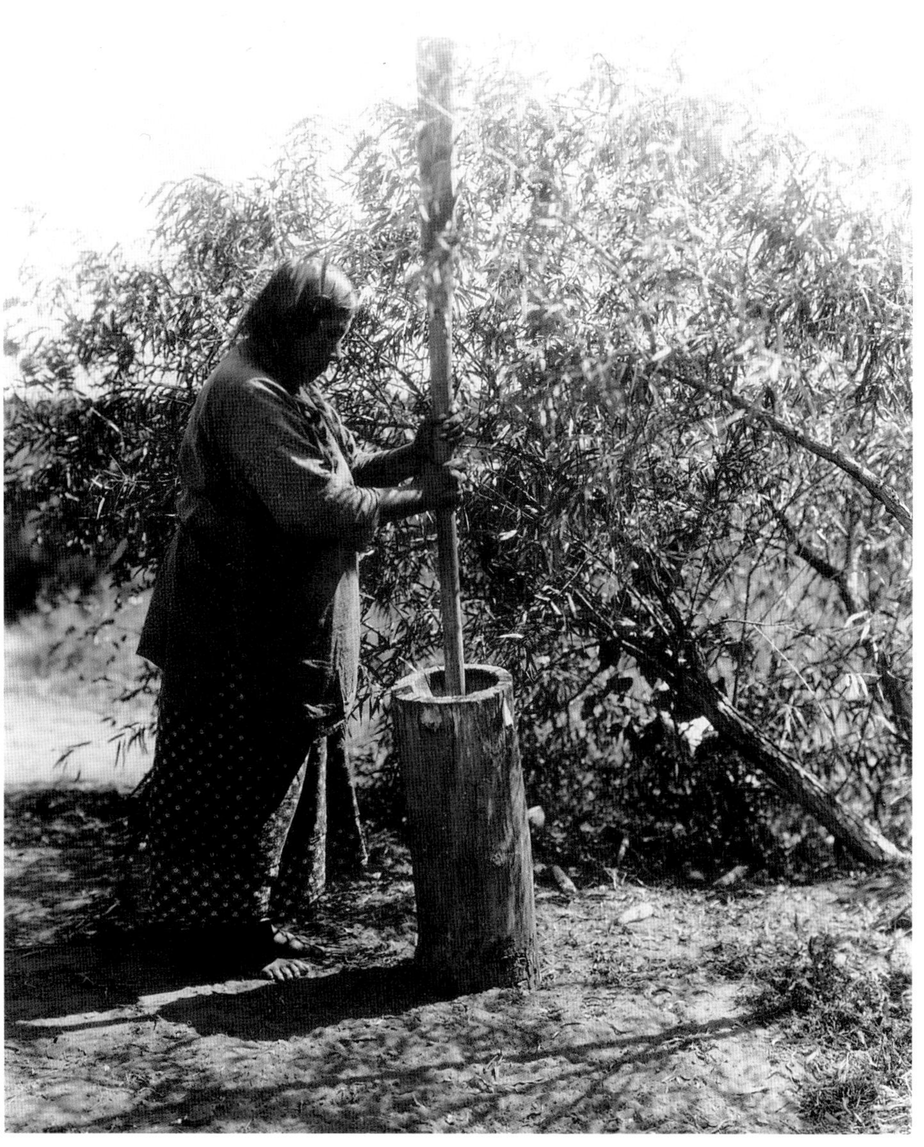

Wichita Mortar, ©1927

The Wichita were primarily an agricultural people, but their culture reflected their location between the Plains and the Southeast. Their villages of as many as 1,000 grass lodges were first described by the Spanish explorer Coronado in 1541–42; an illustration in an 1852 U.S. government report showed a Wichita village on Rush Creek, a tributary of Louisiana's Red River, with grass lodges surrounded by carefully tended plots of maize and other crops—beans, squash, watermelons, gourds, and tobacco. Following the Civil War, the Wichita were given a reservation in Indian Territory, later Caddo County, Oklahoma. While fertile, well-watered soil allowed many Wichita to continue their farming lifestyle, the presence of so many other Indian tribes led to a rapid loss of distinctive Wichita culture. Curtis undoubtedly posed this woman using a traditional wooden mortar and pestle for grinding dried corn. Like the Pueblo tribes of the Southwest, Wichita women also had used grinding stones for corn, as well as for pounding flat strips of squash.

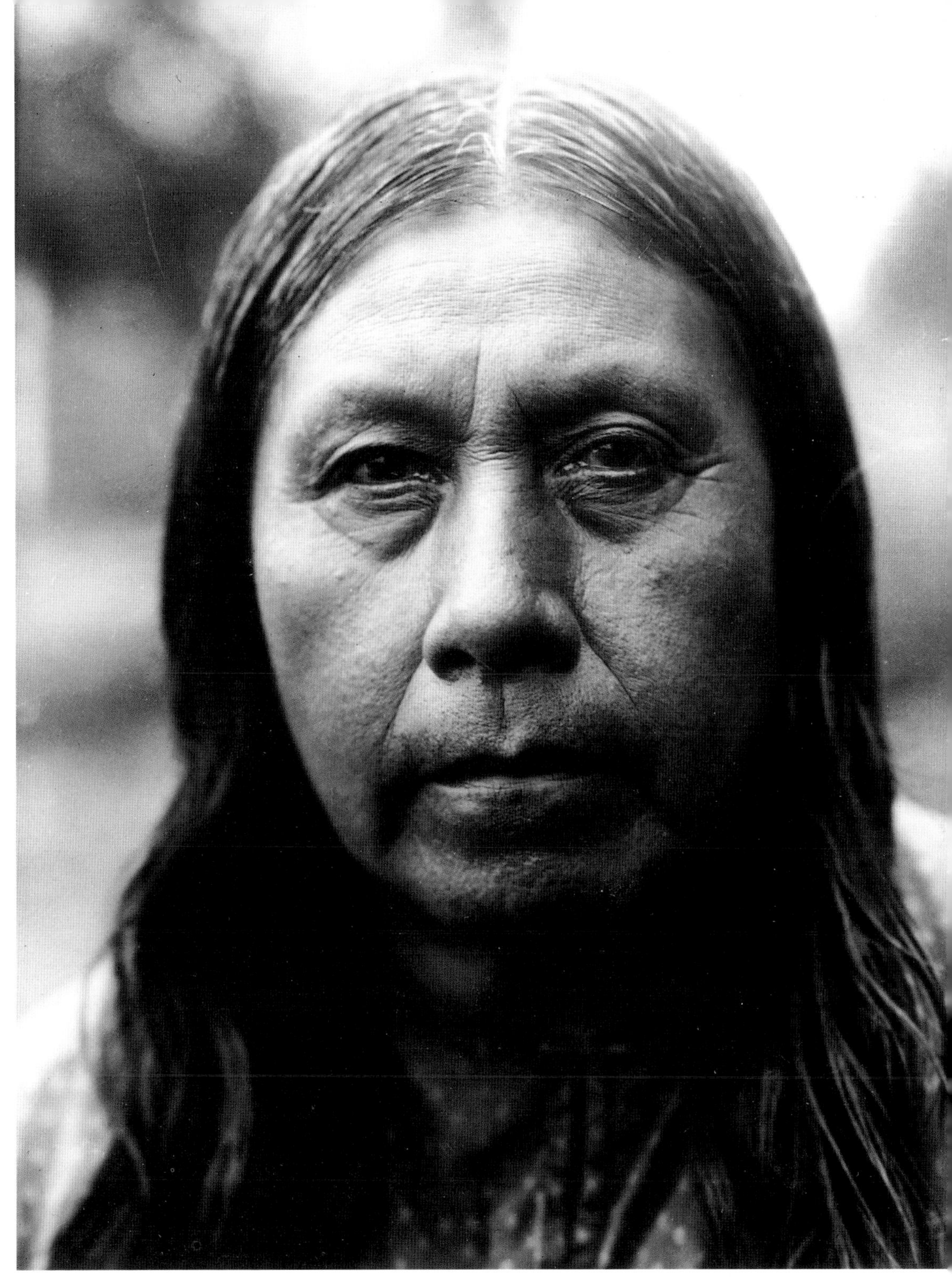

A Wichita Matron, ©1927

Tilling and processing crops were so central to a Wichita woman's life that she was generally buried with her household and gardening implements. The women often grew a surplus of crops, which they traded to other tribes. They dried and stored corn in underground storage places, pressed tobacco into flat loaves, and cut squash into long, thin strips that were then dried, flattened, and woven into mats to facilitate storage and transportation.

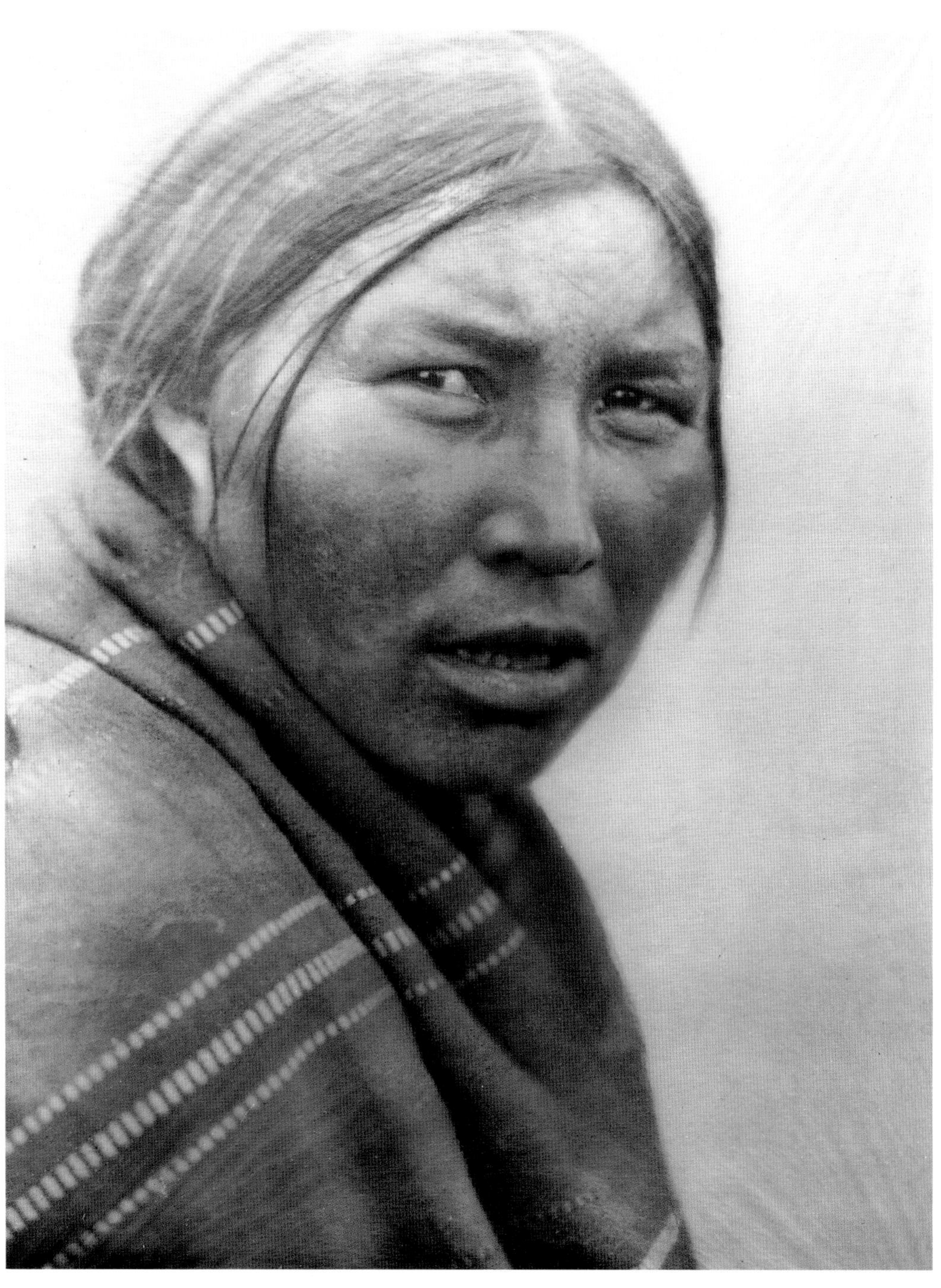

A CREE WOMAN, ©1926

The Cree were an Algonquian-speaking people who lived at the crossroads of the Plains and Subarctic cultures. This woman, named Mawinéhikis (which Curtis said was a common female name among the Cree, meaning "Tries-to-Excel"), was a member of the Western Wood Cree, who lived in the boreal forests north of Lake Winnipeg in Canada. The lake country was heavily forested with black and white spruce and other coniferous trees, as well as birch, aspen, and balsam poplar. Bands congregated on the shores of lakes for two or three months during the summer, when Cree women were depended upon to locate wild plant foods to supplement the hunting, fishing, and trapping of game by the men. During the winter freeze, when traveling, hunting, and trapping were limited, the women concentrated on processing hides and pelts and making or repairing clothing.

Moss for the Baby-Bags—Cree, ©1926

According to Curtis, Cree women gave birth in the kneeling position, supporting their arms on a pole lashed to the tipi pole and attended by women experienced in assisting during childbirth. The newborn was bathed following the cutting of the cord and placed on a bed of dried bog moss (sphagnum) on a piece of cloth. The cloth (formerly tanned skin was used) was tucked in at the bottom and folded over at the sides, and the edges were then laced together with a thong passing through looped eyelets. The infant stayed in this "moss-bag" until it was old enough to crawl; the mother carried the baby slung on her back, held by a tumpline across her forehead. The moss in the bag was renewed several times daily, and quantities of the freshly gathered material could be seen drying on poles or on the ground in any Cree camp. The stump of the umbilical cord was preserved for a long time, wrapped in a bit of hide and tied at the side of the moss-bag. A Cree baby was named when he or she was eight days old by the old man chosen to bestow the name, who was one of a number of tribal elders invited by the baby's father to a naming ceremony in his tipi.

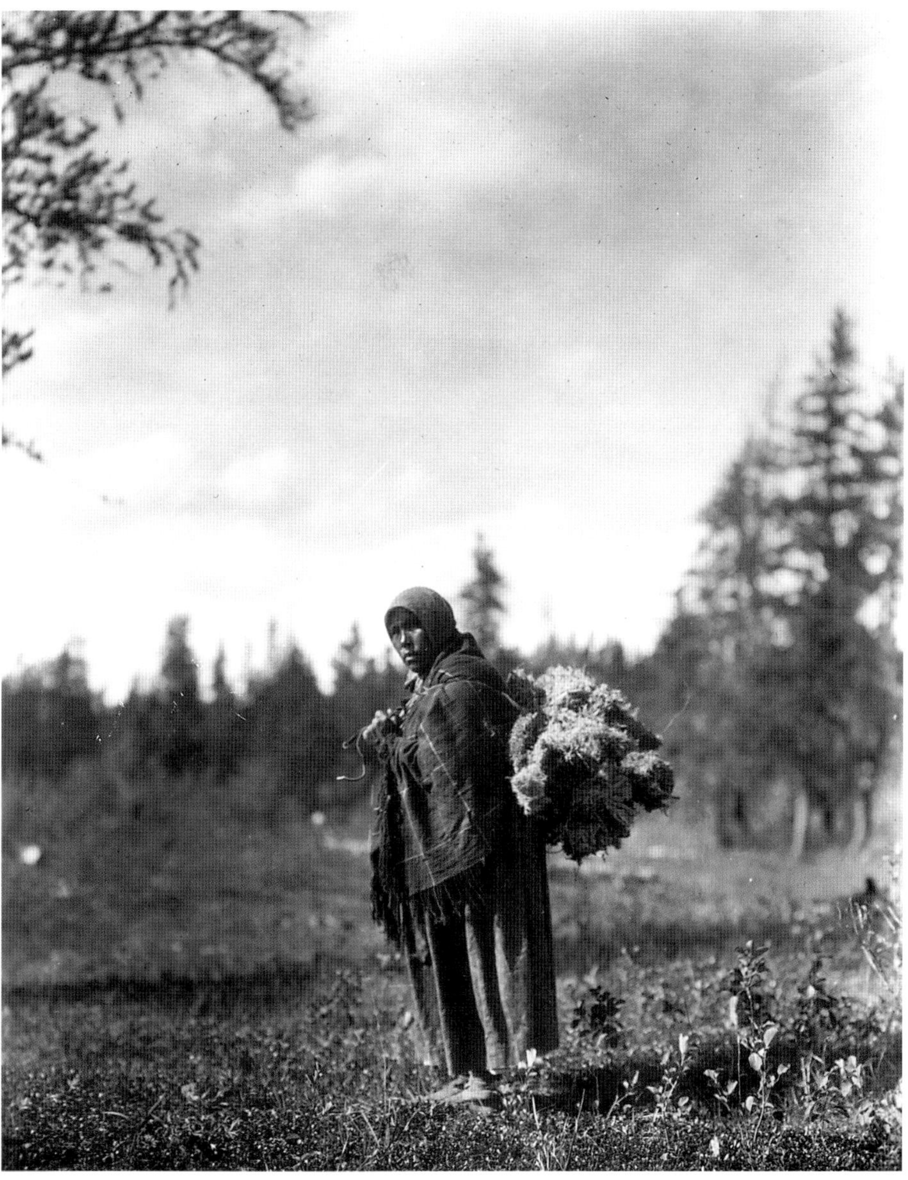

The Southwest

Curtis visited many of the desert-dwelling southwestern tribes, in the present states of Arizona, New Mexico, and parts of western Texas and northern Mexico, including several of the Pueblo tribes, the Navajo and Apache, the Pima and Maricopa, and the Walapai, Havasupai, Yavapai, Yuma, and Mohave. He was most active among the Navajo and with the Hopi, whom he visited seven times between 1900 and 1919. He photographed the women gathering and preparing food, fetching water (a constant concern in this arid region), making pottery and weaving, and dressed for ceremonies.

The eastern Pueblo tribes live in villages along the Rio Grande valley. Curtis spent less time with these groups than he did with the western Pueblos, but he photographed the San Ildefonso, Santa Clara, and San Juan Pueblos, among others. The western groups, in addition to the Hopi towns in eastern Arizona, include the Zuni, Acoma, and Laguna of central New Mexico. The Pueblo peoples were farmers who were successful in maintaining their cultural integrity. With religious beliefs closely tied to food sources, they spent a great deal of their time in ceremonies and rituals revolving around rain and corn. The current economy, however, is largely centered around cash, especially based on arts and crafts.

Speakers of a Southern Athapaskan language that became Apache and Navajo had arrived in the region by 1500. They began to dominate many areas once they acquired horses, and their culture became a mix of Pueblo, Plains, and Spanish traits. There were seven recognized Apachean-speaking tribes: the Kiowa Apache, the Jicarilla Apache (with whom Curtis spent the most time), the Lipan Apache, the Mescalero Apache, the Chiricahua Apache, the Western Apache, and Navajo.

The Upland Yuman–speaking groups of northwestern Arizona, including the Walapai, Yavapai, and Havasupai, were visited only briefly by Curtis. To their south were the Upper Pima and Papago and the River Yuman Maricopa, whom Curtis also visited briefly. Most of his time with the River Yumans along the Colorado River was spent with the Mohave.

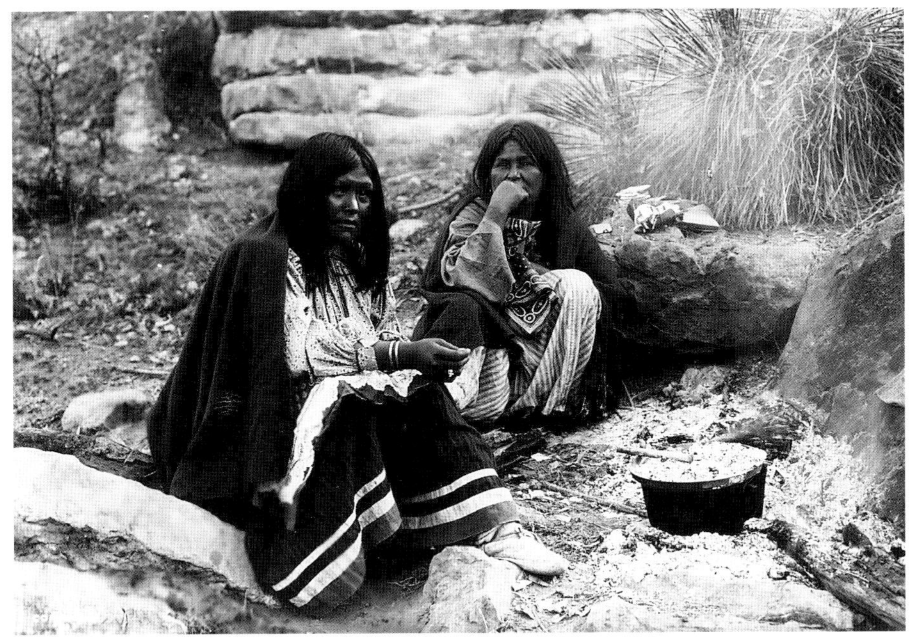

Women at Campfire—Apache, ©1903

According to Curtis, when Apache women finished unloading their horses in preparation for camping overnight, they filled their pitch-covered water baskets at the stream and gathered fuel for preparing the meal. They waterproofed the twined baskets intended to be water bottles by rubbing a mixture of mashed juniper leaves and ground hematite onto the surface and then applying heated piñon pitch to both the inside and the outside. When they were not traveling, the Western Apache lived in wickiups, dome-shaped houses built by the women with mesquite, willow, or cottonwood poles and secured by yucca cord. Except in rain and cold weather, the house was not covered completely, as this would prevent air flow. Wickiups were used only for sleeping; other activities were performed outside. Apache women also made baskets for many different uses.

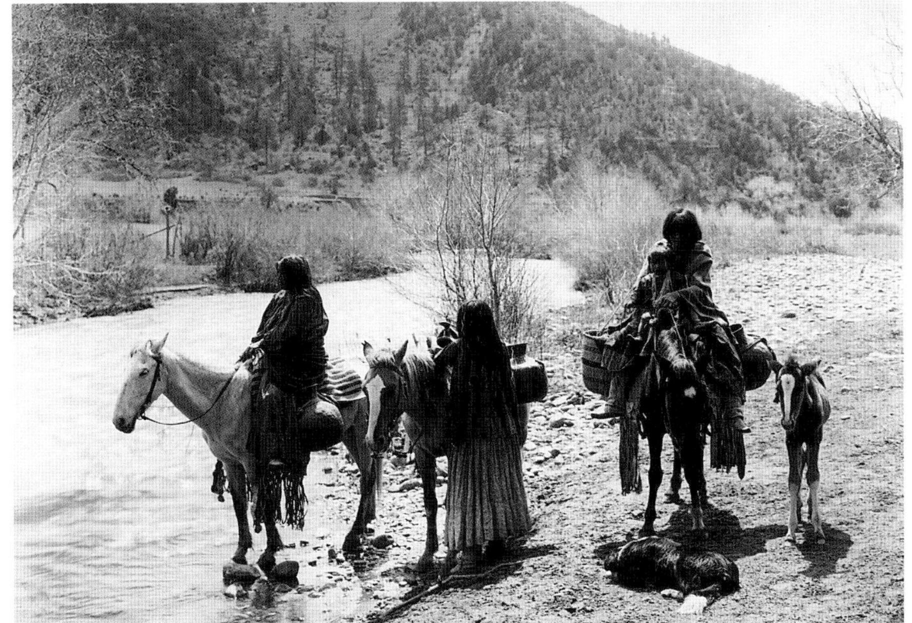

At the Ford—Apache, ©1903

Western Apache women would load many of their possessions onto horses, including children; blankets; a burden basket containing foodstuffs; a pitch-covered, woven water bottle; and a large rawhide carryall containing family supplies and extra clothing. Presumably this was the group that Curtis reported watching as they forded the Black River, in Arizona, on their way to the mountains to harvest mescal tubers, a staple of the Apache groups. They had risen early so as to travel in the cool morning hours. The women harvested the mescal using a pointed stick to uproot the budding plant and a stone hammer to sever its root. They then trimmed the leaves with a hatchetlike knife, producing a cabbage-shaped crown weighing from five to twenty pounds. Mescal plants harvested over several days were roasted for forty-eight hours in rock-lined pits covered with green brush, grass, dry leaves, and a layer of earth to keep in the steam. The hearts were then cut up for immediate consumption while the rest was pounded into large, flat, rectangular cakes and dried.

JICARILLA MAIDEN, ©1904

"This pictures exceedingly well the typical Jicarilla woman's dress: a cape of deerskin, beaded, a broad belt of black leather, a deerskin skirt, and the hair fastened at each side of the head with a large knot of yarn or cloth," said Curtis of this photograph. The girl's clothing would also have included legging-moccasins.

The Jicarilla's Southern Athapaskan language and culture reflected an interesting blend of influences, including their contacts with Plains tribes and the Pueblo groups. The tribe typically lived in tipis and made periodic trips from their mountain home in southeastern Colorado and northern New Mexico to the eastern plains to hunt buffalo. Farming was a family effort. The men prepared the fields and dug the irrigation ditches, while the women seeded, hoed, weeded, and harvested the maize, beans, squash, and other crops.

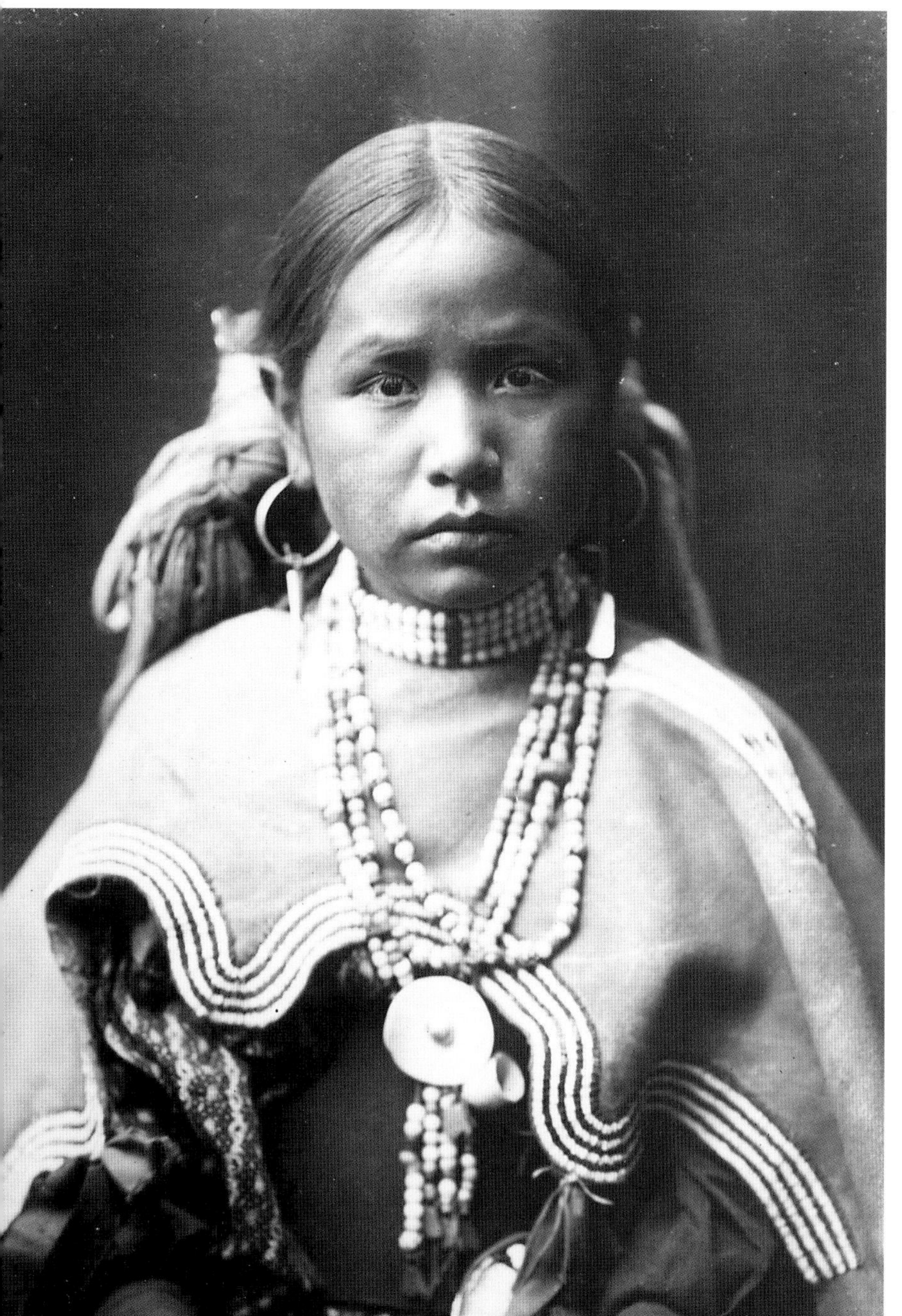

A NAVAJO SMILE, ©1904 *(opposite)*

This portrait is rare among Curtis's work for the relaxed openness of the young woman's smile. Their Athapaskan language and many cultural similarities indicate that the Navajo and the Apache came originally from the same northern source about 1,000 years ago. This woman is wearing the full cloth skirt and velveteen blouse, adapted from Euro-American culture, that became the traditional dress of Navajo women. In addition to their fame as weavers, Curtis said, "The women of the Navajo are for the greater part, the owners of the flocks and invariably, with the children, the herders." Traditionally, the Navajo were a matrilineal tribe in which camps were presided over by "headmothers." The Navajo origin story of Changing Woman, born of darkness and dawn, credits her with creating corn and the first Navajo people. Changing Woman was adopted by First Man and First Woman, who held a puberty ceremony, which is still celebrated for all Navajo girls reaching womanhood.

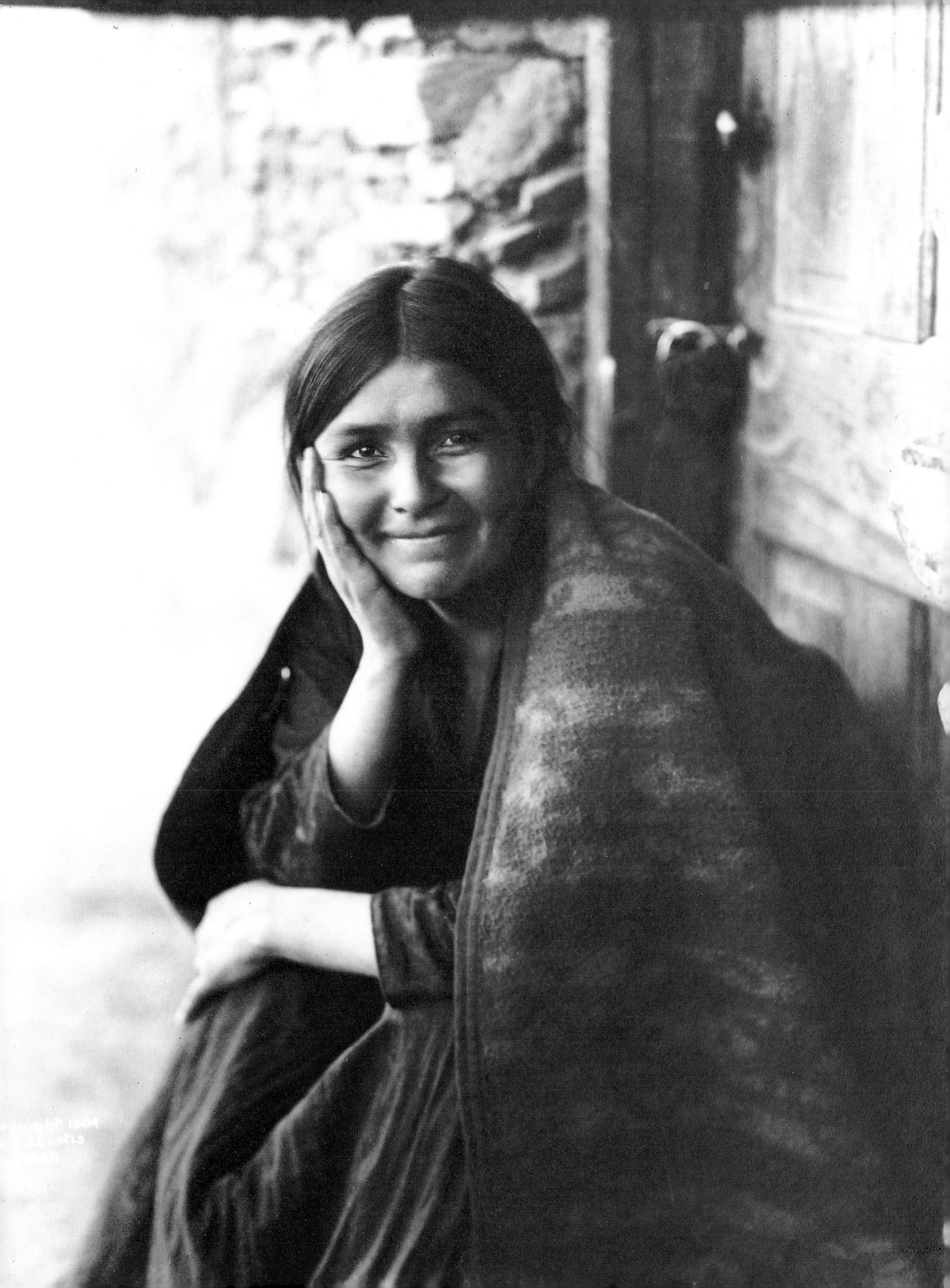

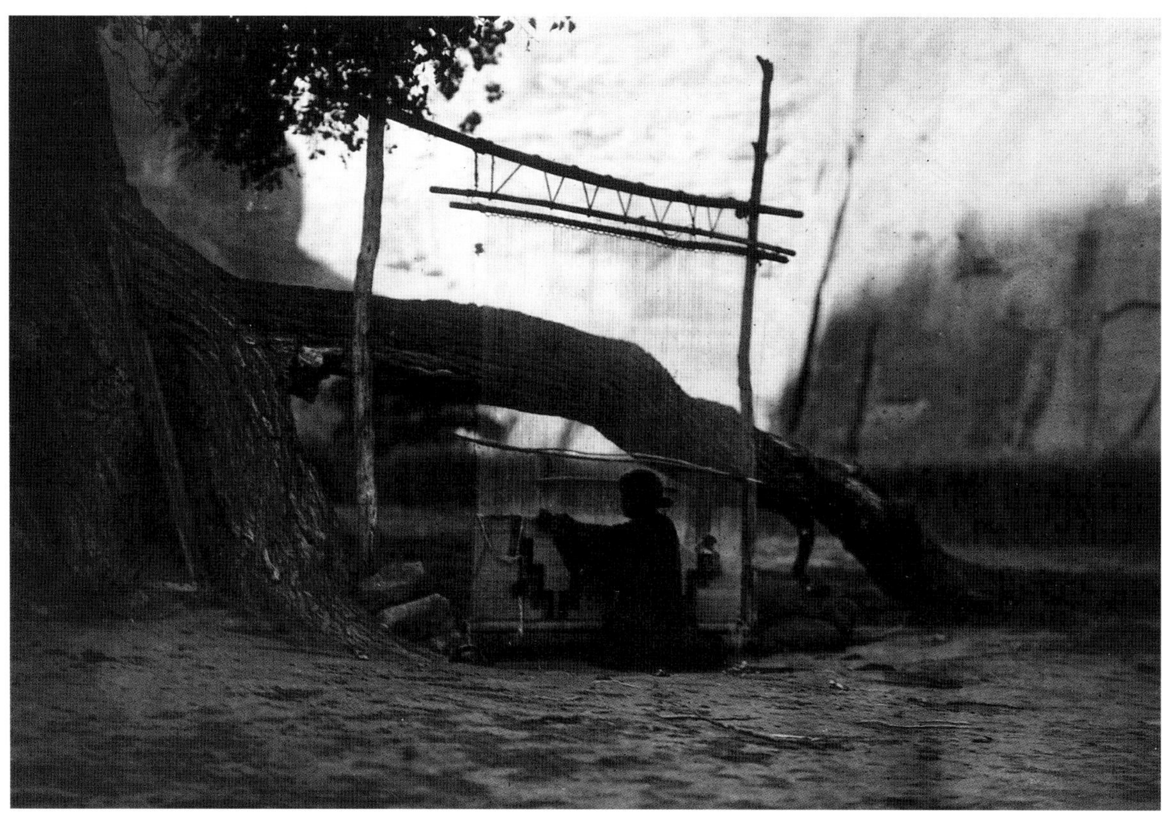

THE BLANKET WEAVER—NAVAJO, ©1904

"In Navaho-land blanket looms are in evidence everywhere," wrote Curtis. "In the winter months, the looms are set up in the hogans, but during the summer they are erected outdoors under an improvised shelter, or, as in this case, beneath a tree." The blankets produced by Navajo women are among the most widely recognized crafts produced by any North American tribe. While many anthropologists believe that the Navajo learned how to weave from the Pueblo, with indirect Spanish influence in designs, the Navajo themselves believe that Spider Woman instructed their women how to weave on a loom at their entrance into this world. Whatever the origin, the Navajo women initially wove cloth of wool or cotton for clothing. The blanket product was developed in the nineteenth century. The Navajo churro sheep's double coats produce long, coarse, greaseless fibers that are perfect for hand-carding and spinning, and their natural colors range from white, through various earth tones, to black. Vegetable dyes produced from plants, bark, and roots gave almost unlimited colors. Today a women's cooperative at the Ramah Navajo Reservation in west-central New Mexico has modernized the traditional methods of blanket production, from raising sheep to weaving.

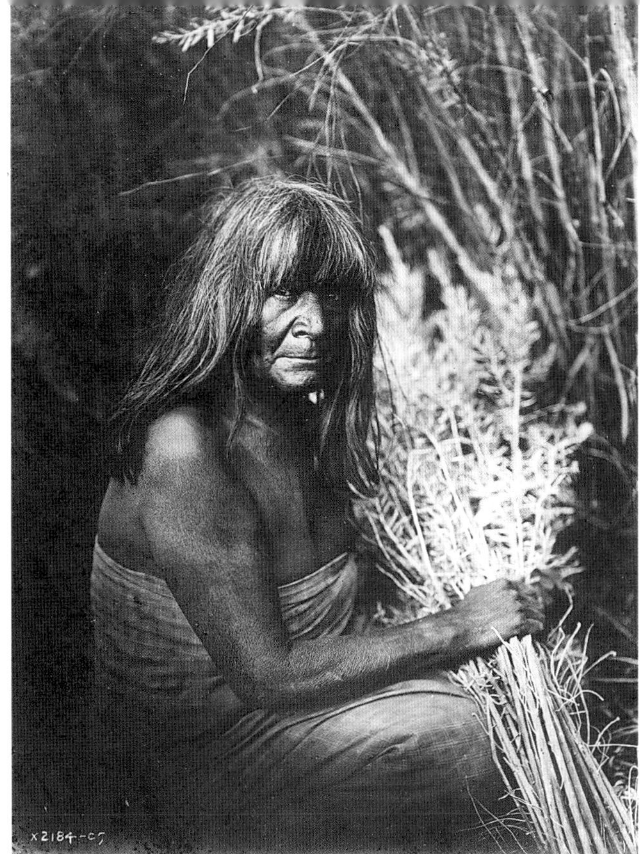

Hipáh with Arrow-Brush—Maricopa, ©1907

"Arrow-brush is extensively used by the tribes of this region as a covering for their houses," wrote Curtis. "In earlier times they lived in circular houses constructed of a framework of heavy poles covered with arrow-brush and coated with mud. In many of the modern rectangular houses, also, the arrow-brush is used, bound together closely with withes, and plastered on the outside with adobe." For this reason, the Western Apache called the Papago, Pima, and Maricopa the "sand-house people."

Following Maricopa custom, Hipáh's face was probably tattooed following her first menstrual seclusion. Maricopa women made pottery using the bottom of an old pot as a mold; they beat the clay into the desired thickness with a wooden paddle and then built up the sides of the pot with clay rolls. The pots were dried in the sun and then fired if they were to be used for cooking or holding water. Smaller pots were decorated with red or white clay slips or black paint made from the woody portions of mesquite trees.

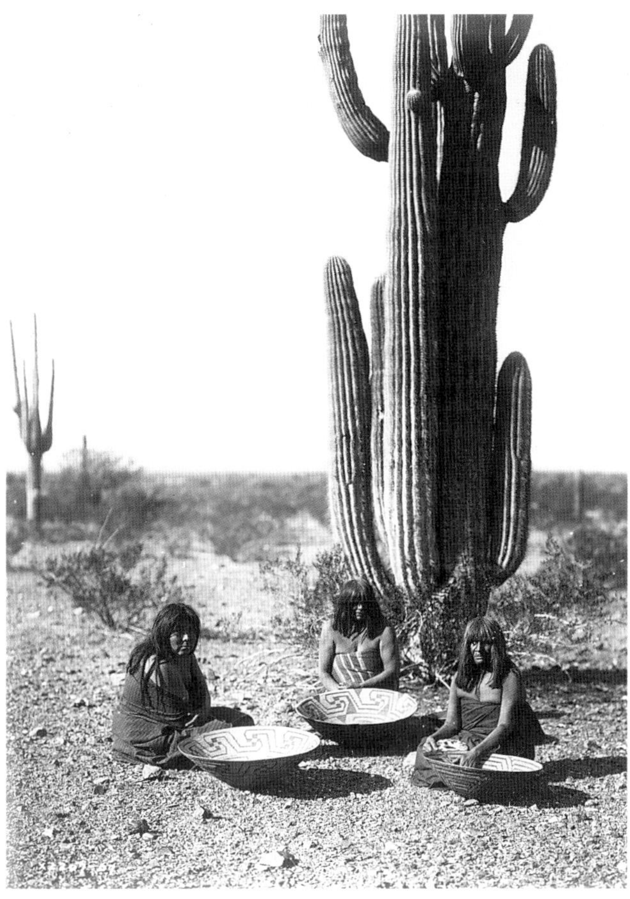

Saguaro Fruit Gatherers—Maricopa, ©1907

While men did the planting and cultivating of maize, beans, squash, cotton, wheat, and melons—the last three crops were introduced by the Spanish—women did the harvesting. They also gathered mesquite beans and cholla buds, ironwood nuts, seeds, berries, and honey—and saguaro cactus fruit. The saguaro cactus can grow as tall as fifty feet. Maricopa women went into the desert in June through mid-July with long poles for knocking the fig-sized fruit from the tops of the cactus. The fruit of the saguaro was eaten raw, dried, and also made into syrup, jam, and ceremonial wine. The wine was made by boiling crushed fruit in water, straining, and cooking again to produce a thick red syrup. Some of this syrup was stored in earthenware jars and allowed to ferment.

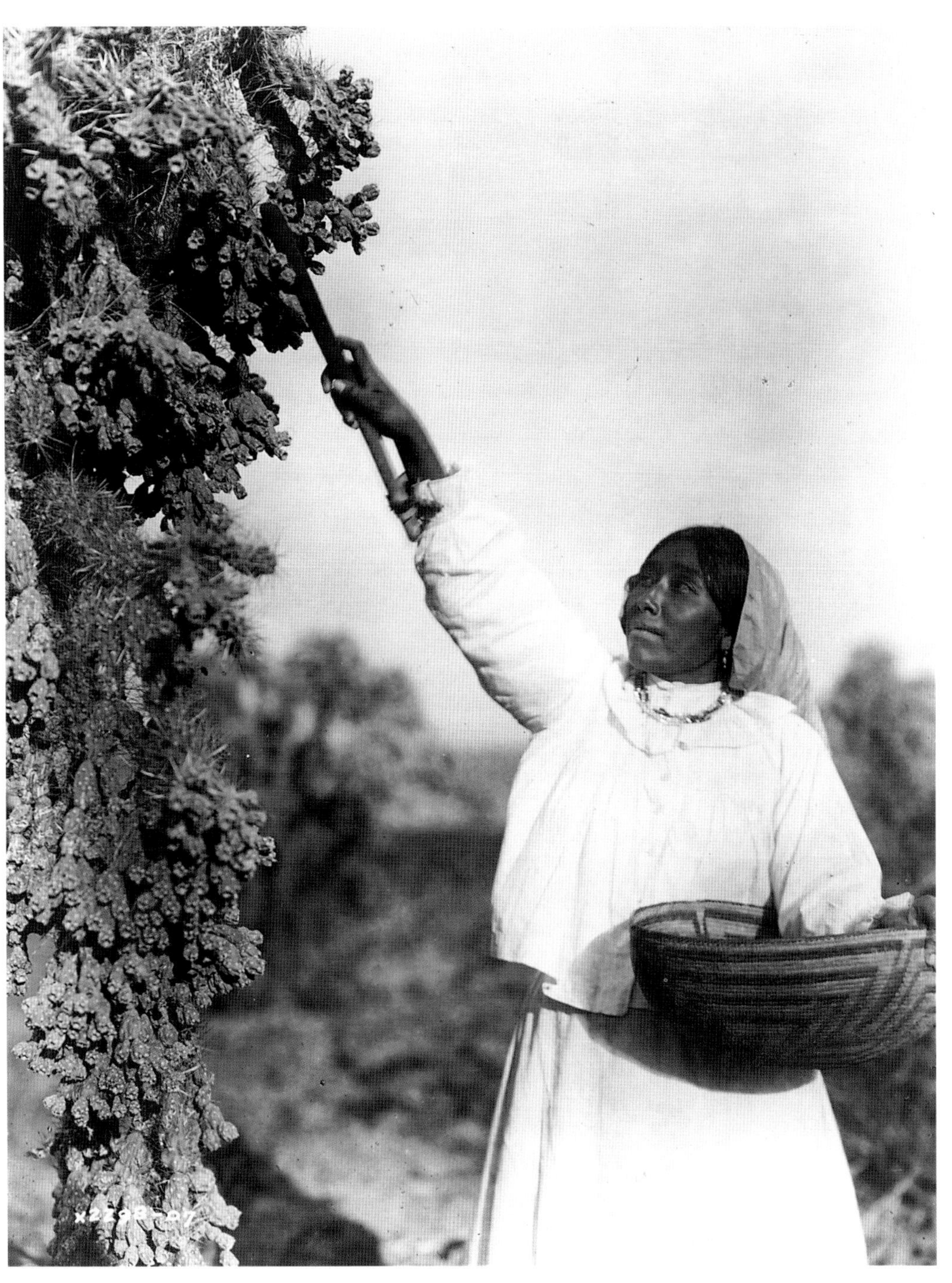

Gathering Hánamh, ©1907

"Hánamh is the Piman name for the cholla cactus and its fruit," wrote Curtis in his caption for this photograph. "The natives gather the fruit of this spiny plant in large quantities, and it forms a food of material importance to the several tribes living within its habitat. In gathering it they use rude tongs made from a split stick. After a basket is filled, the fruit is spread on the ground and brushed about with a small, stiff besom until the spines are worn off, or the spines are burned off in an open fire." The Tohono O'odham (Papago) live in the central Pimeria Alta, Arizona, a region of the Sonoran Desert characterized by high mountain ranges and valleys and low altitude plains. They had winter houses next to permanent water springs in the mountain foothills and summer dwellings on the plains, where they farmed on lands washed by summer rains.

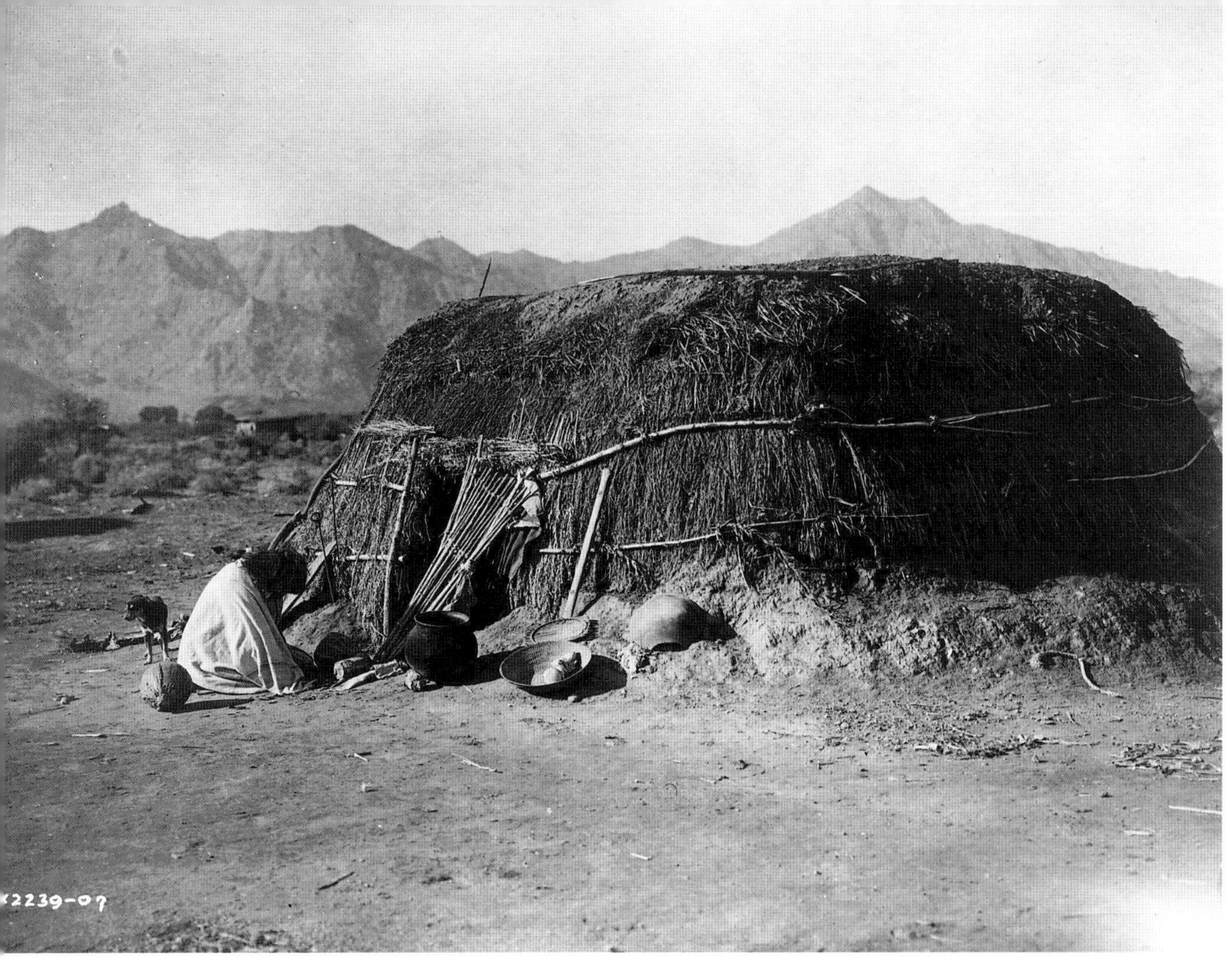

PIMA KI, ©1907

The Pima live in permanent villages along the Salt and Gila Rivers, near present-day Phoenix. Curtis's photograph shows a traditional flat-roofed, round Pima dwelling built of a framework covered with material such as wheat straw, arrowweed, or cattail reeds and then covered with earth. Pottery jars and baskets would contain stores of foodstuffs, particularly corn and mesquite beans. Women generally worked outdoors, as in this photograph. Rectangular structures with arbor roofs located next to most houses served as drying platforms for corn, bolls of cotton, and straw. The women did most of their food preparation, basket weaving, and other tasks in the shade of these arbors. Today the Hoo-Hoogam Ki Museum on the Salt River Reservation highlights the superb Pima basket-making tradition.

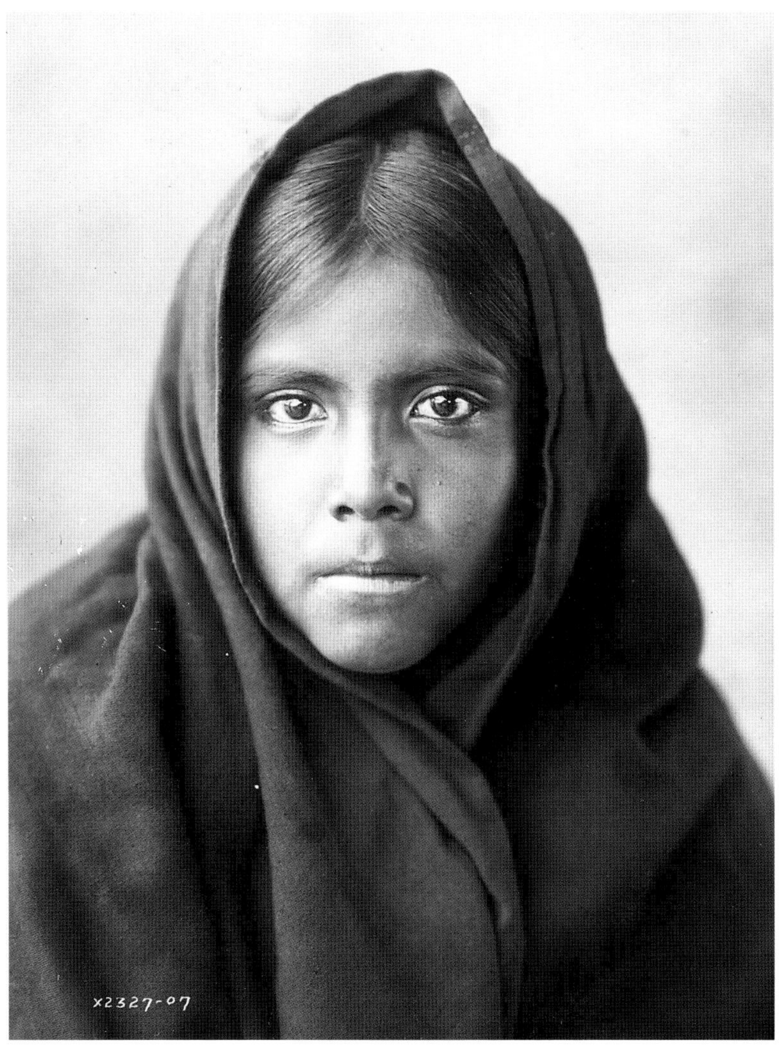

Qahátika Girl, ©1907

This young girl's wide-eyed beauty—which Curtis himself emphasized by framing her face with a shawl—belies what Curtis had to say about her tribe, the Qahátika of the desert Southwest. Marveling at the ability of this Pima group to survive in the desert, Curtis said, "A stranger would regard their sandy waste as beyond human subjection, yet these people manage to wrest an existence from it." However, Curtis also remarked on their lack of courtesy in comparison to their neighbors, the Pima and Papago: "Their never-ending struggle with the hostile desert seems to have left its mark." Curtis reported that Indian tradition explained the separation of the Qahátika from their Pima ancestors on the Gila River by their escape into the desert following an Apache attack. When Curtis visited them before 1907, he found the Qahátika living in five small villages about forty miles due south of the Pima Gila River Indian Reservation in central Arizona. Although they still depended on gathering mesquite beans and cactus fruits, noted Curtis, they also located their villages where drainage from storms allowed them to grow wheat. Like other southwestern tribes, the Qahátika were skilled in pottery and basket making, including the burden baskets that they used for gathering.

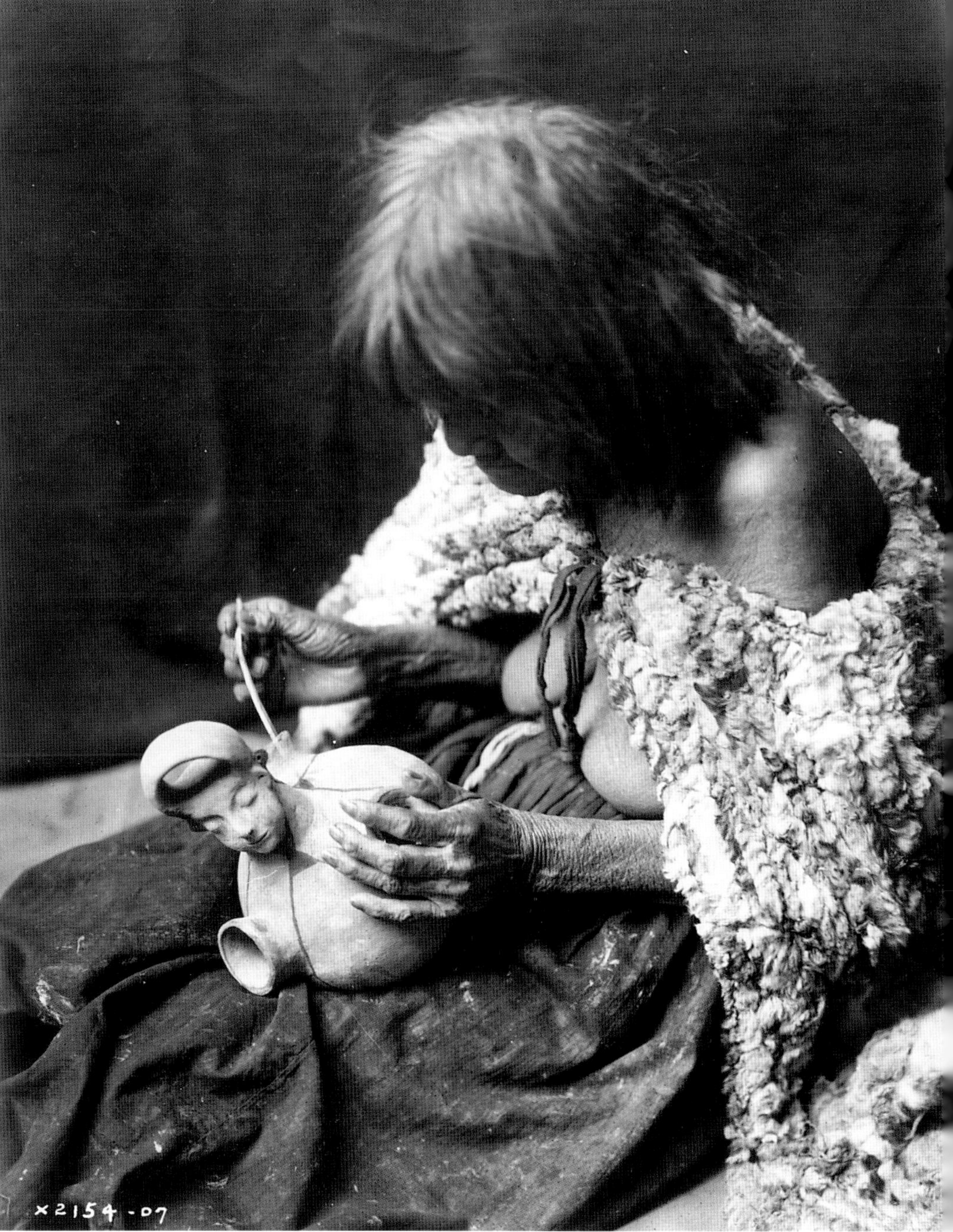

Mohave Potter, ©1907

Curtis's artistry in lighting the subject against a dark background is apparent in this photograph of an elderly Mohave woman absorbed in her work of decorating a pottery vessel, using a yucca stem brush. In addition to the pottery that they made for domestic use, Mohave women also made items for the tourist trade: the four-spouted vessel with a handle in the shape of a human head shown here was probably manufactured for selling to Anglos. Rabbit-skin robes, such as the one worn by this woman, were used by the Mohave in colder weather.

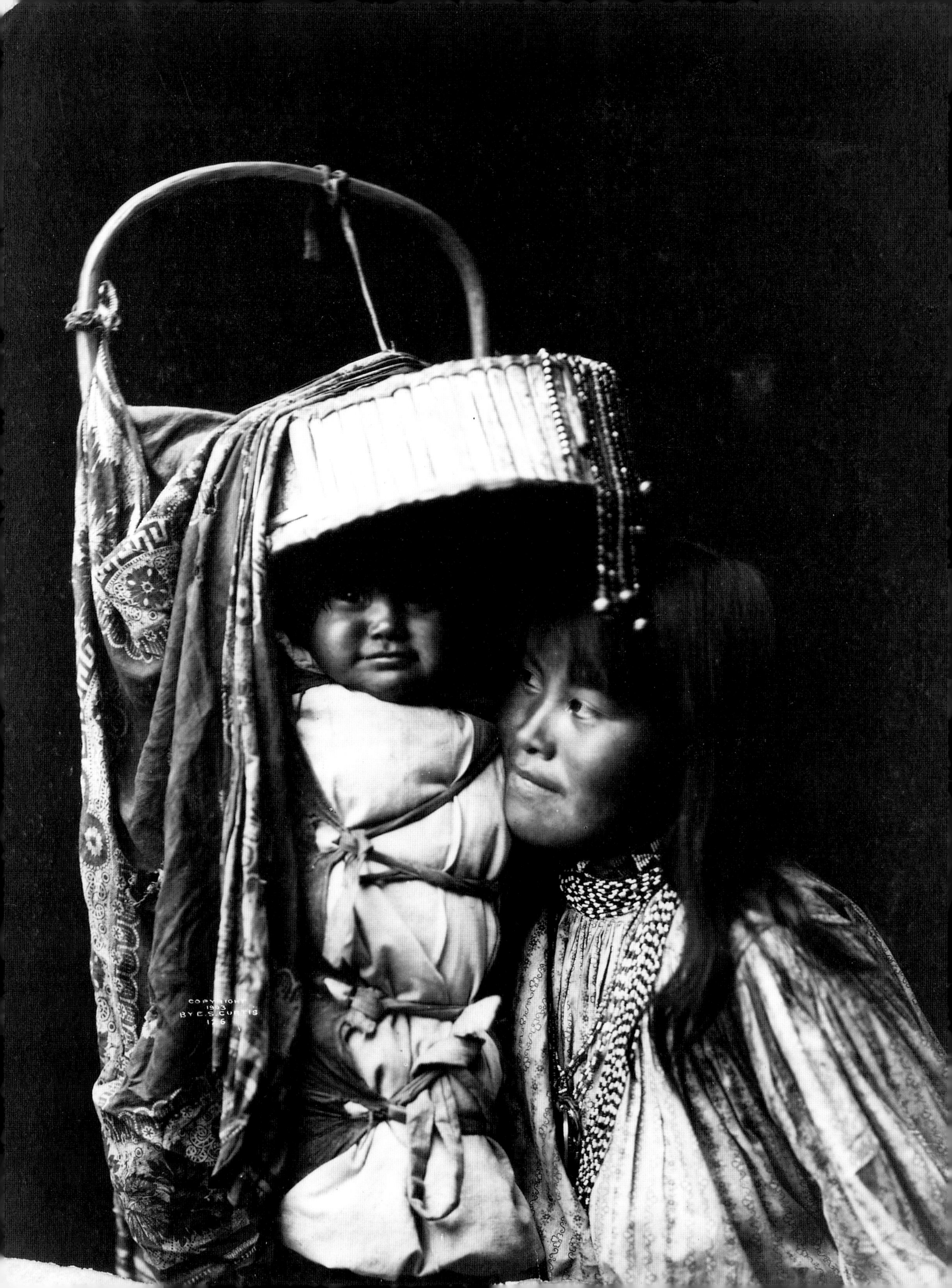
COPYRIGHT
1903
BY E.S. CURTIS
126

"MOHAVE" GIRL AND PAPOOSE, ©1903 *(opposite)*

Curtis took two photographs of this laughing baby strapped snugly into its cradleboard, one with a young woman, possibly its mother, and one on its own. This one, which was mistakenly labeled *Mohave Girl and Papoose,* was not published by Curtis in his twenty-volume work. The other, which he published as *An Apache Babe* in the volume 1 portfolio of *The North American Indian,* he called "a fortunate child picture, giving a good idea of the happy disposition of Indian children. . . ." The baby and its caretaker were in fact Yavapai.

In his chapter on the Apache, Curtis described "the Apache-Mohave, of Yuman stock, whose domain extended along the Rio Verde in central Arizona, immediately adjacent to the territory over which the Apache proper held undisputed sway." The Yavapai were of the same Upland Yuman language family as the Walapai and Havasupai. One of the four Yavapai reservation communities, Fort McDowell Reservation, was designated a "Mohave-Apache Reservation" by the federal government when it was established in 1903, thus contributing to the confusion over their proper name.

Yavapai babies were kept with their mothers constantly, or with other female relatives, while the women went about their daily tasks. Cradleboards—made primarily by the women, in addition to other baskets for their own use and for trading—not only provided a strong, protective frame, but also their hoods provided protection from the sun. Babies in cradleboards were carried on women's backs or on horseback, and they were propped up or even hung from trees.

At the Old Well of Acoma, ©1904

According to Curtis, members of Francisco Vásquez de Coronado's army of explorers in 1540 noted the "cisterns to collect snow and water" on the Acoma mesa. These natural cisterns, where rainwater collected, were located both on the mesa and below it and supplied all of the village's water needs. Curtis's photograph is both an aesthetically pleasing record of an important Acoma women's task and a display for the beautifully crafted pots made by them. Like all other Keresan groups, Acoma remains a closed system and in this way keeps its traditions and culture viable in today's fast-changing world.

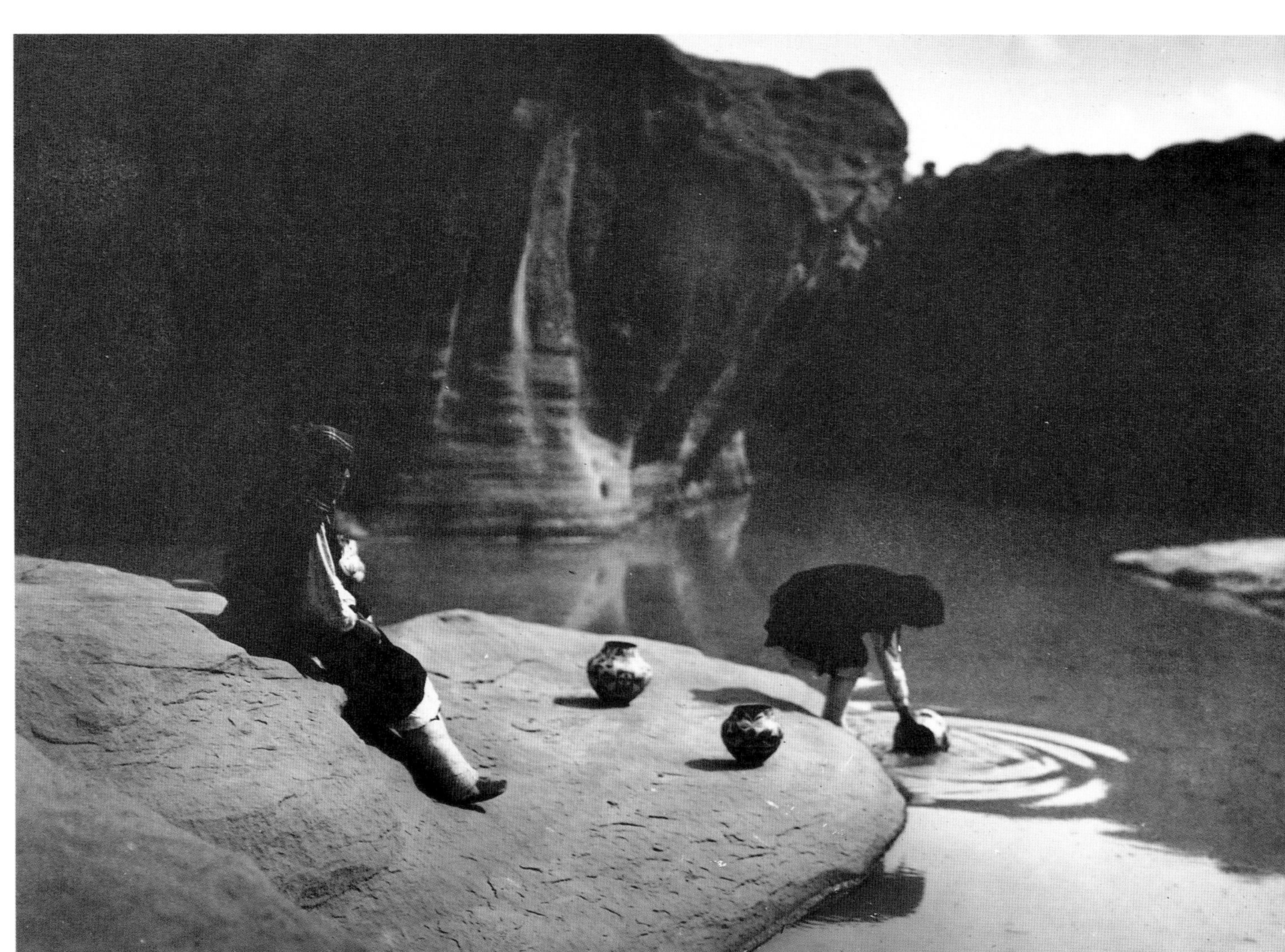

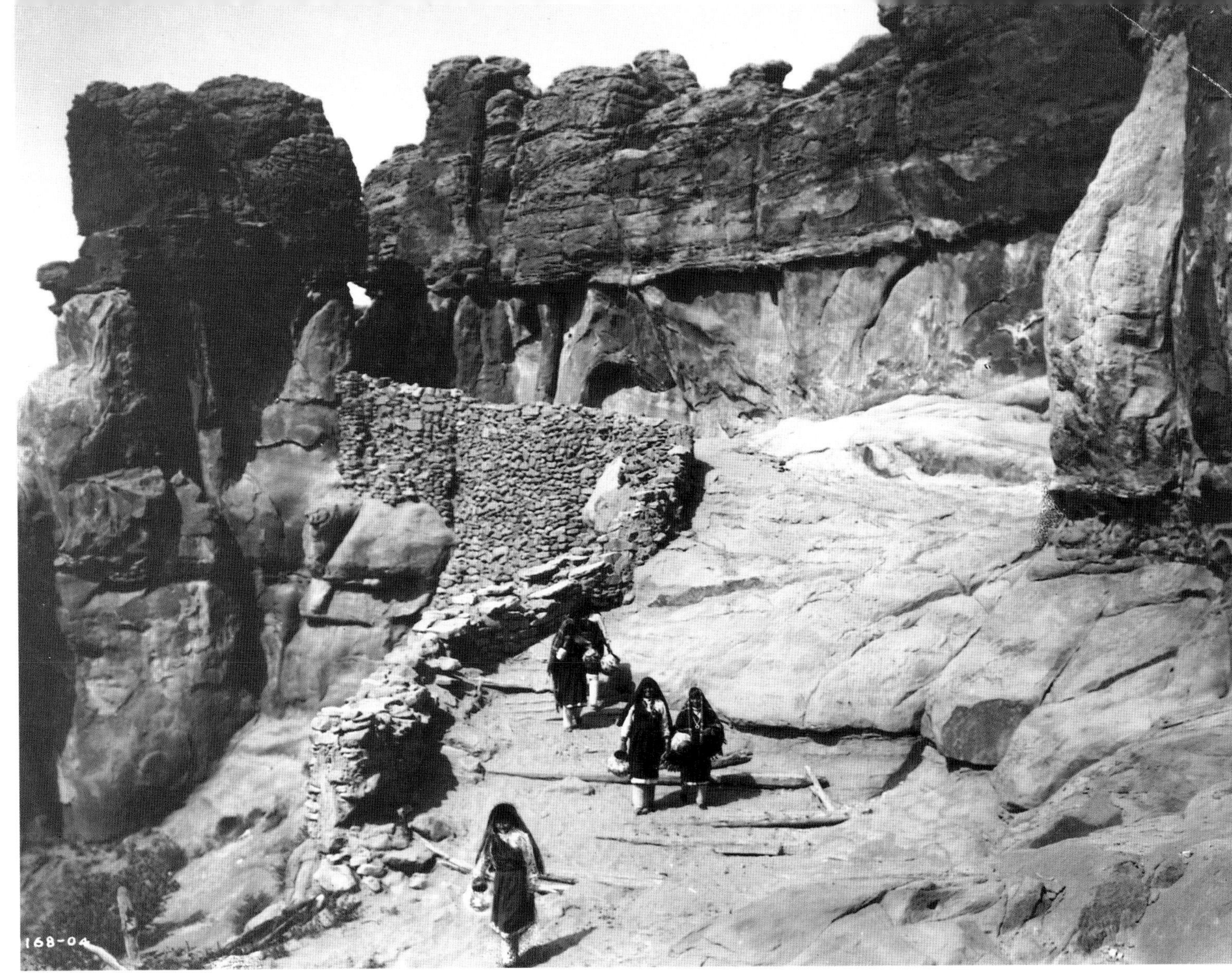

Acoma Roadway, ©1904

The village of Acoma is the westernmost of the Keresan pueblos, built atop a mesa about fifty miles west of Albuquerque, New Mexico. It is the oldest continuously occupied settlement in the United States. Perched some 350 feet above the surrounding valley, it is accessible only by difficult trails partly cut in the solid rock of its precipices, making it a natural fortress against attack. Curtis photographed the southern entrance to the Acoma mesa with women in traditional dress and carrying earthenware pots descending the narrow and rugged trail to the water cistern. When Curtis made this photograph, the Acoma's population was about 750; it is estimated to be around 4,000 today. Most tribal members now live in the farming villages of McCartys and Acomita, located on the plain about fifteen miles from the Acoma mesa on the south bank of the Rio San Jose. However, a few families choose to continue to live on the Acoma mesa, where they are visited by as many as one million tourists a year.

The Hopi

Curtis was particularly enchanted by the Hopi of Walpi, westernmost of the Pueblos and speakers of a Uto-Aztecan language. He first visited them early in his project, when he was young, well funded, and full of energy and enthusiasm. Fascinated by their ceremonialism, particularly the Snake Dance, he visited the Hopi seven times between 1900 and 1919. He made many photographs of Hopi girls in traditional costume with their hair arranged in the complicated and time-consuming squash blossom arrangement that indicated their unmarried status. He also photographed a solemn Hopi bride in her bridal costume and with her hairstyle indicating her new marital status. Winning the trust of the villagers, he took many photographs of their daily life, including young women at work at a mealing bin and a Hopi housewife making piki (corn bread).

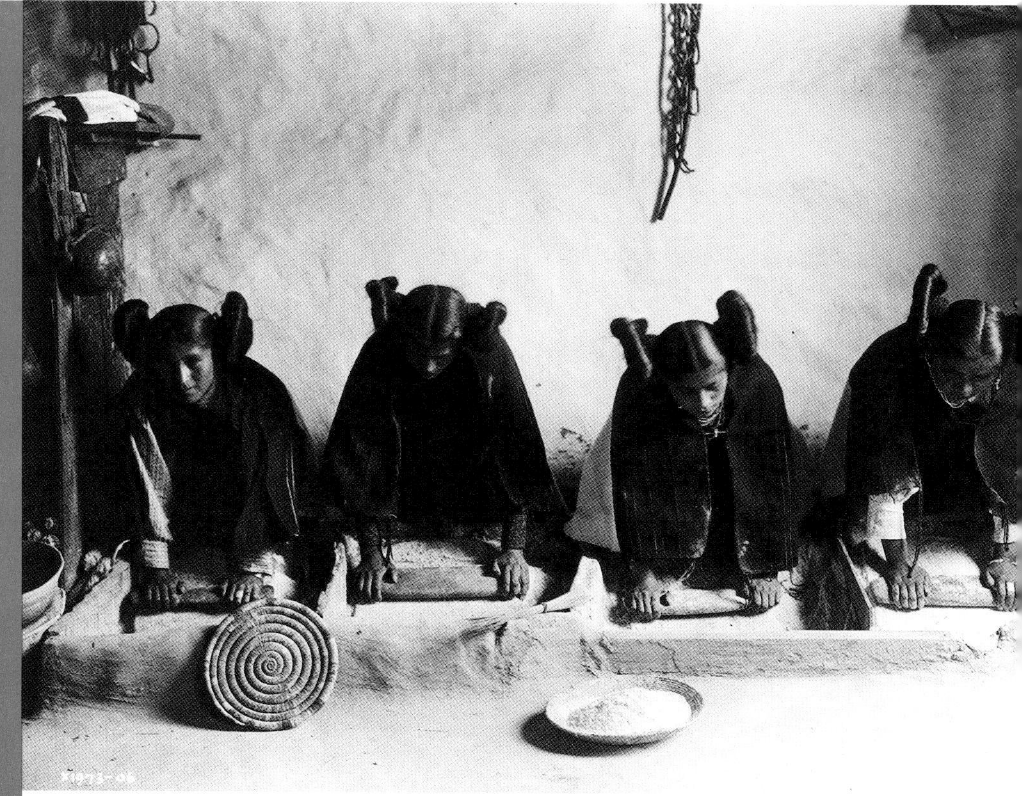

Grinding Meal, ©1907 *(opposite)*

Four unmarried girls—their unmarried status indicated by the distinctive whorls of their squash blossom hairstyles, a fashion that was disappearing when Curtis took this photograph—work together at a traditional mealing bin. Maize was so central to Hopi subsistence and culture that a Hopi girl was required to spend several days grinding corn in her future husband's house to demonstrate that she was qualified to be a wife. Curtis said girls and young women ground the corn early in the morning, often while singing grinding songs. Twenty-five pounds of cornmeal was considered to be a good day's work for a skillful corn grinder. Most pueblo houses included compartmentalized bins, like the one shown here, consisting of a series of flat slabs of sandstone of varying degrees of fineness cemented into the floor, leaving just enough space for the women to kneel with their backs to the wall. The corn was crushed on the coarsest stone by rubbing it with a basalt or lava mano, reduced to coarse meal with a sandstone mano on the second stone, and brought to a fineness almost equivalent to flour with the smoothest mano on a third, and sometimes even a fourth, stone.

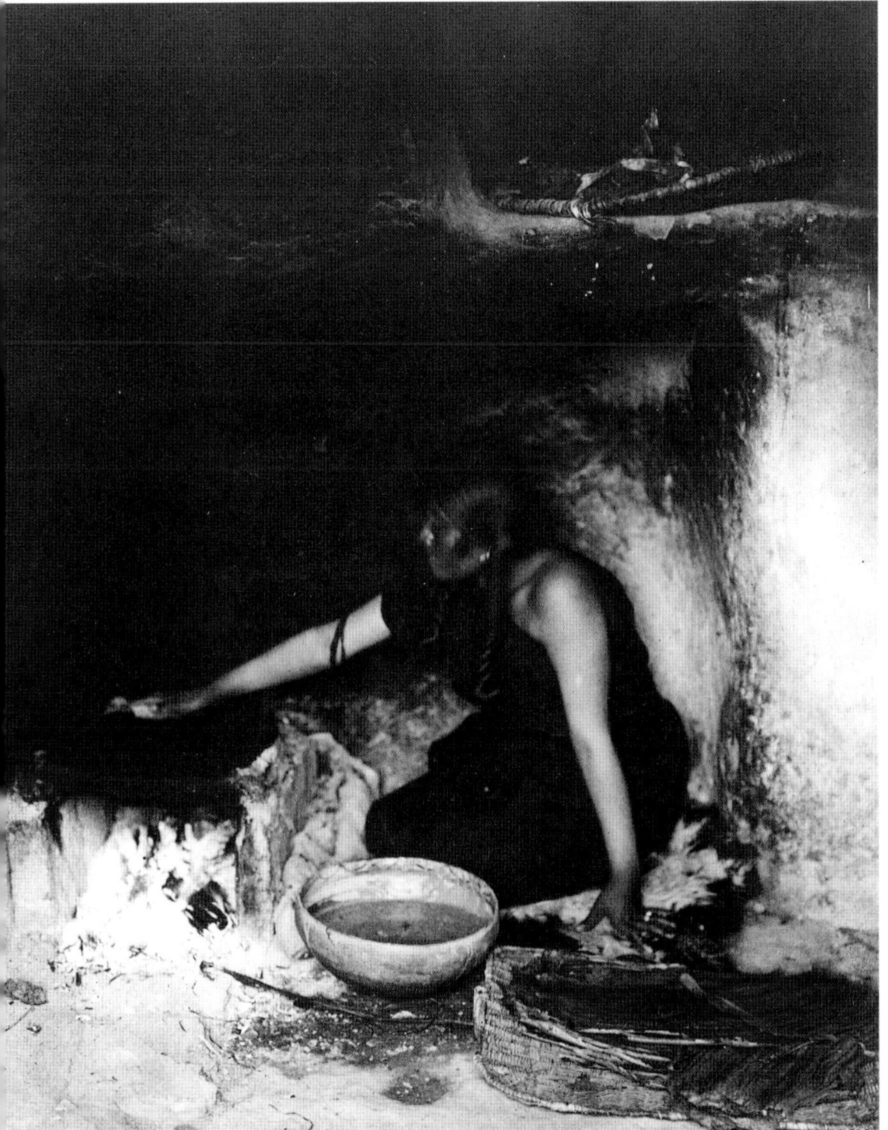

The Piki Maker, ©1906

Piki is wafer-thin bread made from blue cornmeal and baked in sheets. Curtis described how the batter was spread on the baking stone with the bare hand; the quickly baked sheet was then folded and laid on the basket at the baker's left. The baking stone was placed in a small room in the first story of a Hopi house or, in Walpi, "in a cell built in a niche at the edge of the cliff with its roof and hatchway on the same level as the mesa top." A fire was kept burning under the stone all day.

This woman's married status is denoted by her hair, which is parted in the center and wrapped with a long, dark blue cotton string in plaits on each side of her face. She is wearing the traditional blue-black sleeveless tunic of the Hopi women.

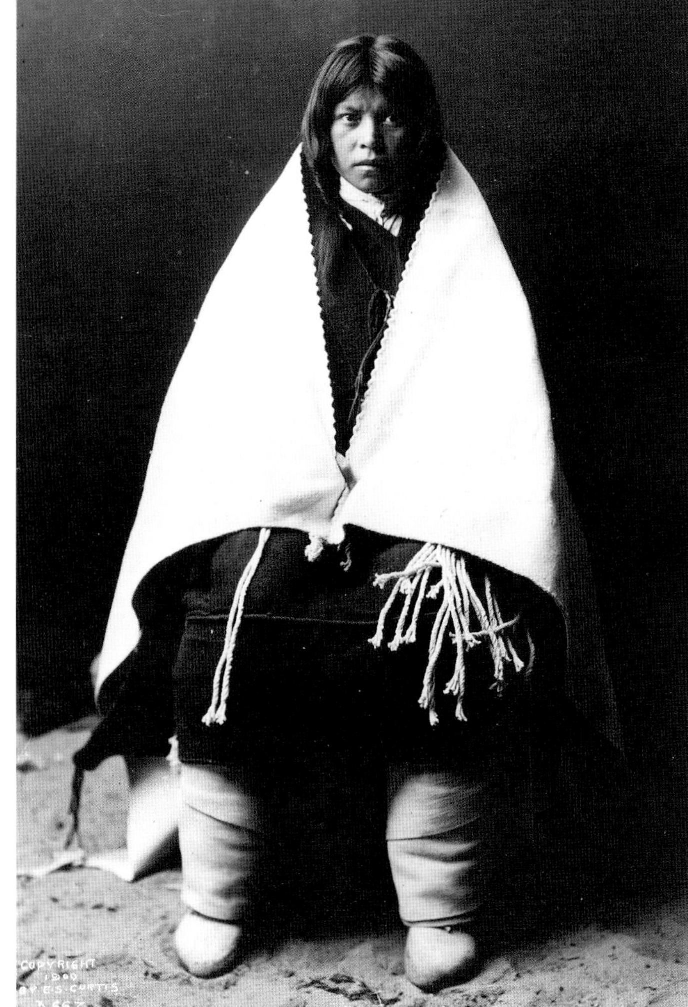

Hopi Bridal Costume, ©1900

A Hopi girl could directly propose marriage to a young man, but regardless of who made the initial proposal, elaborate marriage rites were the responsibility of the bride and of the female relatives of both bride and groom. Wedding preparations for the girl began when she spent several days at her mother's home grinding cornmeal and making piki. She then spent the next three days at her future mother-in-law's house grinding cornmeal from before dawn until late at night. Early on the fourth morning, the female relatives of the young woman brought over all the cornmeal and piki she had previously prepared; then the two mothers washed the couple's heads in one basin and twisted their hair together in one strand. The bridegroom and his male relatives were responsible for weaving one large and one small white wedding robe and a long, wide belt—weaving was a male preserve in the Hopi tribe. The rest of the wedding outfit included white deerskin legging-moccasins. The girl had to work hard and long to make enough cornmeal to pay for the wedding garments. Dressed in her wedding garments, the bride was led back to her mother's house, where her husband joined the household.

Watching the Dancers, ©1906

A group of girls on the highest rooftop in Walpi are looking down on one of the many ceremonial dances held throughout the year. They are described by Curtis as "perched on the point of a rocky island in a sea of sand . . . an irregular, rambling community, built without design, added to in haphazard fashion as need arose, yet constituting a perfectly satisfying artistic whole."

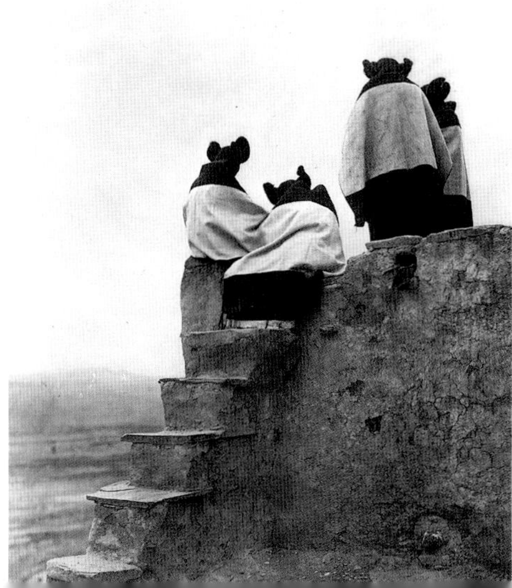

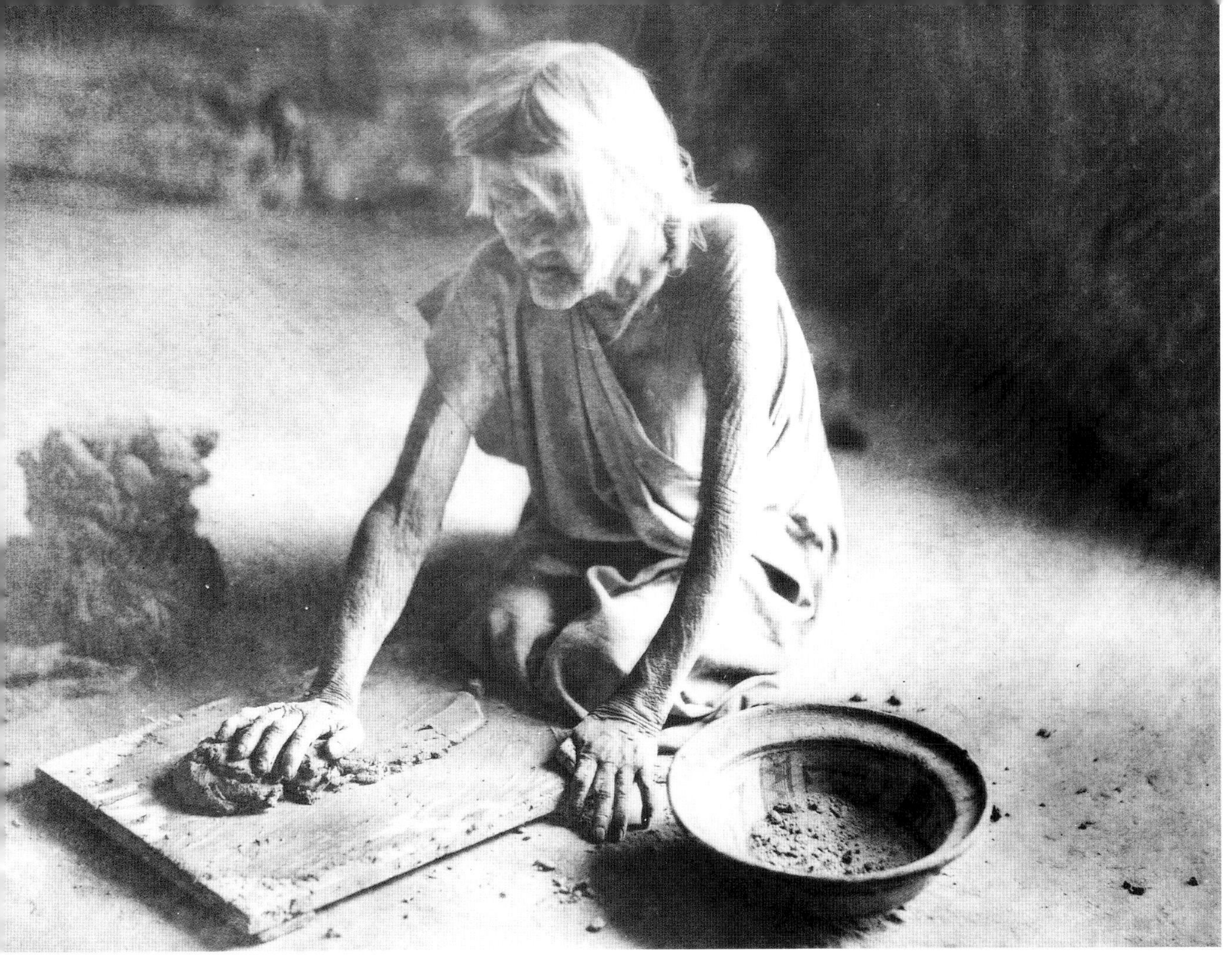

The Potter Mixing Clay, ©1921

Although this photograph was not copyrighted until 1921, Curtis probably took it in 1906, when he photographed the Tewa village of Hano in the eastern part of Hopi territory. Some Tano Tewa had migrated there from south of Santa Fe following the Pueblo Revolt of 1680 to 1692 and became known as Hopi-Tewa. Of this dramatically lit photograph, Curtis said only, "This woman, so aged that her shriveled skin hangs in folds, still finds pleasure in creating artistic and utilitarian pieces of pottery." Writing about Hopi pottery in volume 12 of *The North American Indian*, for which this is a portfolio photograph, he said that the Hano potter's clay was dug from under the rocks about the foothills of the mesa. When thoroughly dry, it was ground on the mealing stones and then soaked in water before it was mixed with pulverized sandstone or potsherds. This mixture was then thoroughly kneaded before it was shaped by hand into a pot.

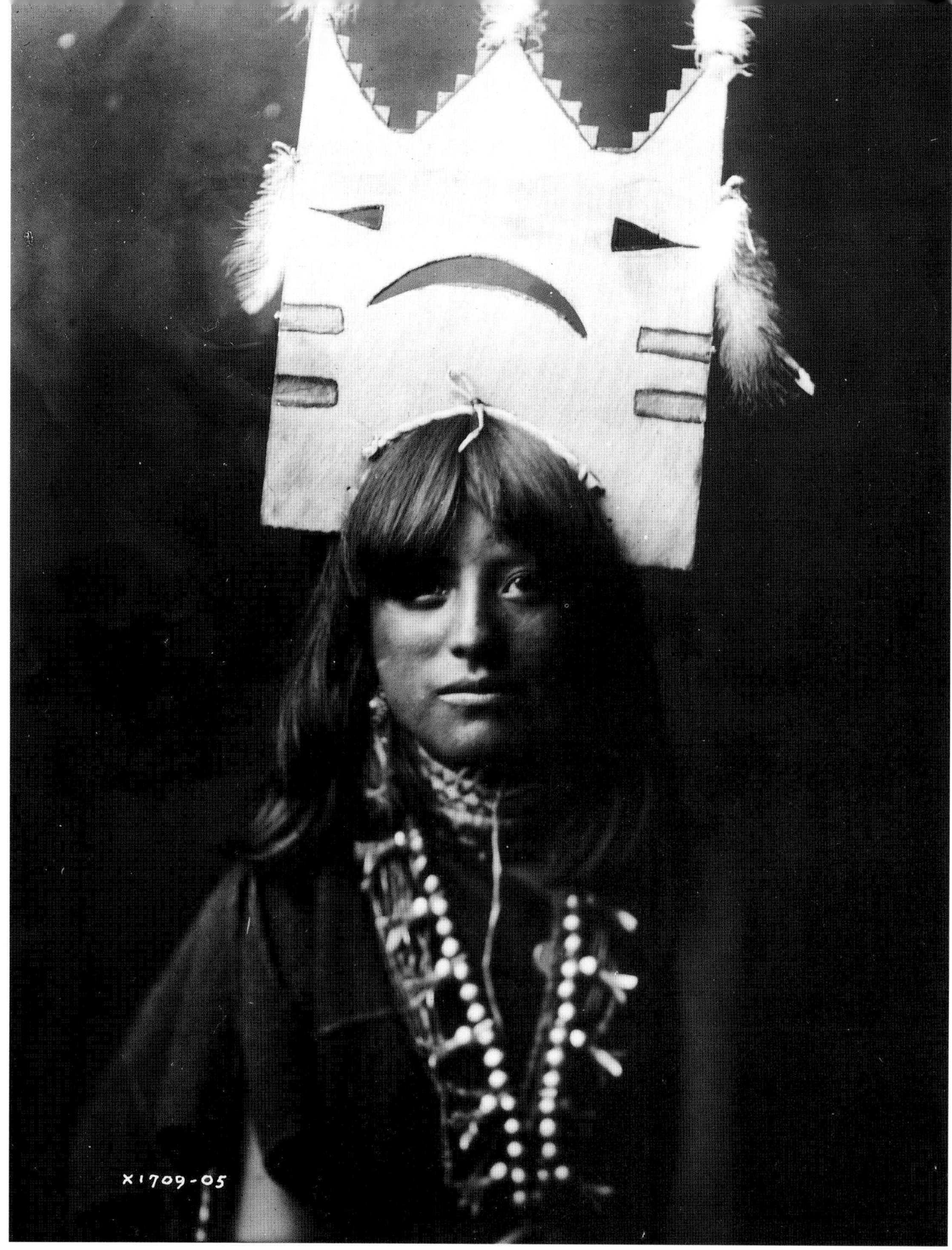

TABLITA WOMAN DANCER —SAN ILDEFONSO, ©1905

Ceremonies are at the heart of the Pueblo way of life and their belief in maintaining balance and harmony between the natural and supernatural worlds. Curtis's caption reads, "The ceremony called Kohéye-liyáre, 'tablita dance,' popularly called the Corn dance, occurring in June and again in September, is characterized by public dancing and singing for the purpose of bringing rain clouds. The name refers to wood 'tablets' worn by female dancers." San Ildefonso played a leading role in the 1680 to 1692 Pueblo Revolt against the Spanish and held out against Spanish reconquest on top of Black Mesa until 1694. Of the Tewa Pueblos, San Ildefonso was the least influenced by Christianity; not until well into the nineteenth century did Roman Catholic ritual begin to merge with traditional religious practices.

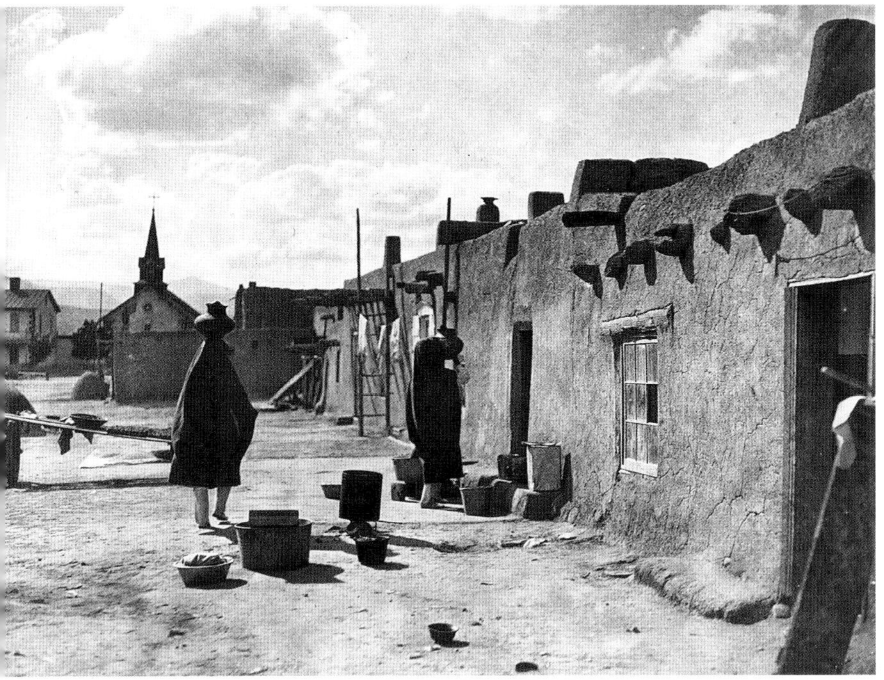

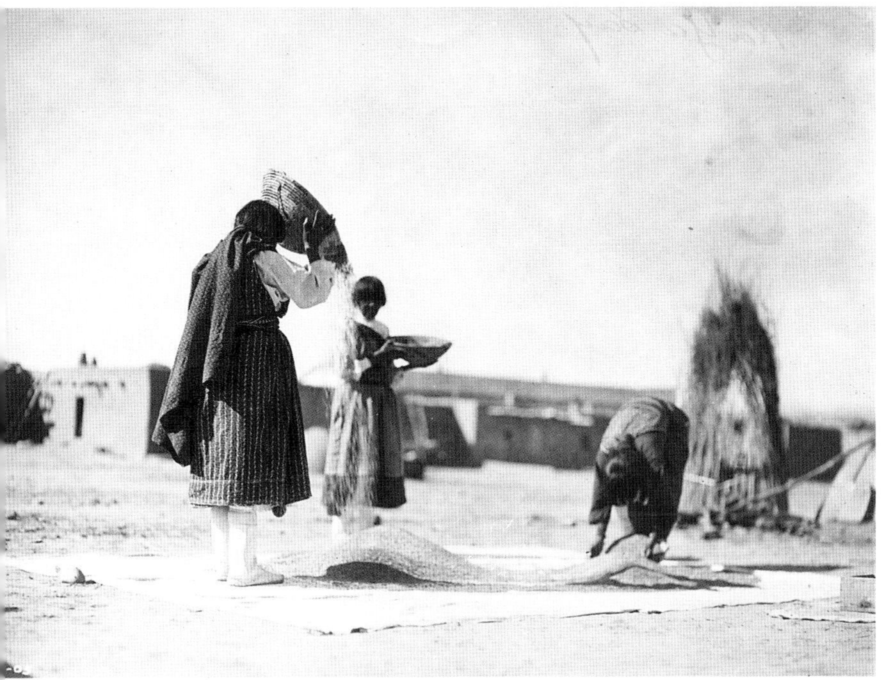

Street Scene at San Juan, ©1925

San Juan Pueblo, largest and northernmost of the six Tewa-speaking Pueblos, is on the east bank of the Rio Grande, about five miles from the town of Espanola. The adobe architecture of the Pueblo can be traced back to the Anasazi, or cliff dwellers, structures of the Mesa Verde area. The Tewa imbued their three-tiered social order of Made People (priests, both men and women), youths (or assistants), and ordinary people with additional meaning by dividing their physical and spiritual worlds into three parts each. The central circle of their physical world includes the village, farmlands, and surrounding lowlands. Four shrines, or kivas, at the perimeter of the village are dedicated to spirits of dead ancestors, the spiritual equivalent of the living. This innermost area is largely the ordinary people's—especially the women's—domain. The second circle, a mediating area between men and women, includes the hills, mesas, and washes and is defined by four sacred mesas. The outer circle includes the higher mountains and is the territory of male hunters and pilgrims, or Made People, and spirits who never left the sacred underworld.

Winnowing Wheat—San Juan, ©1905

Traditional farming life in the San Juan Pueblo included the cultivation of fruits, corn, chiles, squash, wheat, and hay. The women cut apples, peaches, and some squash and pears into thin slices and laid them out to dry in the sun; chiles and beans were laid out flat or hung to dry on strings; the most perfect blue and white ears of corn were blanched in outdoor ovens, braided together, and hung to dry; and wheat was brought by the men into a "corral" area, where the women winnowed it, or cleaned it of chaff, using basket sieves, as shown in this photograph. Although this image indicates a continuation of the traditional farming life in the early 1900s, the San Juan Pueblo had lost 75 percent of its irrigable acreage by 1912. By the 1970s, there was an increasing reliance on tourism and wage-earning income.

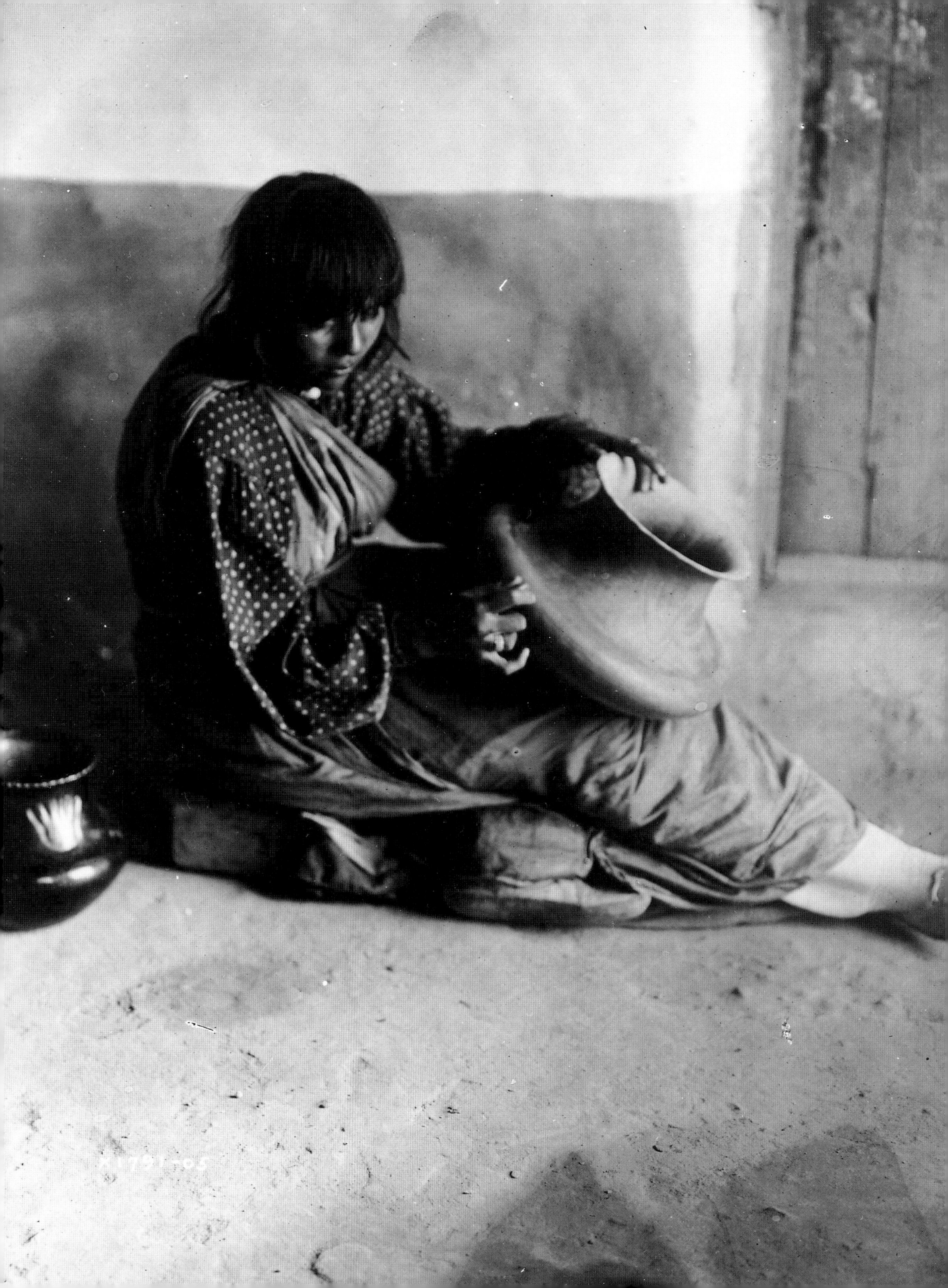

The Potter—Santa Clara, ©1905 *(opposite)*

Curtis attached an intriguing caption to this photograph: "The potter is polishing a vessel. The smooth pebbles used for this purpose are found in small heaps among or near deposits of fossil bones. They are the stomach pebbles of dinosaurs. Tewa women prize them highly, refuse to part with them, and foresee ill luck if one is lost." The modern economy of the Santa Clara Pueblo has become increasingly dependent upon arts and crafts, particularly pottery. Its potters have been, and continue to be, recognized for the extraordinary quality of their work. The highly polished blackware, of which an example sits on the floor next to this potter, has a bear claw decoration, a distinctive Santa Clara design. The black pottery—a traditional craft—is still highly prized and sought by collectors.

As a result of schisms in traditional tribal government, Santa Clara was the first tribe to adopt a written constitution following the Indian Reorganization Act of 1934, a form of government that was generally not adopted by the Pueblo tribes because it separated religious and secular affairs.

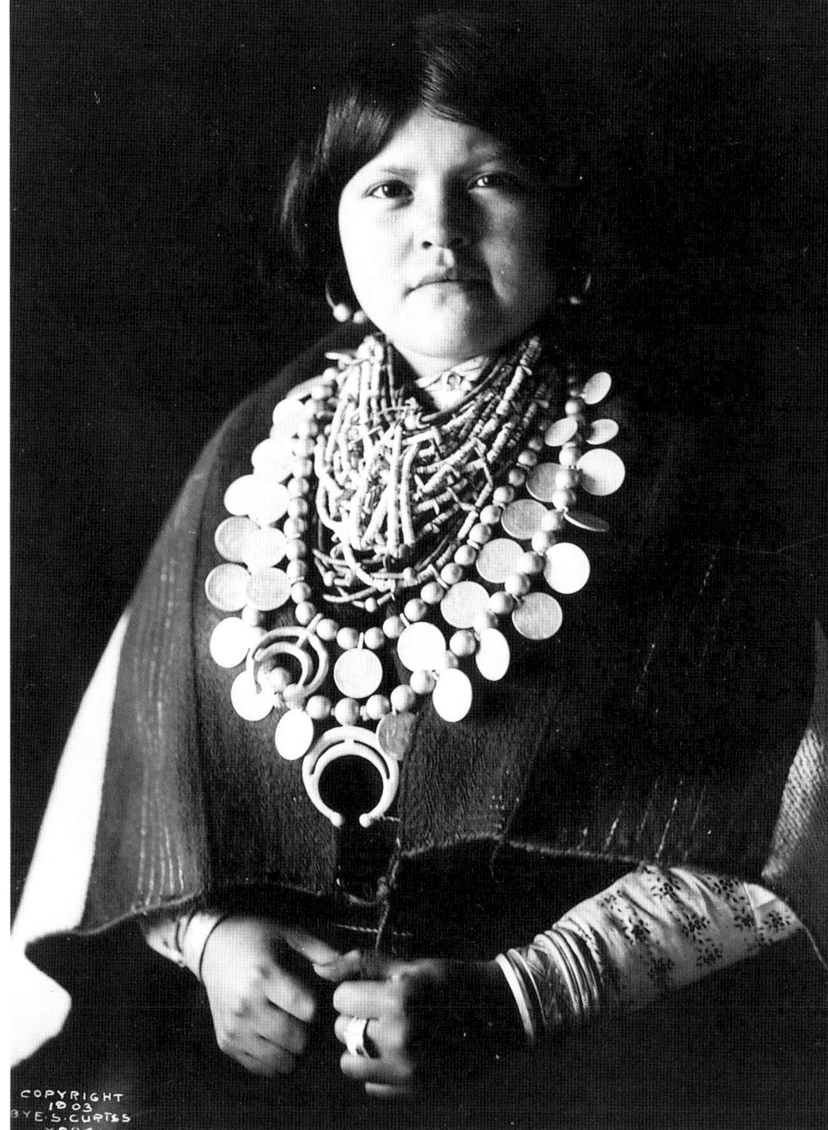

Zuni Ornaments, ©1903

The Zuni have lived in the Zuni River valley in western New Mexico, a tributary of the Little Colorado, since about 800 A.D. This young woman photographed by Curtis is wearing an impressive collection of silver-and-turquoise Zuni-made jewelry, which also included non-native coins. She is also wearing traditional clothes. In the 1960s, the Zuni Pueblo, the largest of the Pueblos, established The Craftsmen's Cooperative Association to facilitate the manufacture and sale of Zuni silver jewelry; 90 percent of the men and women are involved in this major source of income for the community. The men design the patterns and cut the silver, and the women cut and mount the stones.

California and the Great Basin

Curtis went in search of California tribes late in his project, in the 1920s, when his funds and his spirits were low. In many cases, his findings cannot have done much to lift his spirits. Most of the northern and central California tribes had been devastated by Euro-American settlement of the 1800s, and many small tribes of this region had disappeared by Curtis's time.

Traditionally, the tribes of northern and central California lived in villages. Along the coast of present-day northwestern California and southwestern Oregon, the Athapaskan Hupa and Tolowa and the Algonquian Yurok were fishers, hunters, and gatherers; lived in plank houses; and were expert woodworkers and basket makers. Just inland from the Yurok lived the Hokan-speaking Karok, who were culturally very similar. Like their Northwest Coast neighbors, these tribes were concerned with wealth, social rank, and prestige. They were unique in having women shamans, or curers. Further inland lived the Hokan-speaking Achumawi, Atsugewi, Yana, and others.

To the south along the Pacific Coast lived another Hokan-speaking tribe, the Pomo, whose neighbors, the Yuki and Wappo, were linguistically members of the Yukian family. Other tribes in the central California coastal ranges and central valley included the Penutian-speaking Wintun, Patwin, Maidu, Costanoan, Miwok, and Yokuts groups. Each group had headmen and their own mythology and ceremonies. The Pomo were outstandingly skilled at basket making.

Curtis devoted an entire volume of *The North American Indian* to the Indians of southern California and southern and western Nevada—in particular, the Cahuilla and Tipai-Ipai (Diegueño), who inhabited some of the most arid country in the United States. The Washoe, whom he visited during this period, were in fact living in the Great Basin region at the foot of the Sierras and around Lake Tahoe, but their Hokan language and basket-weaving skills indicate that they may have migrated eastward.

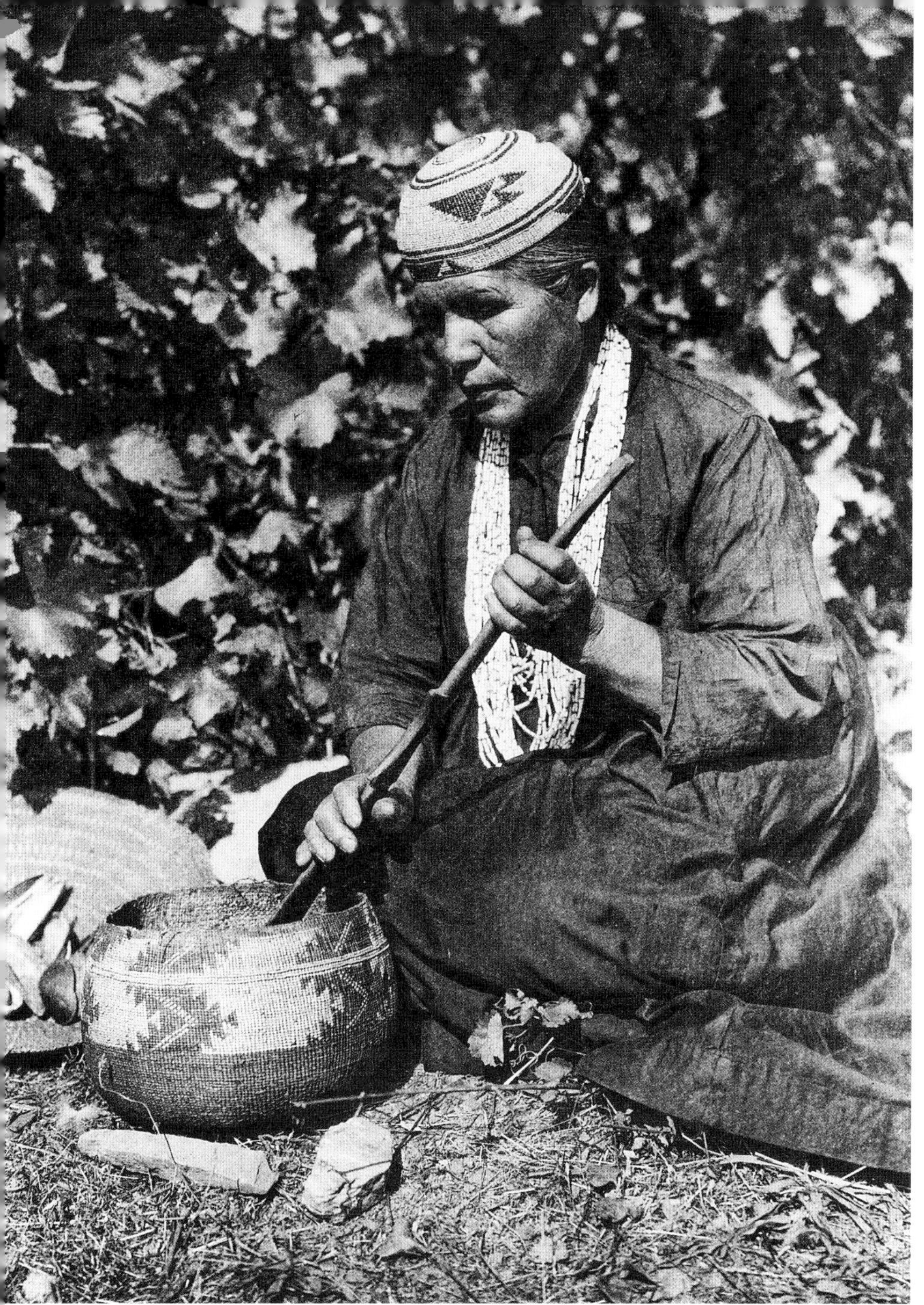

THE MUSH-BASKET—KAROK, ©1923

The Karok lived inland from the coast, establishing themselves in the rich valleys along the middle course of the Klamath River in northern California. A Hokan-speaking tribe, they were culturally assimilated with their Algonquian-speaking neighbors, the Yurok. Although some anthropologists have included the Karok among Northwest Coast peoples, Karok women seemed to share many California tribal customs and skills—the most obvious being the high quality of their basketry. Like the women of other inland tribes of northern California, Oregon, and Washington, Karok women spent much time locating and preparing the numerous edible roots and nuts to be found in the region, the most plentiful of which were acorns. Acorn dough made from ground acorn flour, which had been leached in a pit to remove the bitter tannic acid, was mixed with water and boiled in a large basket with heated rocks to make acorn soup or mush. A good mush-basket could last for years, and examples became highly prized by collectors of Native American arts and crafts.

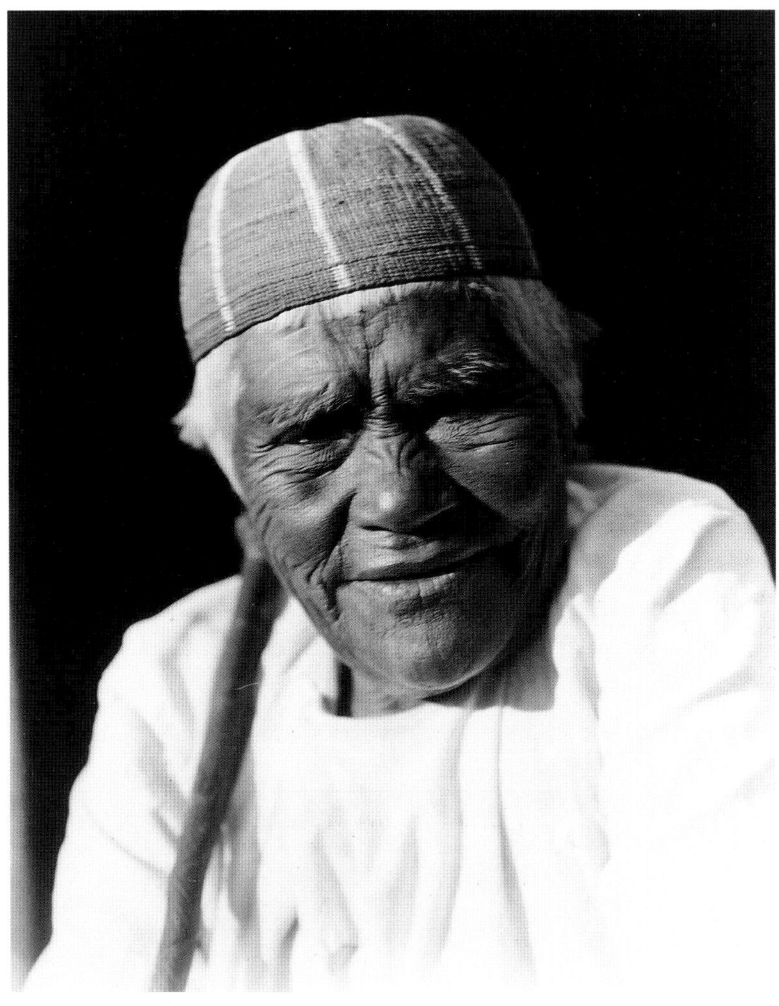

A Yurok Widow, ©1923

The Yurok lived in permanent villages along the northern coast of California, south of the Tolowa. Their homeland—a rich expanse of deer-filled forests and salmon-rich waters—assured the Yurok of a stable livelihood. Individual families and their house sites were the most important social unit. The Yurok placed a high value on wealth. In observing inheritance practices, they would leave heirlooms and family treasures to relatives. Elderly Yurok were said to prepare the boards for the fencing that would surround their own graves. Widows and widowers sat beside the burial plot for several nights after the burial, until the soul of the departed spouse had moved on and to guard against sorcerers who might dig up the fresh grave for death-causing "medicine." Curtis's picture of an elderly Yurok widow, wearing the customary basketry cap, is thoughtful and reverential.

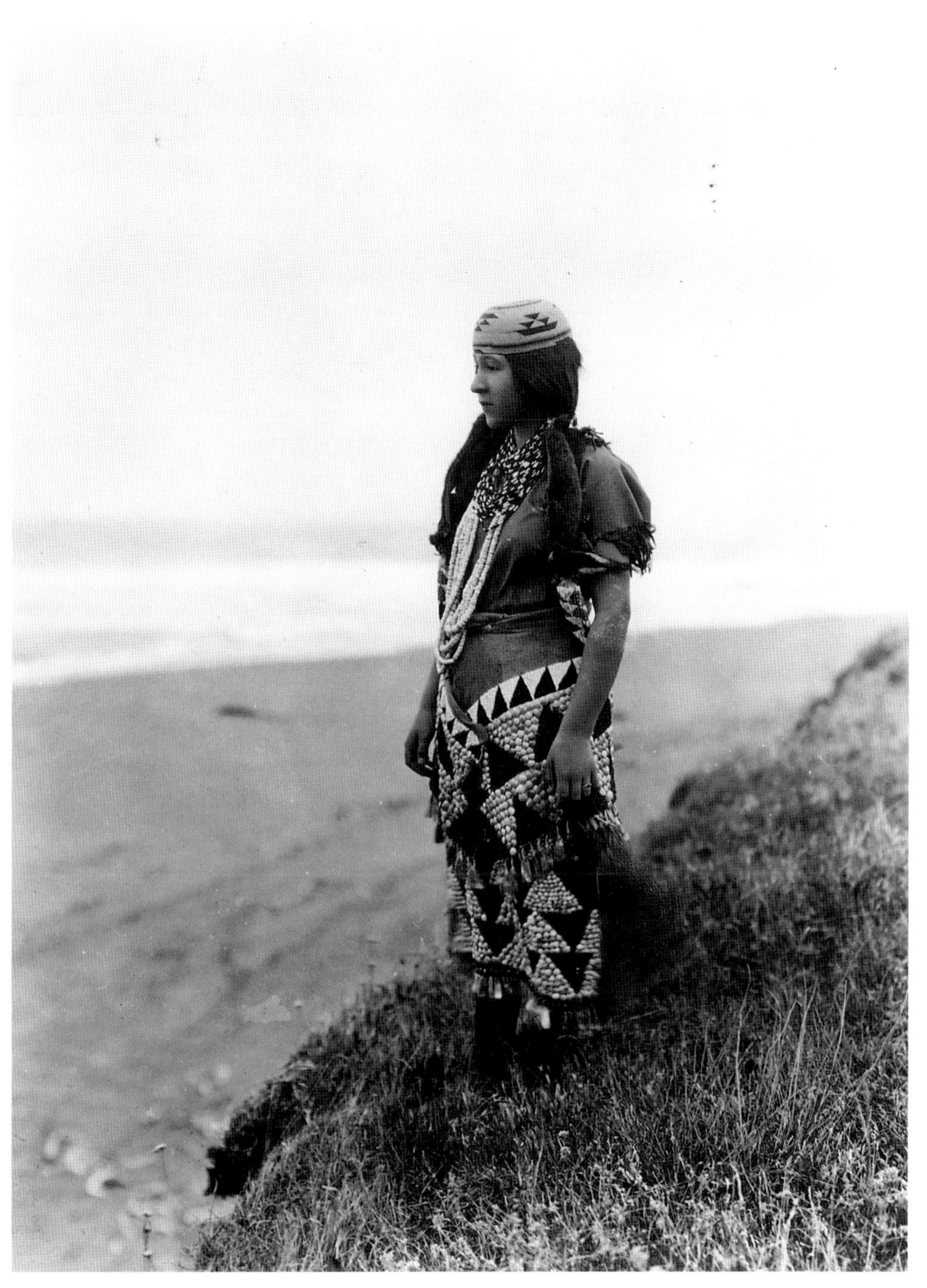

Woman's Primitive Dress—Tolowa, ©1923

This Tolowa woman struck one of Curtis's favorite romantic poses: wearing a "primitive dress" and outlined by a vast backdrop of sky and rugged terrain. The Athapaskan Tolowa, however, were anything but "primitive." They participated in a complex trading network—including trading dentalium shells from Vancouver Island—with their neighbors. Like the Yurok, the Tolowa lived along the precipitous headlands and river mouths of northwest coastal California, where the oceans and rivers yielded a ready supply of fish, shellfish, shorebirds, and sea mammals. The coastal forests provided oak, redwood, and Douglas fir for their plank houses, as well as being a habitat for deer and a source of acorns. Thus, the Tolowa lived in permanent villages of substantial houses and, as this woman's wardrobe suggests, were well clothed—in addition to her fine basketry cap, she is wearing clamshell-bead necklaces and a shell-decorated skirt.

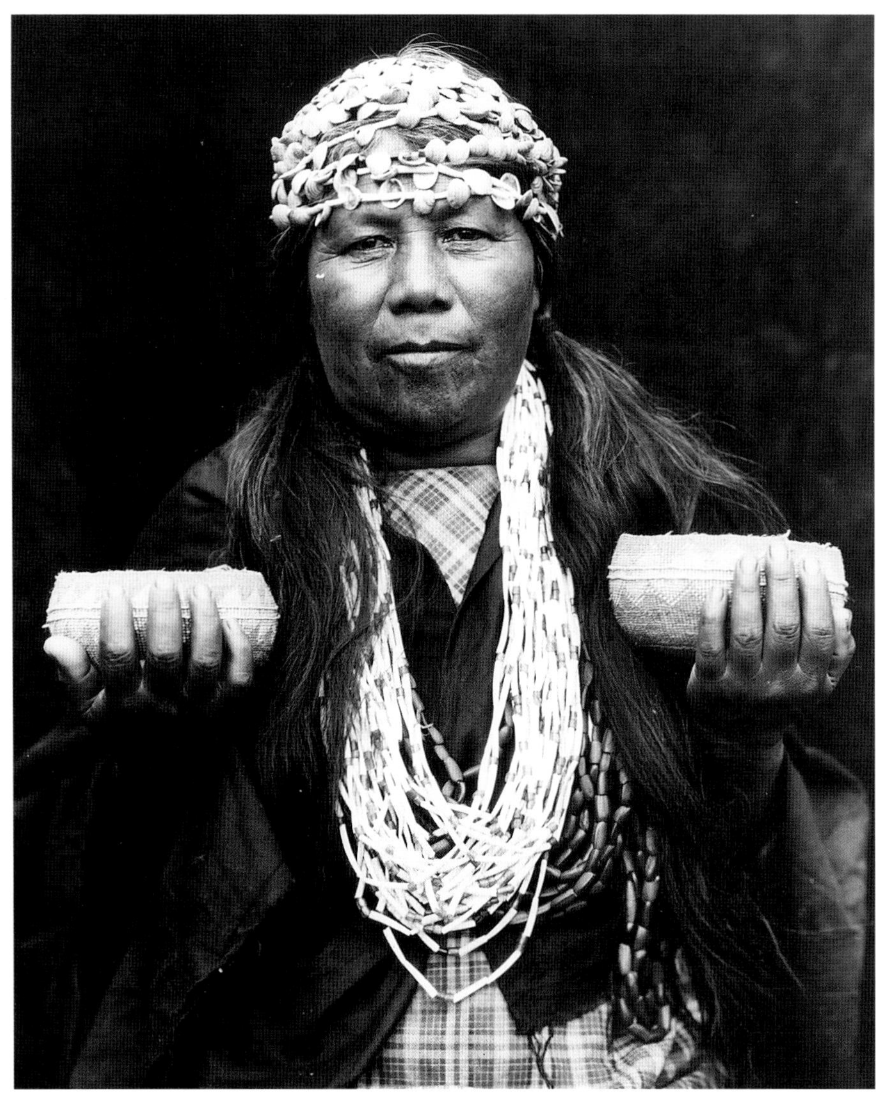

Hupa Female Shaman, ©1923

One of the more venerable members of any tribe was the shaman, or healer. Among the Athapaskan Hupa of northwestern California, most of the shamans were women. With her impressive robes and regalia and her confident demeanor, this female shaman suitably evokes the seriousness of her rank. Shamans derived their powers from the spirit world, powers that could be used for good or ill. These powers—often channeled through an animal spirit—were used to heal the sick members of the tribe; thus, a female shaman was often called a medicine woman. Because illness was said to result from a person's spiritual and natural worlds being out of alignment, the shaman used potions, poultices, incantations, fasting, chanting, and secret rituals to drive out evil spirits and restore the person's inner balance.

HUPA MOTHER AND CHILD, ©1923

The Hoopa Valley, where the Hupa live, is an eight-mile swath of forested land that runs northwest along the Trinity River until it merges with the Klamath River, where the Yurok people live. The Hupa, like the Yurok, share cultural traits with tribes of the Northwest Coast and those in California. This Hupa mother wears a fine example of a woven basketry cap, which the women of the region were renowned for creating from an array of vegetative materials, including hazel, willow, bear grass, and ferns. Her child, wrapped in blankets, is carried in a cradle basket. The principal elements of the Hupa diet, like those of the Pomo and many other California tribes, were salmon and acorns. Without the women's skill at processing acorns, they are inedible, containing tannic acid, which in large doses is poisonous. After the women gathered the acorns, they were stored and dried out and then shelled; later they would pound the inner kernels in bedrock mortars. Then they sifted and winnowed the pieces to a fine-grained meal. To extract the tannin, they began a long process of leaching the meal with water. The acorn gruel could then be made into soup, mush, or cakes, the staples of existence.

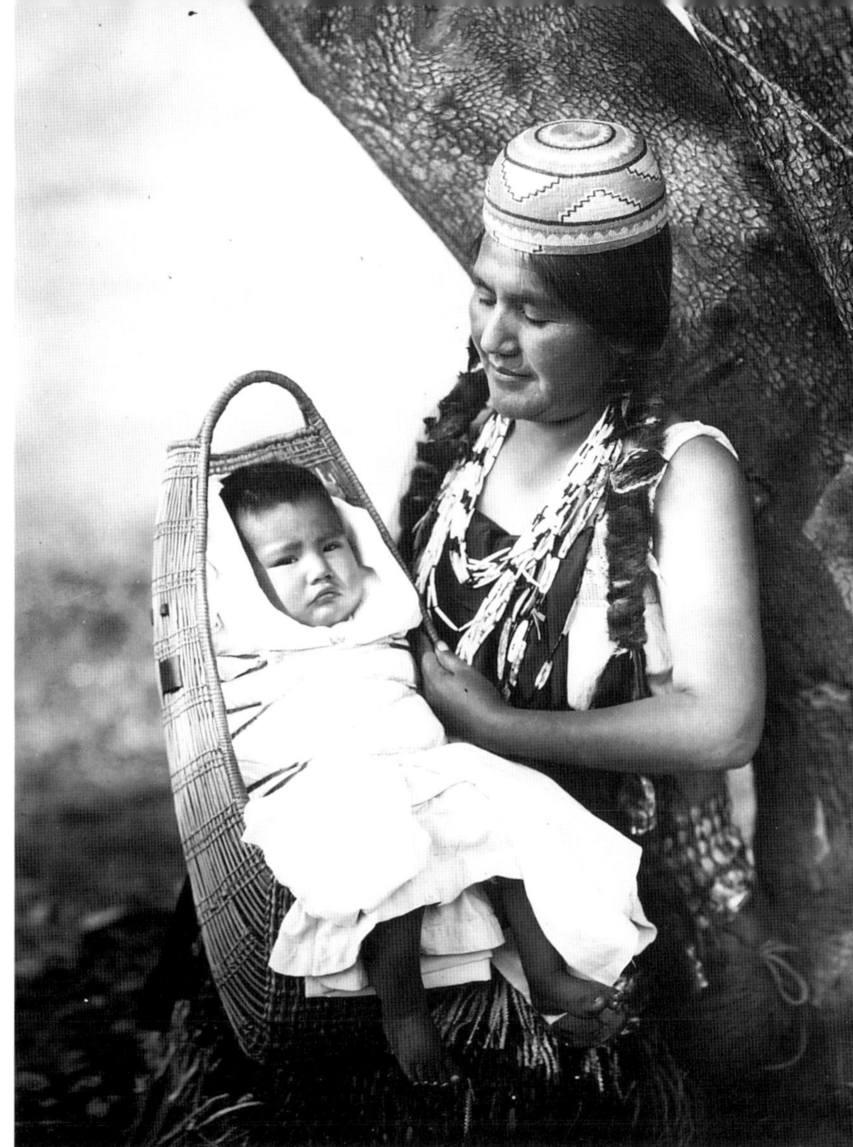

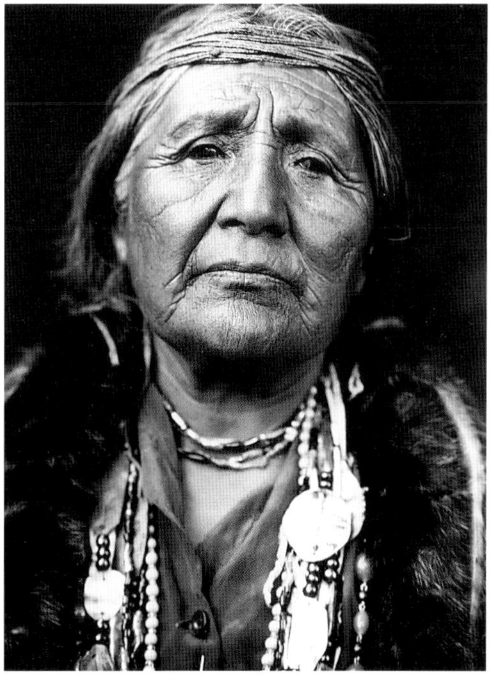

HUPA WOMAN, ©1923

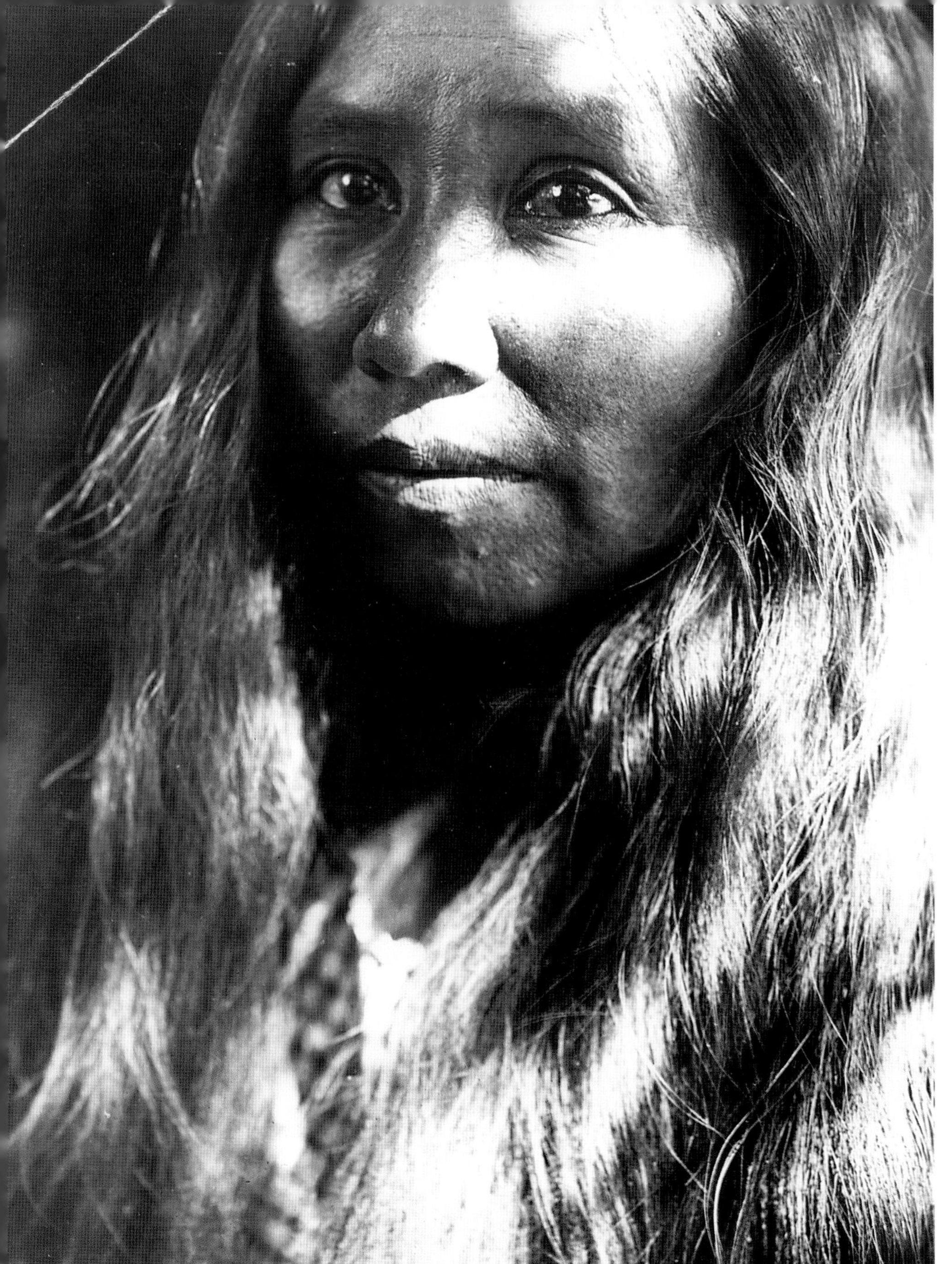

A Kato Woman, ©1924

The Cahto (spelled Kato by Curtis) were an Athapaskan-speaking group made up of about fifty villages in pre-contact times, located in the western foothills of northwestern California. They hunted, fished, gathered plants and acorns, and made expeditions to trade baskets, arrows, and clothing with the neighboring Wailaki and into Coast Yuki territory to gather shellfish and seaweed. Men and women originally wore a tanned deerskin apron wrapped around the waist. Curtis photographed this unidentified young woman—one of his most unguarded portraits—with luxuriant loose hair and unadorned face; however, he observed that both sexes generally wore their hair knotted and held back by close-fitting knitted hairnets made of iris, while women usually wore grass hoop earrings and tattooed their faces and chests. Cahto girls marked puberty with a six-day ceremony, during which they observed certain taboos, followed by a quiet, abstemious life for five months.

ACHOMAWI MOTHER AND CHILD, ©1923

The Achumawi (spelled Achomawi by Curtis) lived along the Pit River basin in northeastern California and, together with the Atsugewi, were known as the Pit River Indians. Periodic victims of raids by the more populous and powerful Modoc and Klamath, captured Achumawi were sometimes sold on the intertribal slave market along the Columbia River in Oregon. Sometimes they would be adopted into the victorious raider's group. According to the 1910 U.S. Census, approximately 1,000 Pit River Indians survived, some of whom were living on the Round Valley Reservation. Beside child-rearing, Achumawi women were responsible for gathering fruits, berries, roots, and seeds in the areas from Pine Creek in the south to Goose Lake, straddling the Oregon border. About the time Curtis took this photograph, ethnologist A. L. Kroeber published *Handbook of the Indians of California* (1925). Of the Achumawi, Kroeber wrote, "War for the fun of the game, or for gain, was foreign to their ideas."

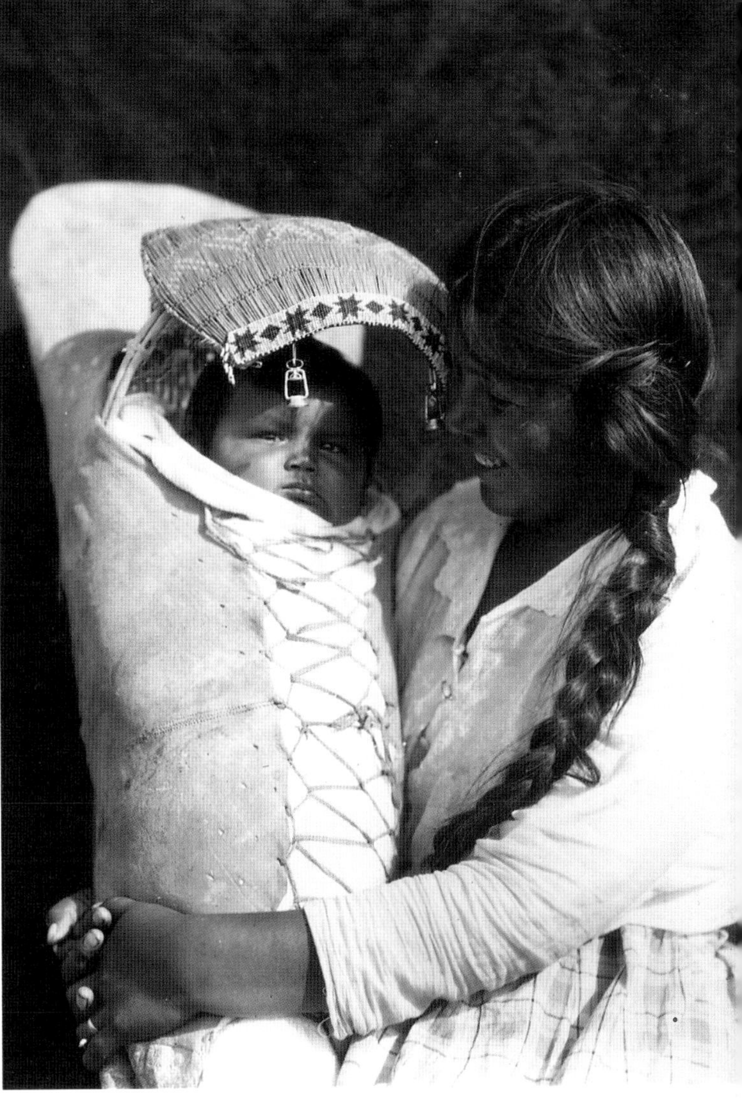

ACHOMAWI BASKET-MAKER, ©1923

California tribes were known for their highly developed textile arts, of which their basketry was of the highest quality. The Achumawi were no exception. While not as accomplished as the Pomo basket weavers, distant neighbors to the south, Achumawi women nonetheless wove utilitarian baskets from many available materials and for every imaginable purpose. Cooking, for example, could be done in large, tight-meshed baskets by dropping heated rocks inside with the desired ingredients, including liquids. The Achumawi still adhered to some of their traditional customs when Curtis arrived with his camera; for instance, half of the Achumawi shamans were women. Collectors of Native American artifacts had, by then, created a market for baskets separate from their utilitarian purpose. The Achumawi woman pictured hard at work here may have had that market in mind.

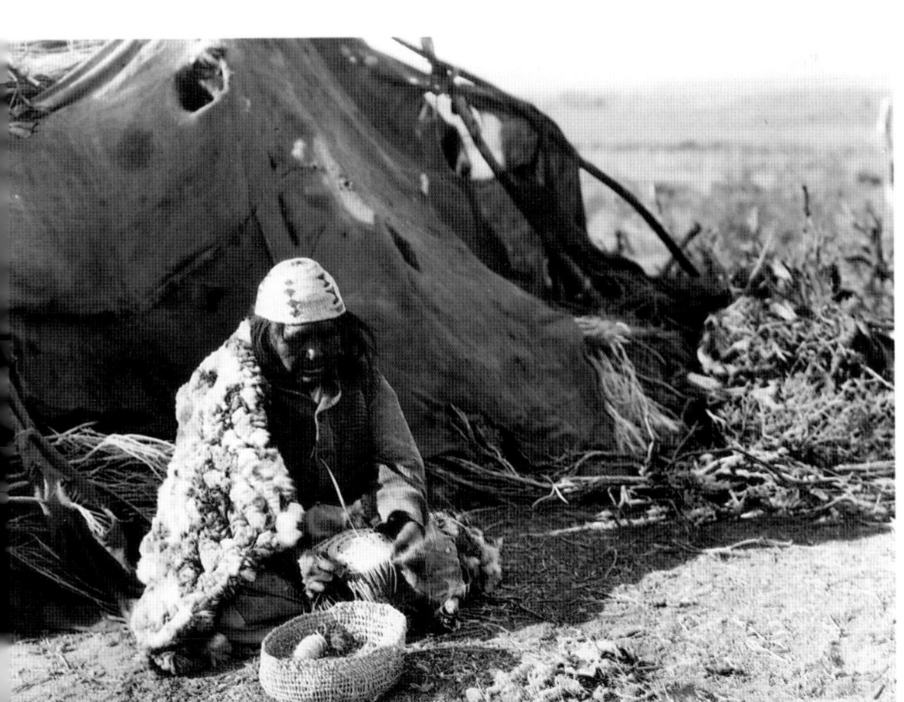

THE POMO

The groups commonly known today as the Pomo inhabited an area that embraced eighty miles of California coast north of San Francisco and Bodega Bays and extended inland into the mountain ridges and canyons of what are now Mendocino, Sonoma, and Lake Counties. Before the arrival of Europeans, the tribes of northern California, in general, were among the most populous native peoples in North America not engaged in agriculture. The intermittent contact with white settlers and traders before the 1850s had been hard on the Pomo, with unfriendly relations on all sides—the Russians from the north, the Spanish from the south. However, the massive influx from the east, unleashed by the discovery of gold at midcentury, was truly devastating. Disease reduced the number of Pomo, thus creating hardship and disintegration of their communities. Stories are told of the wanton cruelty of white cattle-ranch owners, whose forced labor camps further decimated the Pomo numbers.

By the time Curtis arrived in the 1920s—late in his career—Pomo women had, out of economic necessity, begun working as domestic help for white town dwellers. Curtis devoted half of volume 14 of The North American Indian *to the Pomo and was particularly fascinated by the diverse year-round activities of this highly adaptive people.*

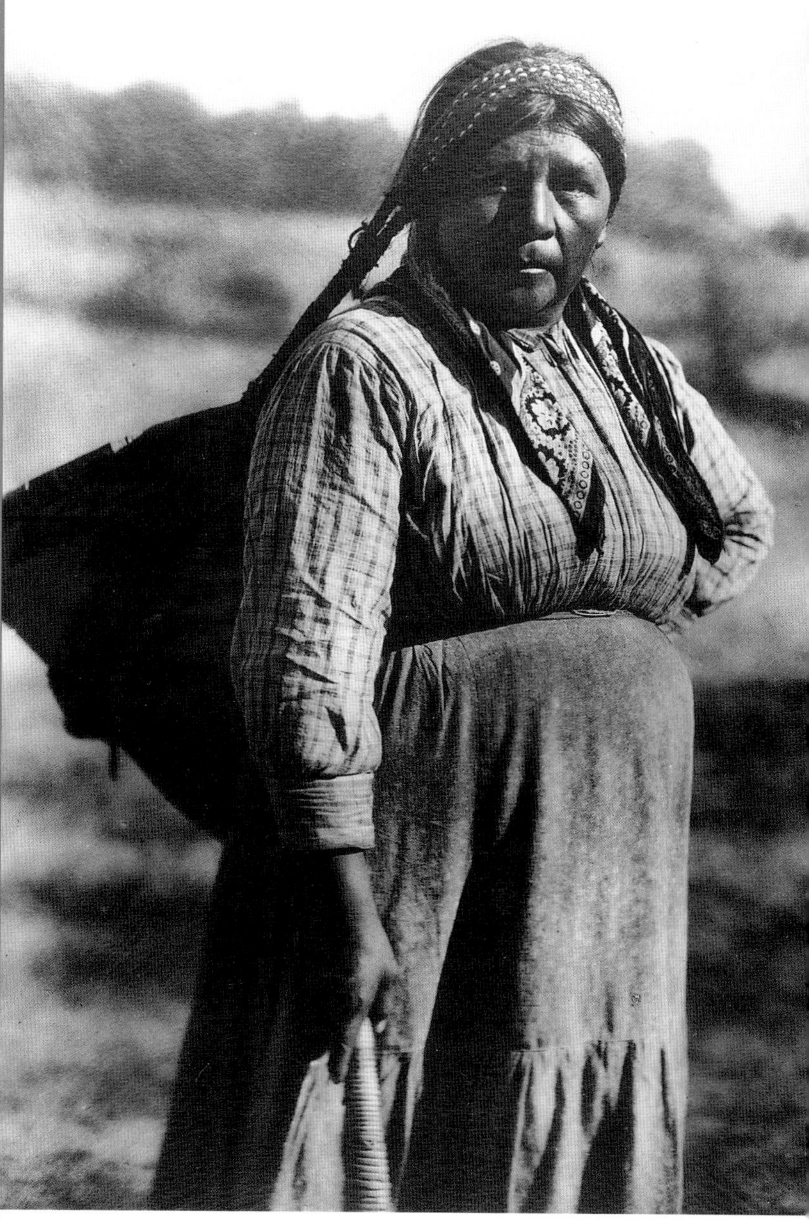

THE BURDEN-BASKET—COAST POMO, ©1924

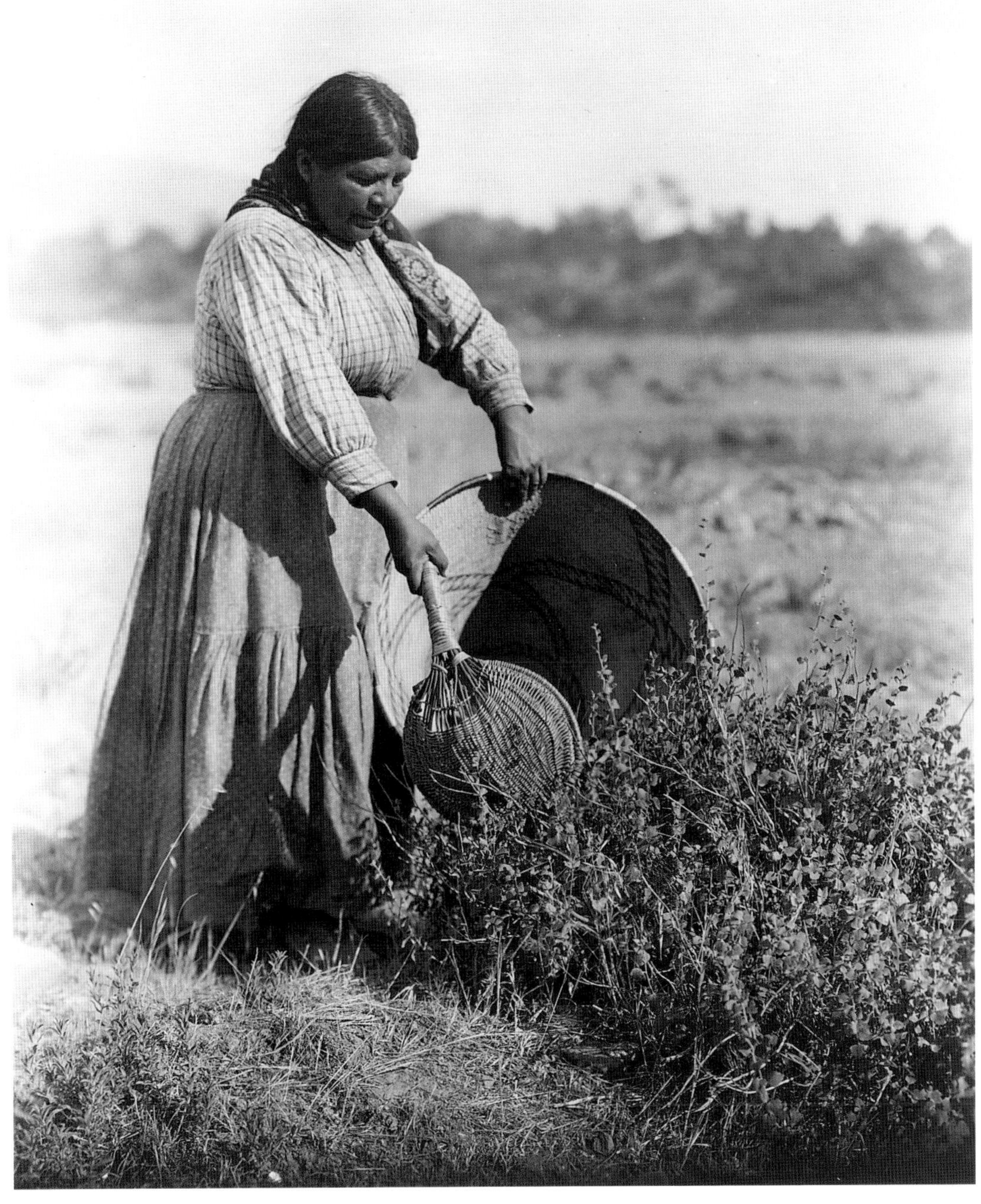

GATHERING SEEDS—COAST POMO, ©1924

Cecilia Joaquin, a Central—called Coast by Curtis—Pomo speaker from the Sanel community at Hopland, demonstrated the use of the burden basket (opposite) and seed beater for Curtis. Her tight-meshed burden basket is held in place by a tumpline that stretches across her head, allowing her to gather wild seeds more easily. She is using the seed beater to knock and scrape the seeds from wild plants and scrub into the open burden basket. Because gathering food was a year-round undertaking, Pomo women spent a great deal of time searching for seeds, nuts, and acorns among the coastal headlands and inland meadows. While the basketry of the Pomo was of a stellar quality, it also served several essential functions. Pomo men made more utilitarian loose-mesh baskets for carrying wood and fish, and the women became true masters of sophisticated basketry and design. They appropriated over thirty different kinds of wild plant material for this purpose. Basket weavers normally used the twining or coiling technique.

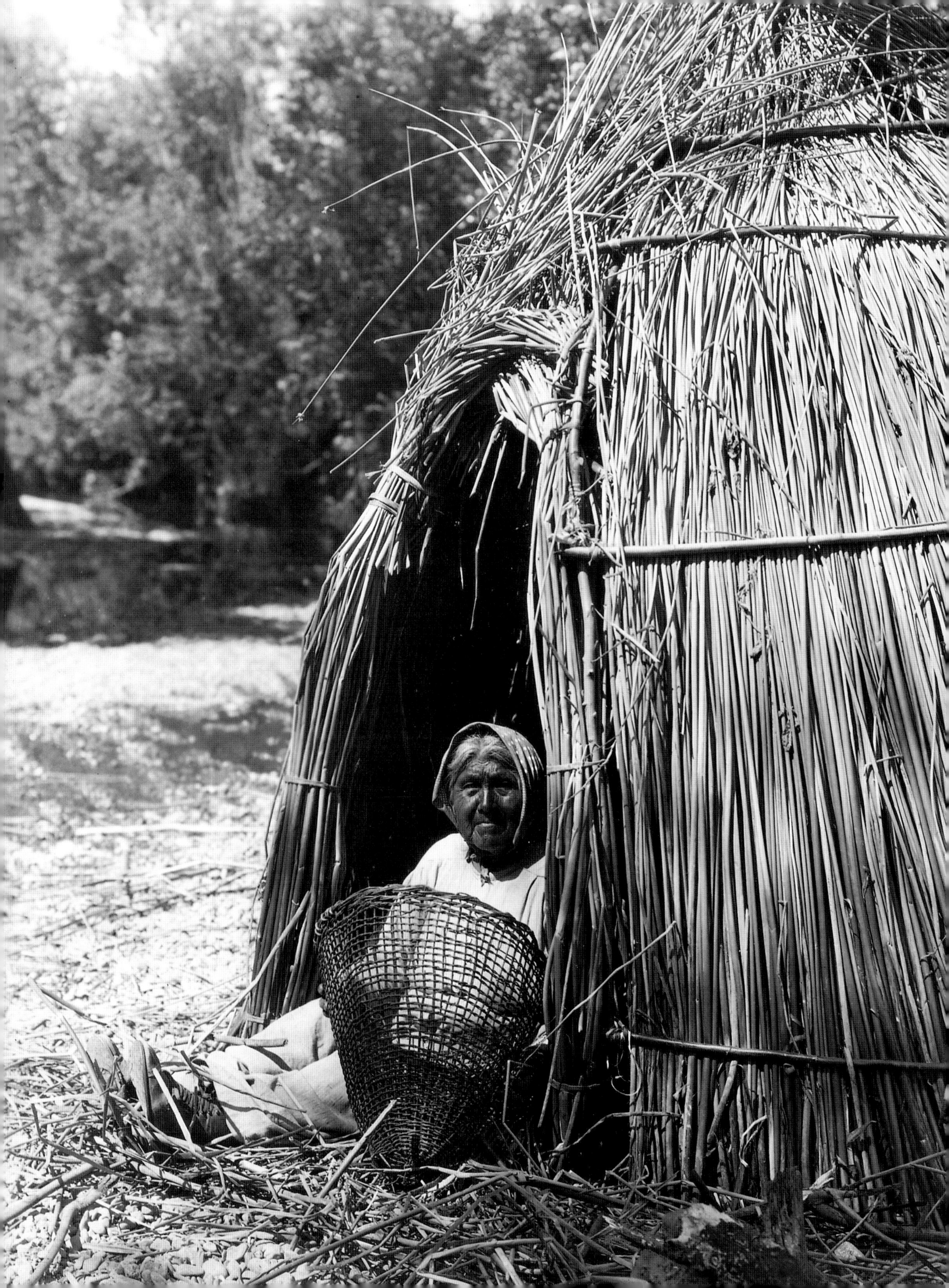

Construction of a Tule Shelter—Lake Pomo, ©1924

(opposite)

The Pomo's extraordinary basket-weaving skills were transferred, on a larger scale, to their watercraft and architecture. This was especially true of the Eastern Pomo—called Lake Pomo by Curtis—who lived in the Clear Lake basin, inland of the coastal mountain range. The shallow waters of lakes and surrounding marshlands were covered with a ready and fast-growing supply of thick grasses and reeds. The most common was tule, or bulrush *(Scirpus californicus)*, which the Pomo women wove into large, thick, and impermeable mats. These sections were then hoisted and lashed together with split grape vines, like hollowed-out haystacks. The temporary, quickly built, but substantial tule huts made for an ideal domicile, especially during the spring and summer lakeside encampments. It is likely, however, that by 1924, most Pomo were not living in tule shelters and the one pictured here had to be built for the occasion. The Eastern Pomo woman in the doorway proudly displays an open-mesh burden basket. Other inventive uses that women found for tule were as skirts, mantles, moccasins, leggings, serving mats, bedding, and diapers. The Eastern Pomo also ate the tender shoots and roots of the tule.

A Chukchansi Matron, ©1924

Before European contact, life for California tribes was, according to anthropologist Clark Wissler, "a kind of Indian paradise where food of some kind was always at hand and climate comfortable." However, like many tribes who spoke the Penutian dialect and lived in the Central valleys, the Yokuts people—of which the Chukchansi were one branch—were devastated by the encroachment of white settlers. It is estimated that between 1769 and 1836—the peak of the Spanish mission system—the Indian population in the valleys between San Diego and San Francisco declined from 72,000 to 18,000, due to change in diet, disease, slaughter, and forced labor on the ranches that sprang up on the ancestral lands of people like the Chukchansi. The Chukchansi were found in the San Joaquin Valley and the western foothills of the Sierra Nevada Mountains. They lived by gathering and hunting; the women did most of the former. They also made an assortment of basketry, including tight-meshed, cone-shaped baskets for collecting seeds, wild plants, and scrub, as well as water bottles, seed beaters, cooking vessels, winnowing trays, and cradles. By the late nineteenth century, clothing styles of the area's native populations were very similar to those of the white settlers. By 1924, the Chukchansi, like this matron, were culturally indistinguishable from the general population of California.

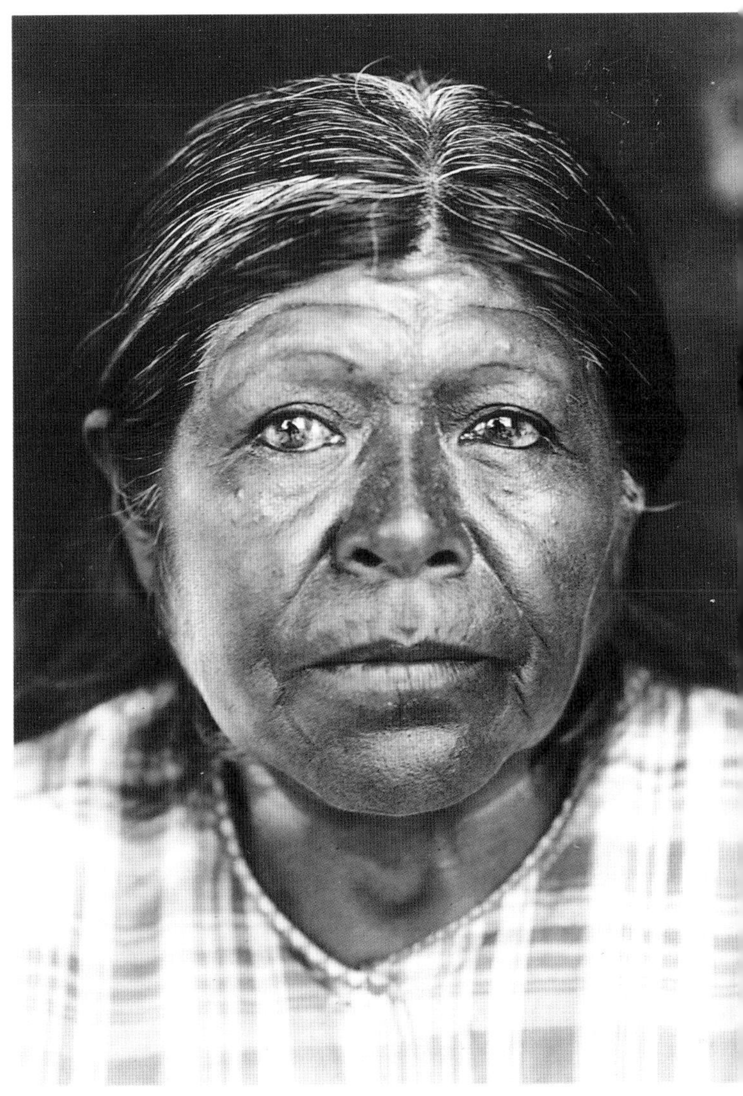

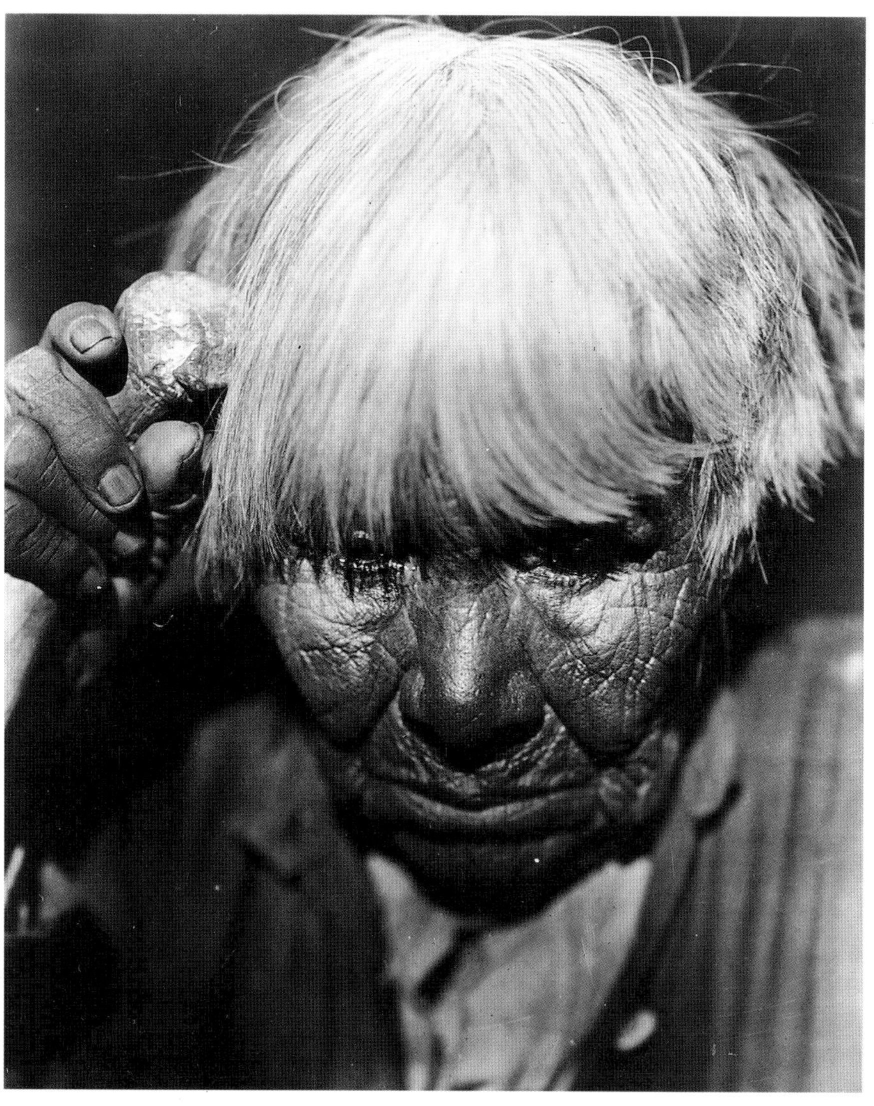

Old Woman in Mourning—Yuki, ©1924

This poignant portrait of an elderly Yuki woman in mourning was taken, like his *Yurok Widow*, toward the end of Curtis's North American Indian project, when his money was running out and he was ailing. The Yuki were a once-populous northwestern California tribe living on the Mendocino coast and inland along the Eel River. Their bountiful location allowed time for an elaborate ceremonial life, which centered around the creator god Taikomol ("he who walks alone"). When a Yuki died, his body was wrapped in skins and placed in a fetal position with the head facing east, in preparation for the journey to the hereafter. In mourning, women were required to cut their hair and coat their heads with pitch. The property of the dead was burned or buried, signifying that their souls had departed; their name was not to be uttered again. For the Yuki in 1924, death was an all too regular event. Their population, which had been as high as 6,800 in 1850, had dwindled to a few hundred by the turn of the century. The remnants were living on the Round Valley Reservation in Mendocino County, along with the Wailaki and with the Nomlaki and Pomo, their one-time enemies. As a result of allotment, at least 70 percent of Yuki land on the reservation was lost to nonnatives. Only about fifty Yuki people lived on the reservation in 1993.

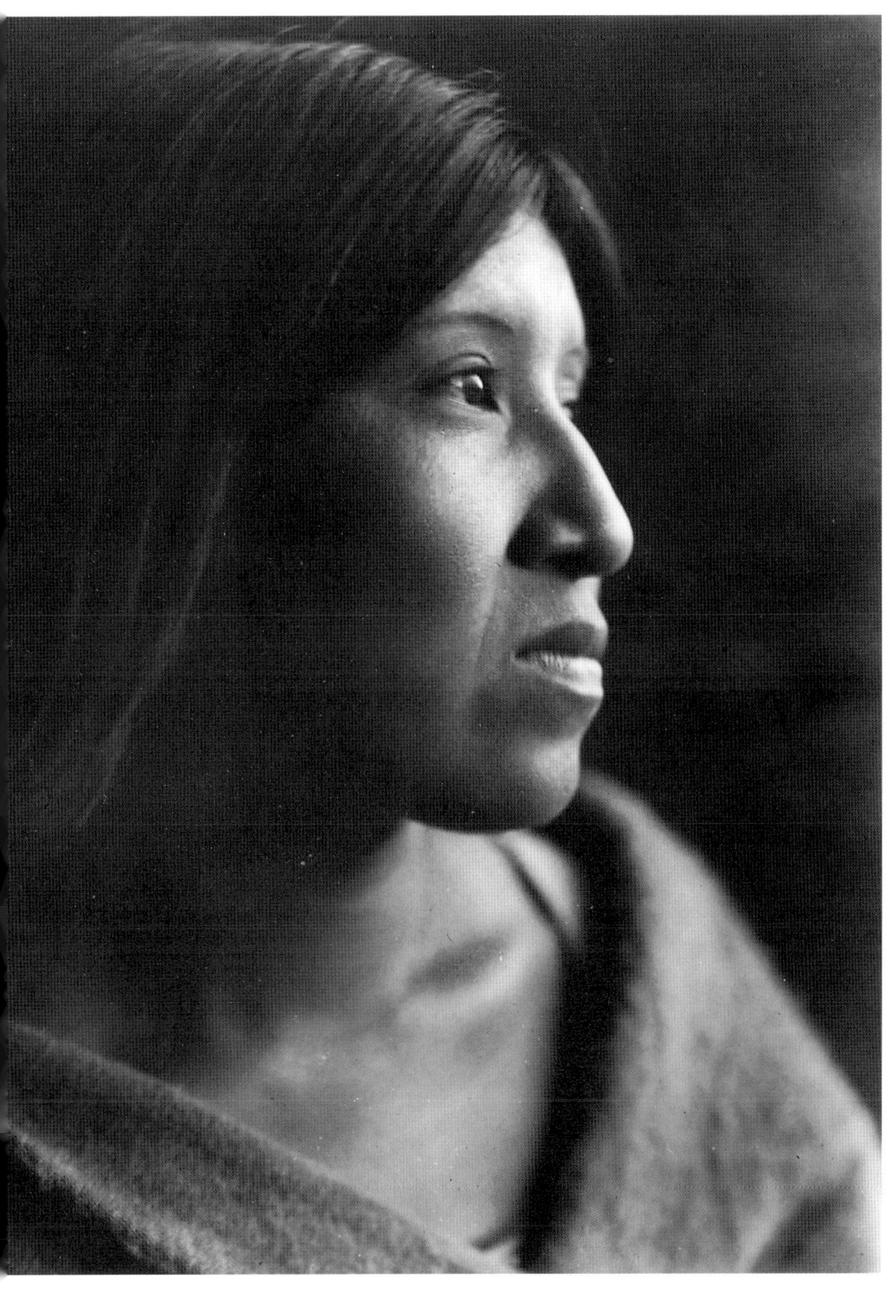

A Desert Cahuilla Woman, ©1924

Cahuilla territory around Palm Canyon—better known today as Palm Springs, California—included some of the most arid country in the United States. The Cahuilla women gathered acorns, beans, seeds, nuts, bulbs of cactus, berries, roots, and greens and were also able to grow some maize, beans, and squash. Because of their knowledge of medicinal plants and herbs, many Cahuilla women became accomplished healers and midwives. According to Curtis, a Cahuilla girl became a woman through an elaborate puberty ritual. At the start of her first menses, she was laid on a bed of brush and herbs in a heated trench, covered with a blanket, and kept there for three nights while men and women danced and sang songs; then she was kept in seclusion for a month, on a diet of acorn mush and warm water, under the watchful eye of an elderly female relative. Marriage was usually arranged by the two fathers, and the woman was persuaded to accept her parents' decision. Sometimes prepubescent girls were pledged; they were then considered to be married even if they remained at home.

Cahuilla descendants today live on or near ten small reservations in southern California and have founded the Malki Museum on the Morengo Reservation to encourage interest in Cahuilla culture, language, and traditions.

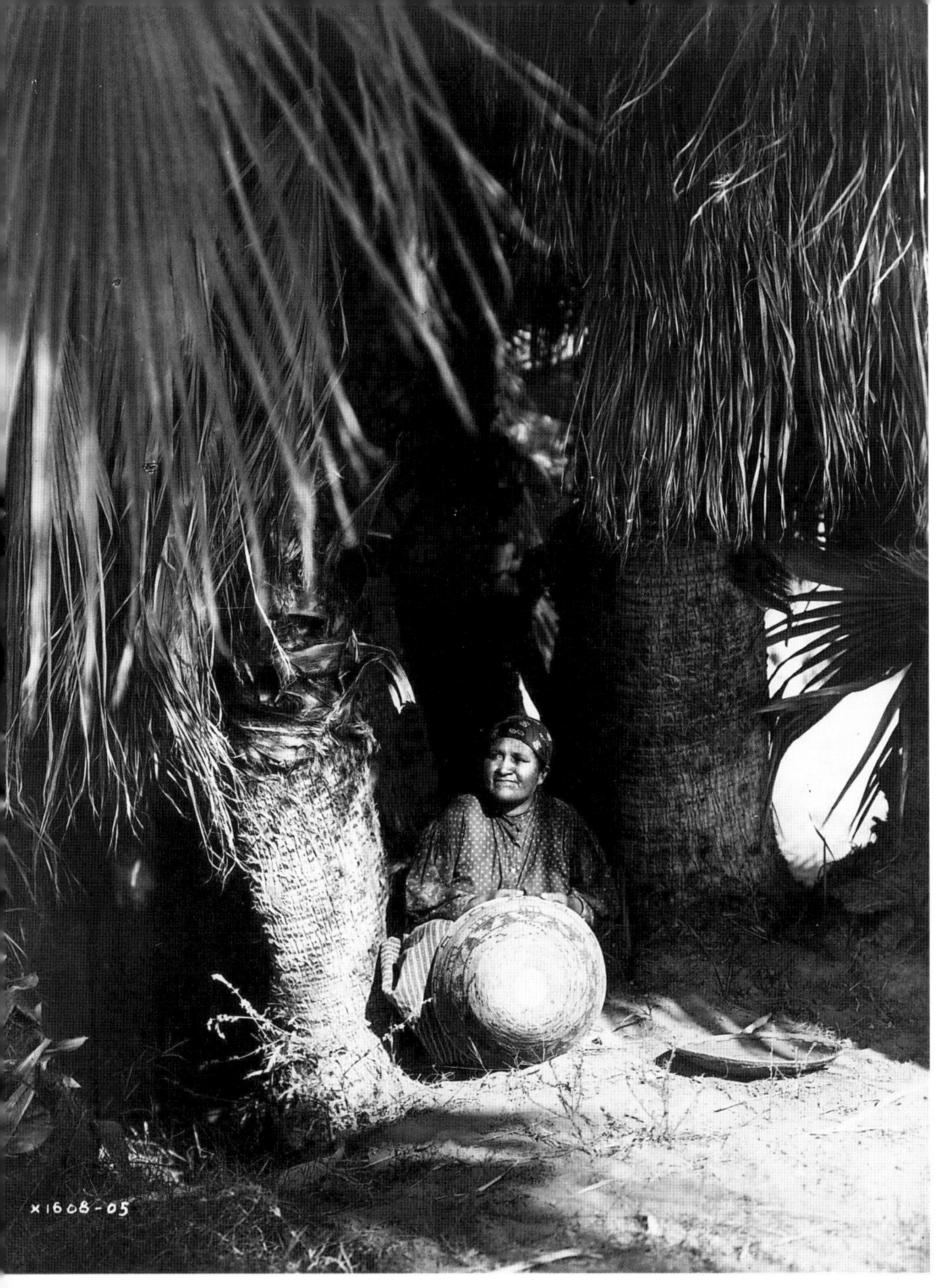

Under the Palms— Cahuilla, ©1924

The western part of Cahuilla territory bordered on the Colorado Desert, an arid region to which these people were well adapted. Although they ranged widely for food, the Cahuilla built permanent villages near water sources and in areas that were protected from high winds. Palm Springs (one of their villages), for example, provided water, shade, and wind protection. Curtis clearly admired the Cahuilla people and spent a great deal of time among the few hundred who remained.

The Cahuilla woman caught "under the palms" proudly displays one of her baskets. Cahuilla women made baskets by the coiling method and used them for winnowing, carrying, storing, and parching seeds. The women were also the exclusive makers of pottery, an art that may have been learned from the Pueblo Indians. They worked local clay into ropes, which they coiled round and round and then smoothed by rubbing with a curved stone on the inside and a wooden paddle on the outside, leaving the products to dry in the sun.

The Harvester—Cahuilla, ©1924

The Cahuilla occupied a land area diverse enough to embrace what Curtis called "wide environmental differences"; this meant they inhabited the oak-covered mountains, the low-country valleys, the desert, and an even more arid region in the Salton Sink, much of which was below sea level. Cahuilla men hunted and trapped rabbit and other small game, while the women gathered any of six varieties of acorn, as well as piñon nuts, seeds, berries, and some greens. Curtis reported seeing a large-scale harvesting of seedpods from the mesquite tree and the screw mesquite. After the women harvested these "mesquite-beans," they broke them up and soaked the seeds (called *kahat*) in water to make a drink. They dried the pods, parched them in hot embers, and ground them into a meal; they also roasted the mesquite blossoms in pits and squeezed them into balls for eating.

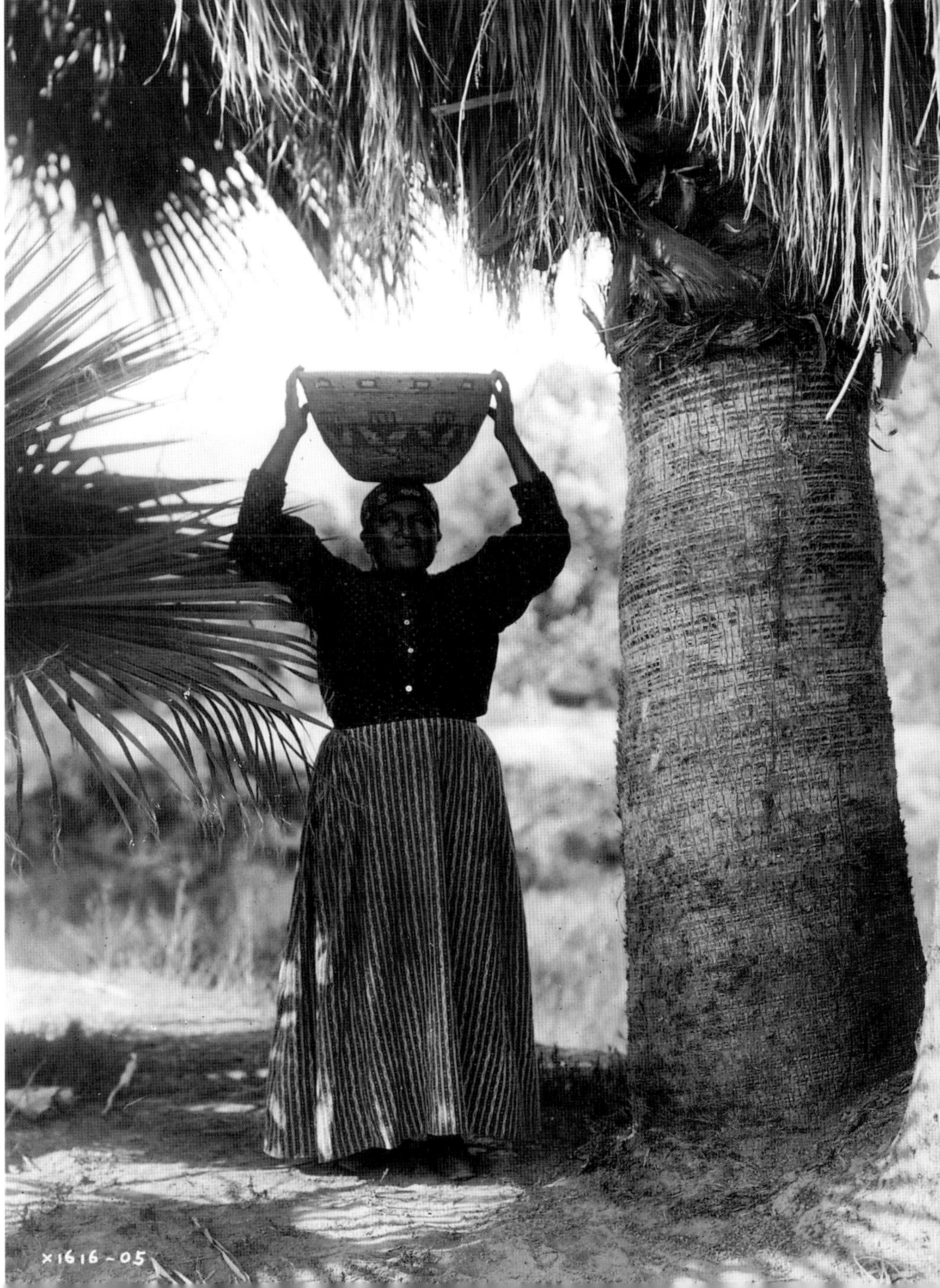

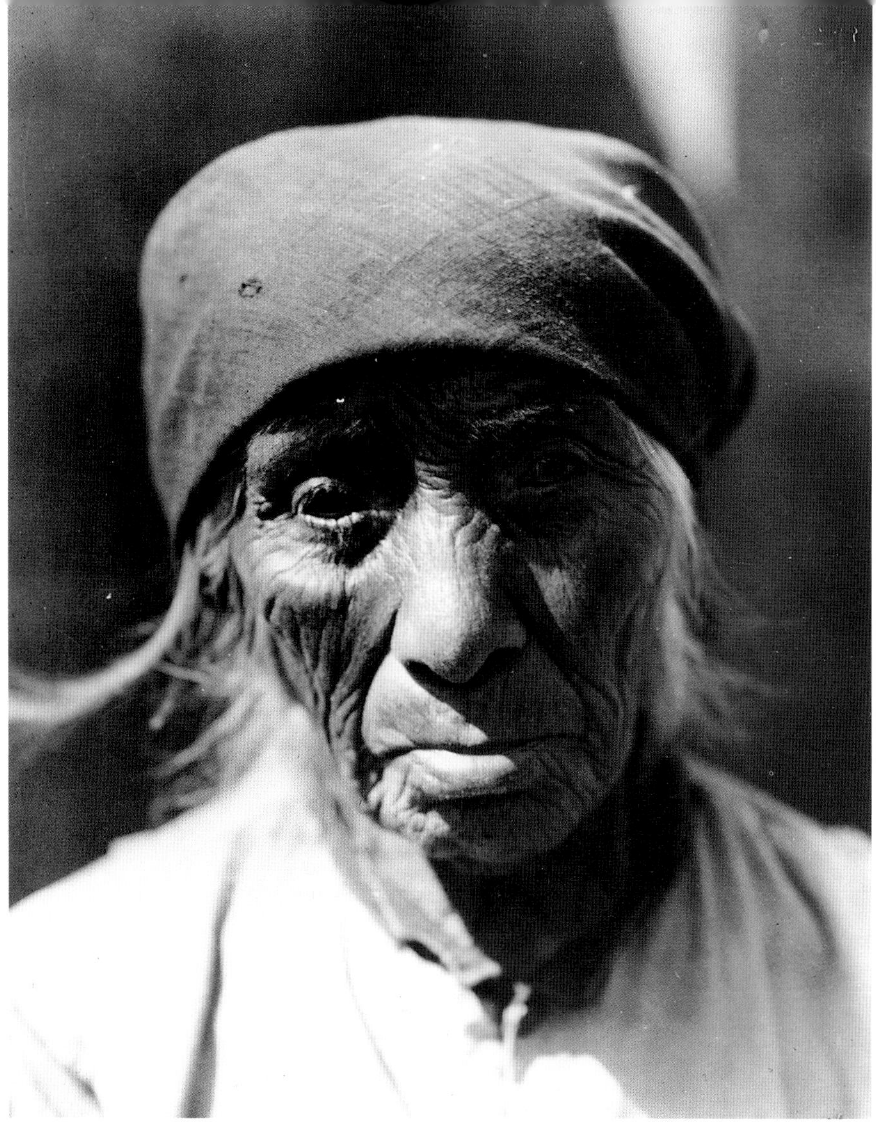

A "SERRANO" WOMAN OF TEJON, ©1924

Because the Serrano were linguistically related to the Kitanemuk, Curtis misidentified this woman as a Serrano. It was an understandable mistake. No archaeological, and very little ethnological, research had been done on the peoples of this area at the time. Of course, that she lived at Tejon—a place where the few Kitanemuk of this time lived—is indisputable. The Kitanemuk lived along the El Paso and Tejon Creeks, in the vast area north of the Mojave Desert and east of the San Joaquin Valley, through which these waters run. In the mid-1800s, a U.S. Army base was set up near here (Fort Tejon), and a Tejon ranch was set aside in 1853, although it was abandoned in 1864, sixty years before Curtis visited. This woman—a young girl at that time—may have witnessed these changes firsthand.

Whether Serrano or Kitanemuk, the life of women was as harsh as the territory. Their existence was dependent on limited and seasonal food sources—piñon nuts and pronghorn antelopes, primarily—found among the few hundred square miles of their land. At puberty, a girl was isolated with one of her female relatives and given special instructions and restrictions to help her through this spiritually dangerous period. After four months, she rejoined the family. Perhaps as a reflection of their hard-won status, Kitanemuk women had a central place in tribal mythology. In their creation story, the world is formed by five brothers and one sister, who is the wisest of the siblings. She is the one who teaches children how to survive, and all living people descend from her.

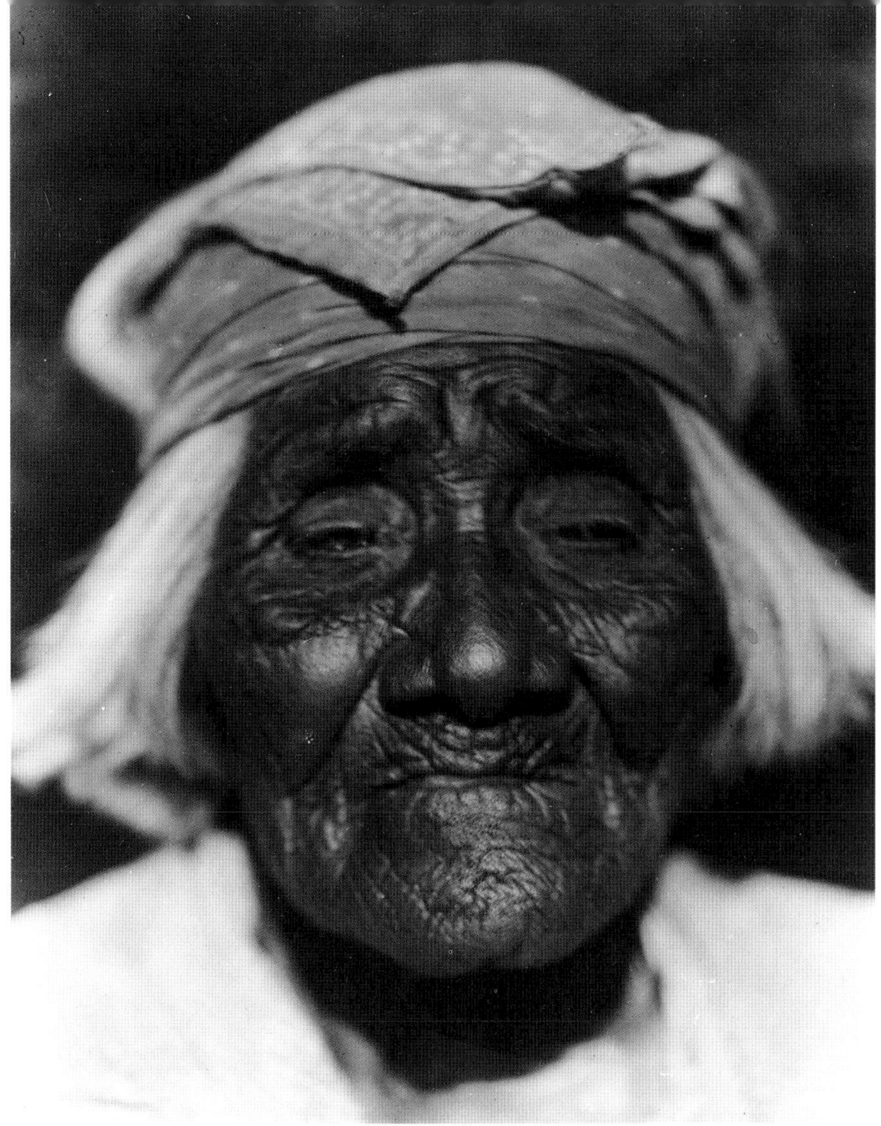

A Santa Ysabel Woman—Diegueño, ©1924

The people who were called Diegueño by the Spanish lived from the southern coast of California well into Baja California, Mexico. Linguistically, they were Yuman speaking and, like the Yuman tribes of Arizona, they were fearlessly independent, despising the name that had been affixed to them by the Spanish. The name, San Diegueño, derived from groups of Indians living near the mission of San Diego de Alcalá, the first of the twenty-one missions built by Spanish Catholic missionaries between the years 1769 and 1834. The mission system subjugated native peoples of south and central California, treating the different nations with varying degrees of brutality and culture-destroying insensitivity. The Diegueño called themselves Tipai-Ipai, or "people." They refused to submit to Spanish control and were described as "proud, rancorous, boastful, . . . passionately devoted to the customs of their fathers, and hard to handle," according to documents cited by historian Alvin Josephy Jr.

Diegueño House at Campo, ©1924

Even under the reservation system, the Diegueño (or Tipai-Ipai) managed to adhere to some of their traditional ways—much to the delight of an increasingly dispirited Curtis in 1924. This temporary summer house at Campo—a town five miles north of the Mexican border in central San Diego County—was probably similar to the structures they had lived in prior to the Spanish incursion. Tipai-Ipai women gathered the poles and brush thatch that were used to construct these shelters. The Tipai-Ipai hunted, gathered a variety of wild plants, and did some farming. One of their dietary supplements was agave, or baked mescal, which was gathered in spring. Tipai-Ipai women wore only an apron in traditional culture, but by the time Curtis photographed them, they wore clothes similar to those worn by Euro-American women.

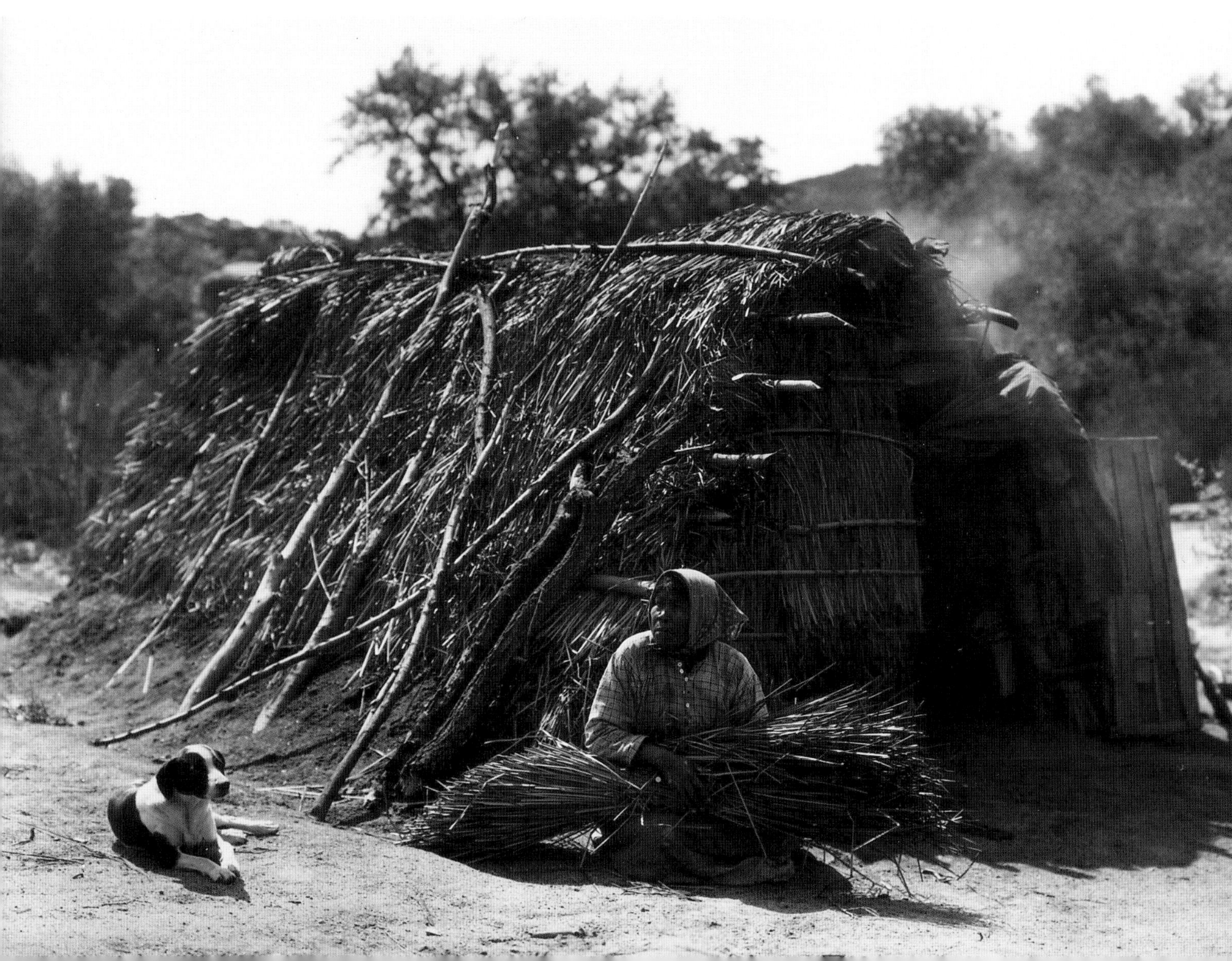

Datsolali, Washo Basket-Maker, ©1924

The Washo—now spelled Washoe—were the only tribe inhabiting the Great Basin whose language was not part of the Numic family; their language is part of the Hokan stock, similar to the languages of California tribes. Perhaps it is no coincidence that the Washoe were excellent weavers of baskets and other utilitarian objects. In her time, Datsolalee (the correct spelling), also known as Louise Keyser, was one of the greatest of Washoe basket makers. When her family's fortunes were at rock bottom, Datsolalee took some basket-covered bottles to sell at a store in Carson City, Nevada. So impressed were the proprietors with her work that they agreed to buy anything she offered them and even encouraged her to experiment. Luckily, her efforts coincided with a large-scale demand for Washoe products. Datsolalee made fine-coiled, perfectly symmetrical, harmoniously colored baskets that were prized by collectors. She called one of her most famous and complex baskets, comprising 56,590 stitches, *Myriads of Stars Shine Over the Graves of Our Ancestors.* Curtis photographed her a year before she died. (She lived from about 1835 to 1925.) Describing a photograph that he called *A Washo Gem,* Curtis said, "Her work has rarely been equalled in the fineness and regularity of the stitches, in perfection of symmetry and in the softness and harmonious blending of shades in the straw-color background and the brown and black patterns."

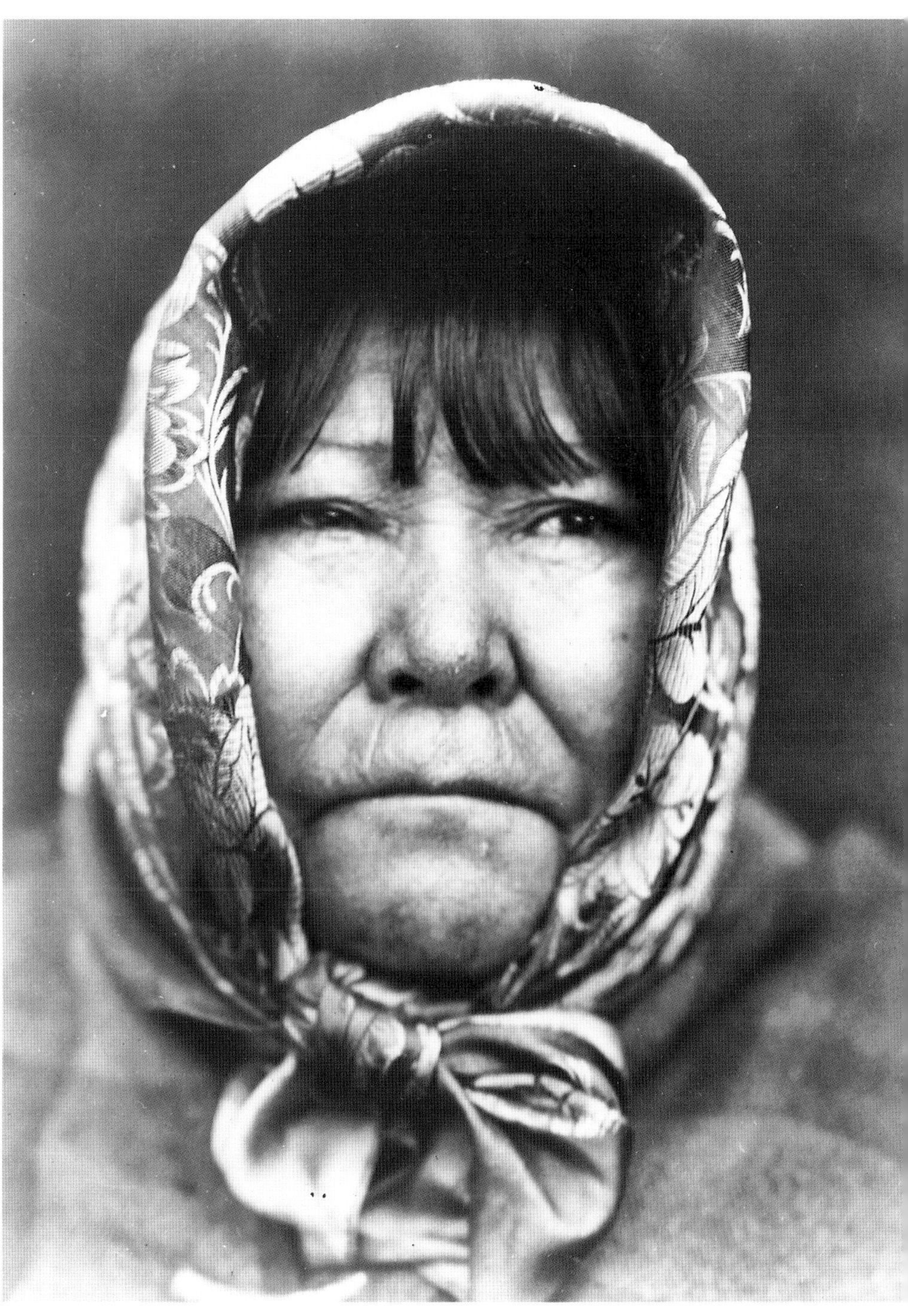

The Plateau

The Plateau region lies north of the Great Basin region and east of the Cascades, in the Snake and Columbia Rivers drainage area.

From east to west, the environment ranges from forested mountains, to vast arid plateaus covered with spiky sagebrush and salt grass, to the narrow grassy valleys of the salmon-laden tributaries of the Snake–Columbia system, to the lakes and marshes of southern Oregon. Traditionally, the Plateau tribes relied on seasonal fishing and local game and gathered and processed roots, berries, nuts, and seeds.

Beginning in the eighteenth century, when they began to acquire large numbers of horses and were able to travel to the Plains, the tribes of the eastern mountains and plateaus—Nez Perce, Flathead, Upper Pend d'Oreille, Kalispel (Lower Pend d'Oreille), Nespelem, and Kootenai—became influenced by the buffalo culture of the Plains tribes. However, they were living on reservations by the time of Edward Curtis's visit. His photographs of the women of these tribes show the influence of the buffalo culture in their dress and ornamentation. Curtis was fascinated by the story of the Nez Perce's courageous stand against Euro-American encroachment; he recounted this history at length and photographed and talked with Chief Joseph, whom he admired greatly.

The many groups living farther west along the Columbia River and its tributaries—including the Yakima, Cayuse, Spokane, and Okanagon—had also made resistance to white encroachments, which Curtis described. Some of his photographs depict women at work digging for and processing roots, staples in the Plateau tribes' diet.

Along the Columbia River near Celilo Falls, Chinookan tribes had lived in permanent villages, subsisting principally on salmon and acting as middlemen in trade between tribes to the north and south of the Columbia River. Curtis studied the Wishram at one of the few remaining Chinookan villages. He also visited the Klamath on their reservation in southern Oregon, which they shared with the Modoc.

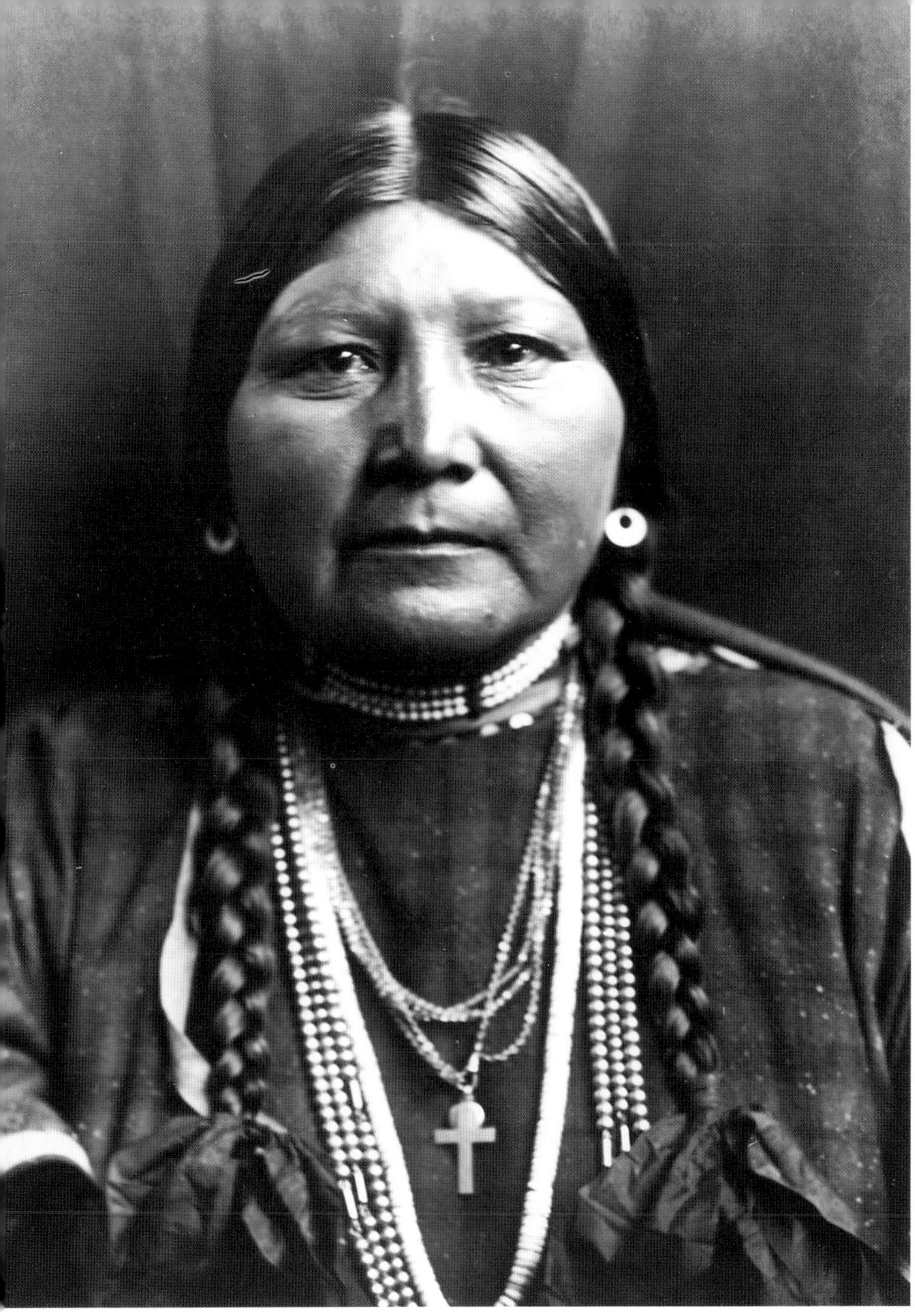

Nez Percé Matron, ©1910

This Nez Perce woman (the accent is generally not used today) was, in all likelihood, a young girl during the 1877 Nez Perce War—or more accurately, the Nez Perce flight from war. That 1,700-mile diaspora, led by Chief Joseph, is now an American legend. This woman's memories probably included the aftermath and settlement on the reservations. While a few Nez Perce were allowed to stay in their homelands in the valleys of the Clearwater River, the majority were placed under military "super-intendency" at Fort Lapwai in Idaho. Her crucifix indicates the influence of Catholic missionaries. According to statistics from 1910, 60 percent of the Nez Perce were Catholics, and 15 percent were Presbyterians. Nez Perce women and men each owned property separate from one another and were in complete charge of their own economic activities. Each was free to pursue wealth—above and beyond the fulfillment of their basic duties.

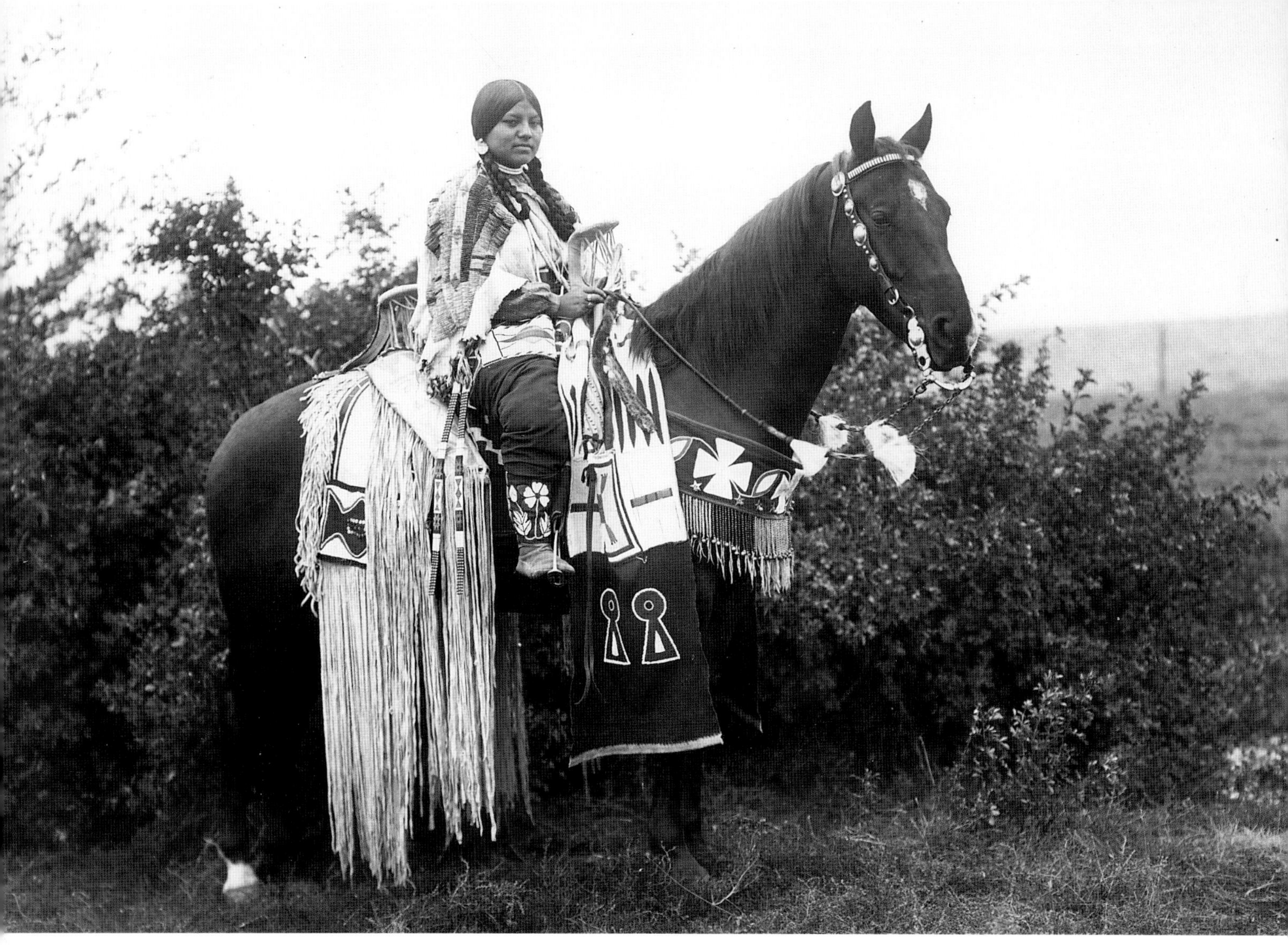

HOLIDAY TRAPPINGS— CAYUSE, ©1910

"Wealthy members of the tribes living on the Umatilla reservation in Oregon spare no expense in bedecking themselves and their mounts on gala occasions," said Curtis of this photograph. "The articles of adornment are usually of deerskin, or of commercial blankets on which designs are worked in beads." Before their relocation to the Umatilla Reservation in northeastern Oregon—where Curtis found some of the remaining 400 Cayuse—the Cayuse lived in the plateaus of eastern Oregon and Washington, near the headwaters of the Walla Walla, Umatilla, and Grande Ronde Rivers. After they acquired horses in the middle of the eighteenth century, the Cayuse were able to travel to the Plains to hunt large numbers of buffalo. Eventually, they were so good with horses that their tribal name became associated with Indian ponies in general. A Cayuse or Nez Perce family might own as many as 1,500 horses. The importance of their equestrian way of life can be seen in the great care with which their horses were dressed. The Cayuse language is considered to be an isolate within the Penutian family.

JERKING MEAT—FLATHEAD, ©1910

The Flathead are a Salishan-speaking tribe in western Montana whose name was erroneously derived from a head-deforming process employed by their western neighbors. They were given that name by early fur trappers, and although they preferred to be called Salish, the name Flathead stuck. Living on the margin of the Plateau and the Plains regions, they were influenced by both lifestyles, roaming east to hunt deer and bison once the gathering season was over. In order to quickly and efficiently preserve the kill, Flathead women "jerked" the meat by cutting it into long strips, which were then dried. The resultant jerky (which derives from *charqui*, a Spanish adaptation of a Peruvian Indian word) was light, easy to carry, and long-lasting. An extremely skilled woman could butcher three buffalo carcasses a day, producing as much as forty-five pounds of dried meat and fifty-five pounds of pemmican (ground meat mixed with fruit) from a single buffalo. While these Flathead still used tipis, many had adopted nontraditional cloth tents by 1910 and had abandoned hunting parties. When Curtis visited, 615 Flathead were living on a reservation south of Flathead Lake, near Dixon, Montana, which they shared with the Kootenai tribe.

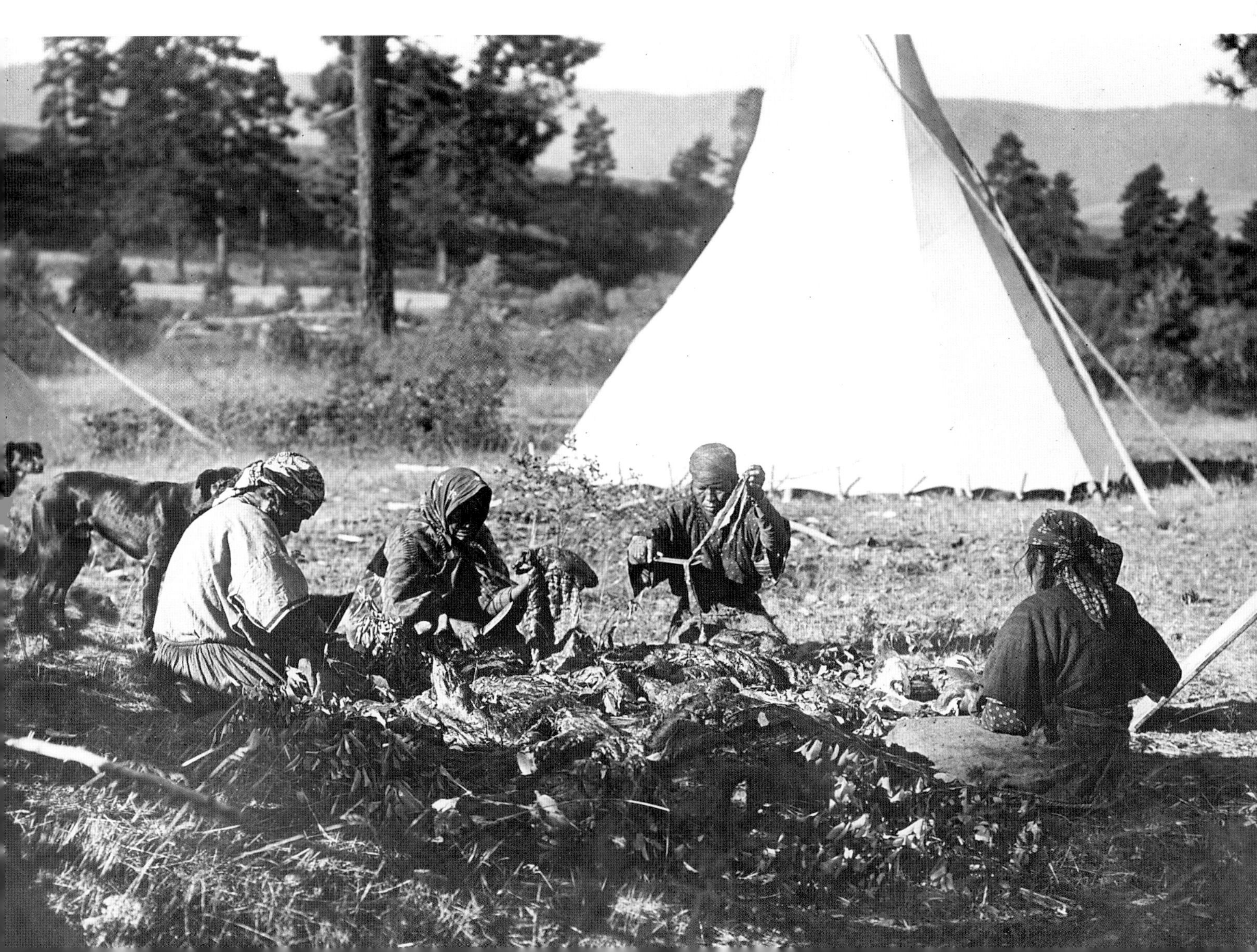

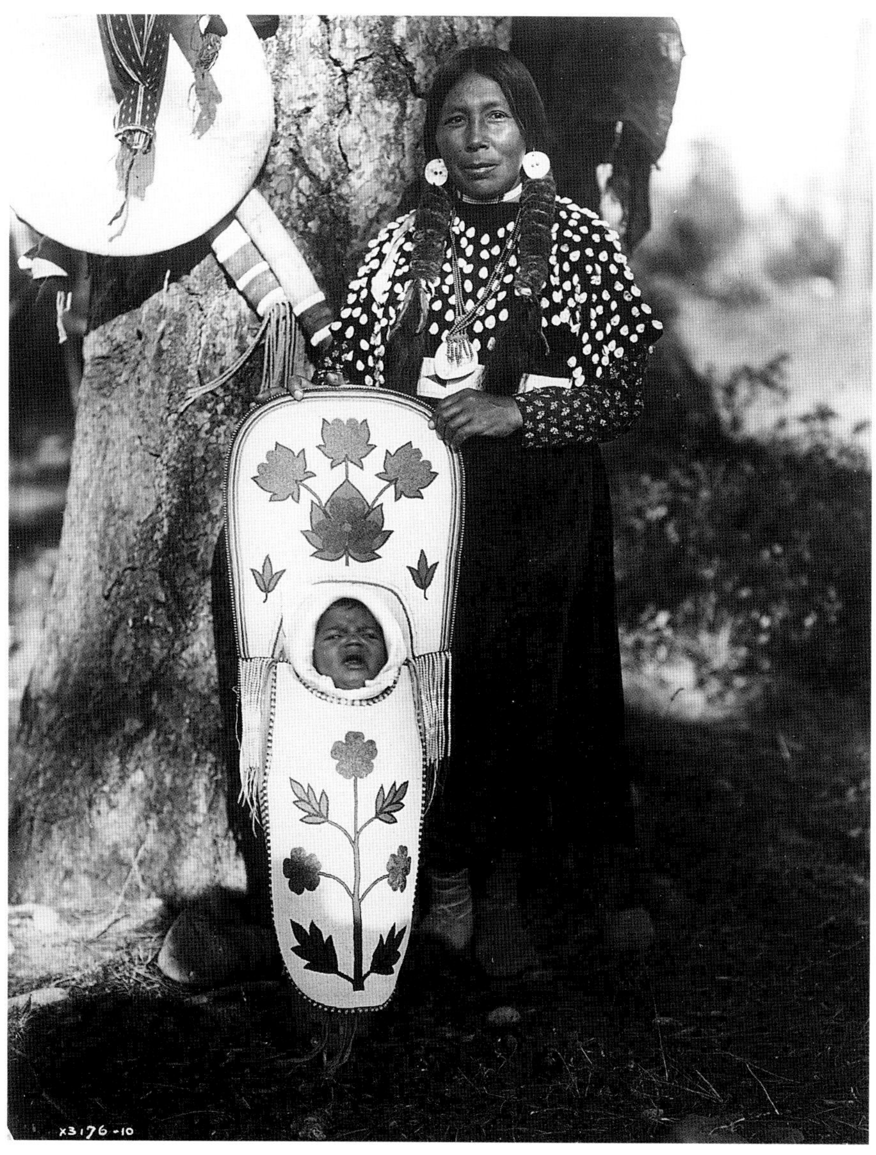

FLATHEAD MOTHER, ©1910 The Flathead refer to themselves as Salish, and since 1935 have been associated with the Kootenai and known as "The Confederated Salish and Kootenai Tribes." They live in western Montana around the area of Flathead Lake, an area of singular beauty. This Flathead mother, in traditional dress, displays the ornately embossed and beaded cradleboard used to carry her infant during travel. Rabbit furs were often used as diapers for infants.

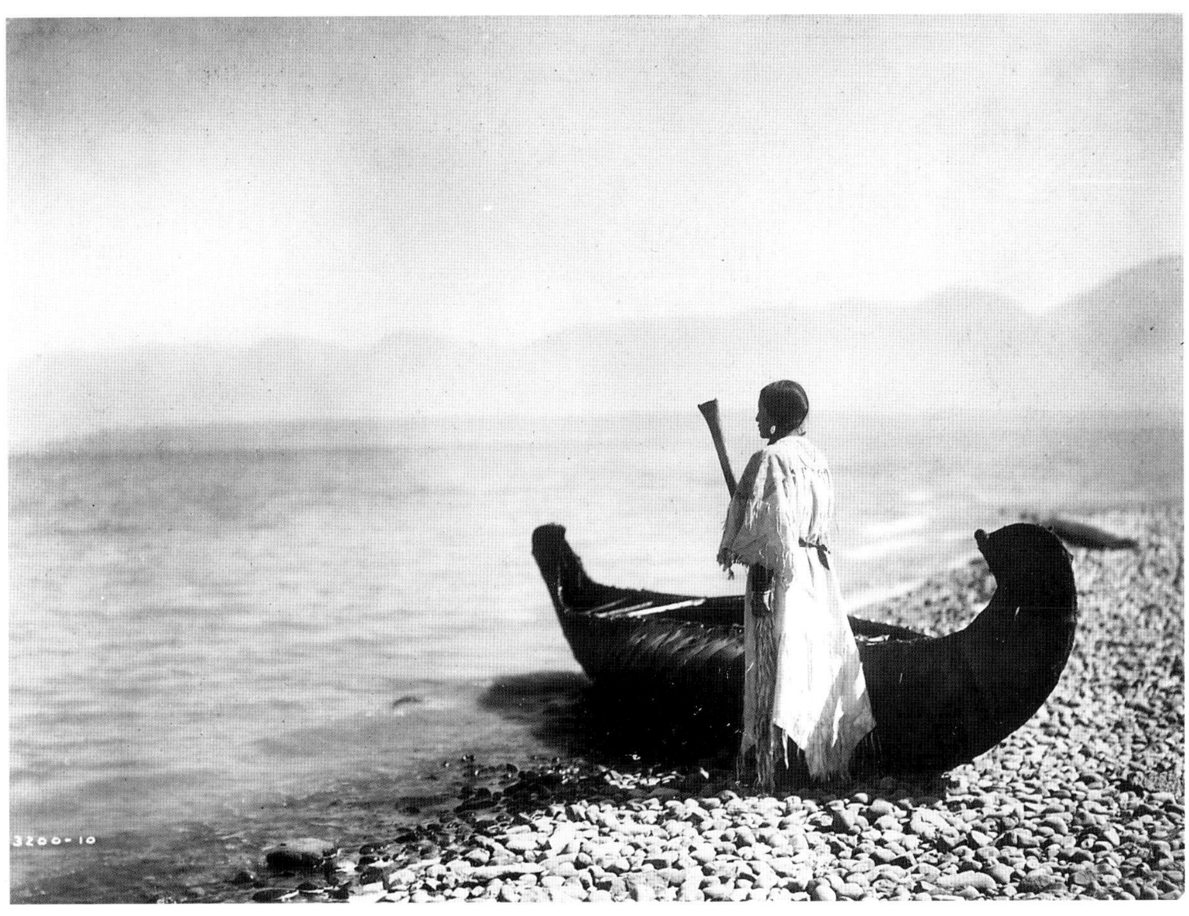

KUTENAI WOMAN, ©1910

The Kootenai (the spelling used today) speak a language unrelated to that of any other Plateau people. Aboriginally, they lived farther north, in the Canadian boreal forests. Following large game, they moved southward, establishing themselves along the Kootenay River valley. They were excellent hunters, fishers, and gatherers, fully exploiting the bounty from the Kootenay River area. The men hunted and fished and took care of the horses, while the women gathered plants and other foodstuff, prepared the food, and cared for the children. The "sturgeon-nosed" canoe was a Kootenai signature, and this woman's pose with one against the watery backdrop is Curtis at his most sentimental.

DUSTY DRESS—KALISPEL, ©1910

This young woman's name, according to Curtis, was Skohlpa, which the *Kalispel Dictionary* (published in 1879) defines as "dusty dress." Her cloth dress, cut in a traditional pattern, was ornamented with cowrie shells. For this portrait, Skohlpa wound her braids with otter fur, with weasel skin dangling from each. The light bands on her hair were made with clay. In the summer, Skohlpa joined other Kalispel women in gathering camas. This pulpy root was such a staple to her people that one of their common names derives from it (Kalispel, meaning "camas people"). The group was also known as Pend d'Oreille, referring to the large shell ear pendants worn by members of the tribe. At puberty, according to Curtis's research, a Kalispel girl was sent into the hills without food to pray for six to eight days. She could gather berries but was not allowed to eat them. Instead, she prayed to them: "When I am a woman, may I have success in gathering berries like you!"

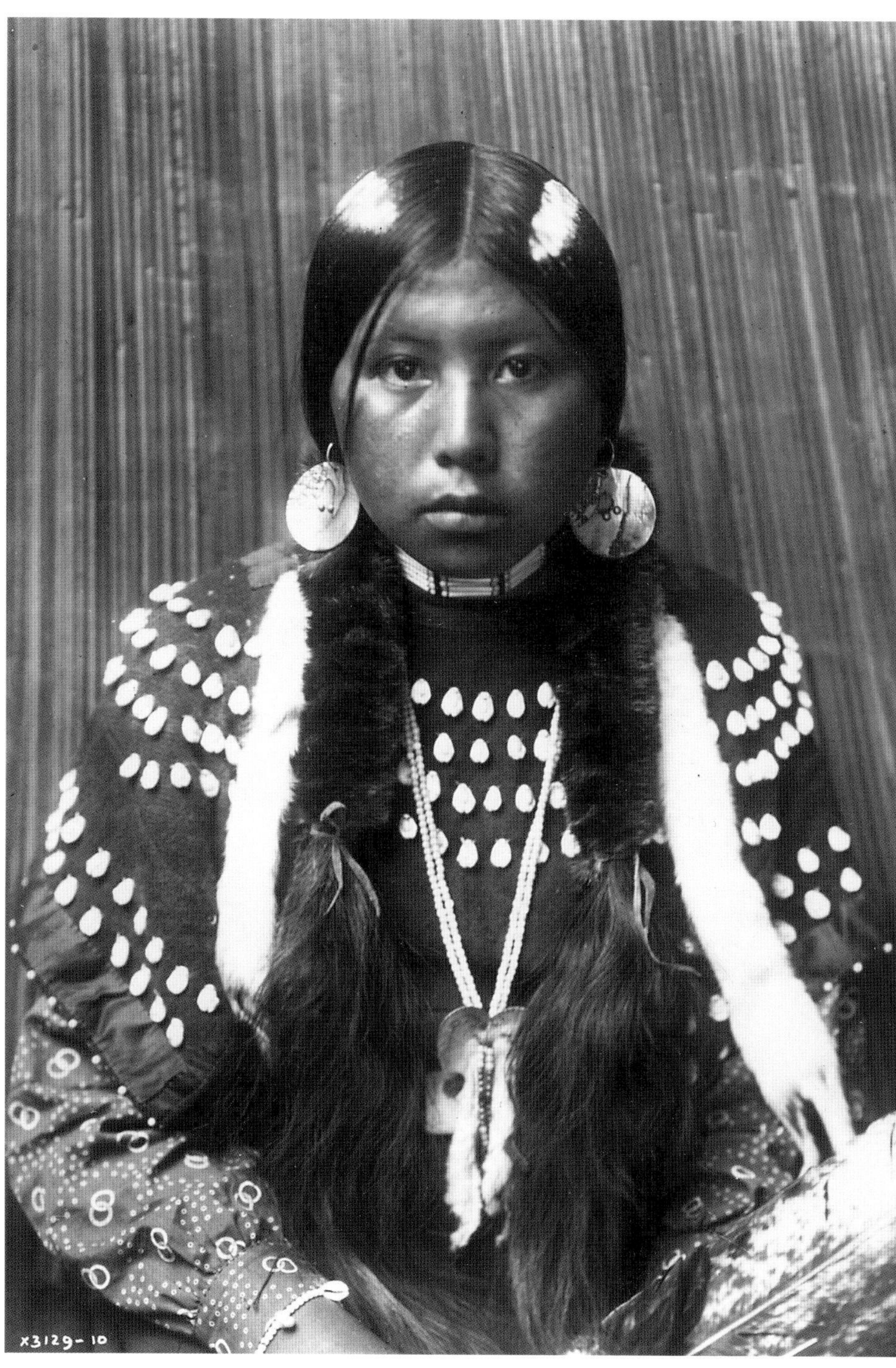

Nespilim Girl, ©1905

In a caption for this posed portrait of a young woman standing coyly among the foliage, Curtis remarked that in the early nineteenth century "various explorers noted that the bands dwelling along the upper course of the Columbia, among which the Nespilim were included, wore practically no clothing, excepting as the cold made some protection necessary." Critics of Curtis's research have noted that occasionally the same clothing and props appear on subjects from different tribes. In this case, the deerskin "wing" dress worn by this young woman was also shown on a Cayuse woman in the photograph titled *In the Forest*. The Nespelem—the current spelling—and Sanpoil, traditional neighbors, today live on the Colville Reservation with eleven other distinct tribes. In nineteenth-century traditional culture, the spring cycle saw villages break up into groups of several families to dig roots and to fish for salmon. Women gathered camas bulbs, bitterroot, piñon, and berries. Men caught the fish, which the women prepared for eating or storage.

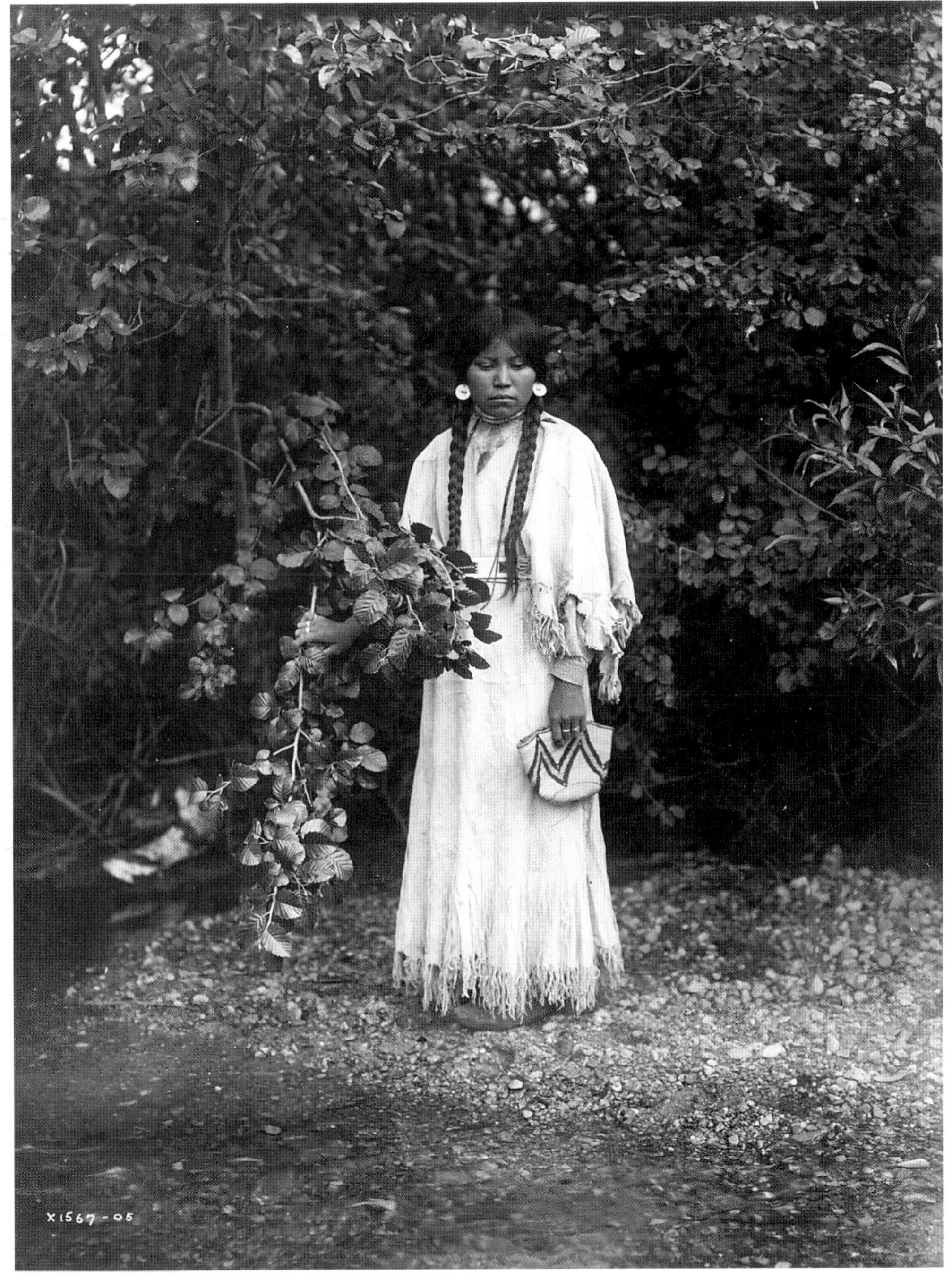

The Wishram

The Wishram, an upper Chinookan tribe called Wishham by Curtis, were blessed with one of the best locations in North America for salmon fishing and trading, along the Columbia River. The culturally similar Wasco were their neighbors. The bounty of salmon, in fact, brought them prosperity and became a staple of their widespread trading before epidemics decimated the tribe. Many Plateau tribes—including the Yakima, Spokane, Columbia Salish, Klikitat, Walla Walla, Umatilla, Cayuse, Palouse, Nez Perce, and Klamath—met at Celilo Falls to exchange goods, with the Wishram and Wasco sometimes acting as middlemen. They bought and sold blankets, robes, horses, shells, canoes, slaves, dried salmon, furs, skins, dried roots, and many other commodities.

Because of the ready supply of salmon and its attendant wealth, Wishram families were sedentary. Their villages along the Columbia River were permanent settlements, and their homes were substantial semisubterranean structures fashioned from vertical planks and with bark roofs.

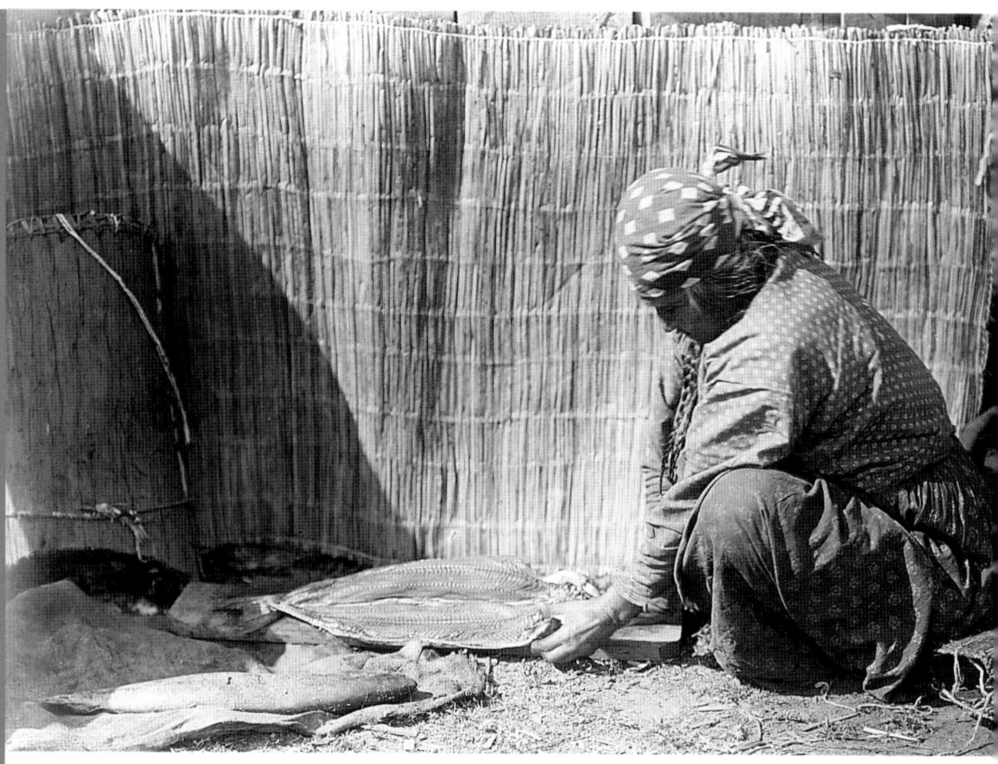

PREPARING SALMON—WISHHAM, ©1909

One means by which the Wishram preserved salmon, efficiently and almost indefinitely, was by filleting and then drying the fish in the sun. They also slowly smoked the salmon over an enclosed cedarwood fire and then pressed the smoked fillets together in bales, to be stored for the seasonal downturn in the salmon catch. All of these vital functions were delegated to Wishram women, who in general dominated the actual trading of salmon to outsiders. One Chinook explained, "The women could talk to white men better . . . and were willing to talk more."

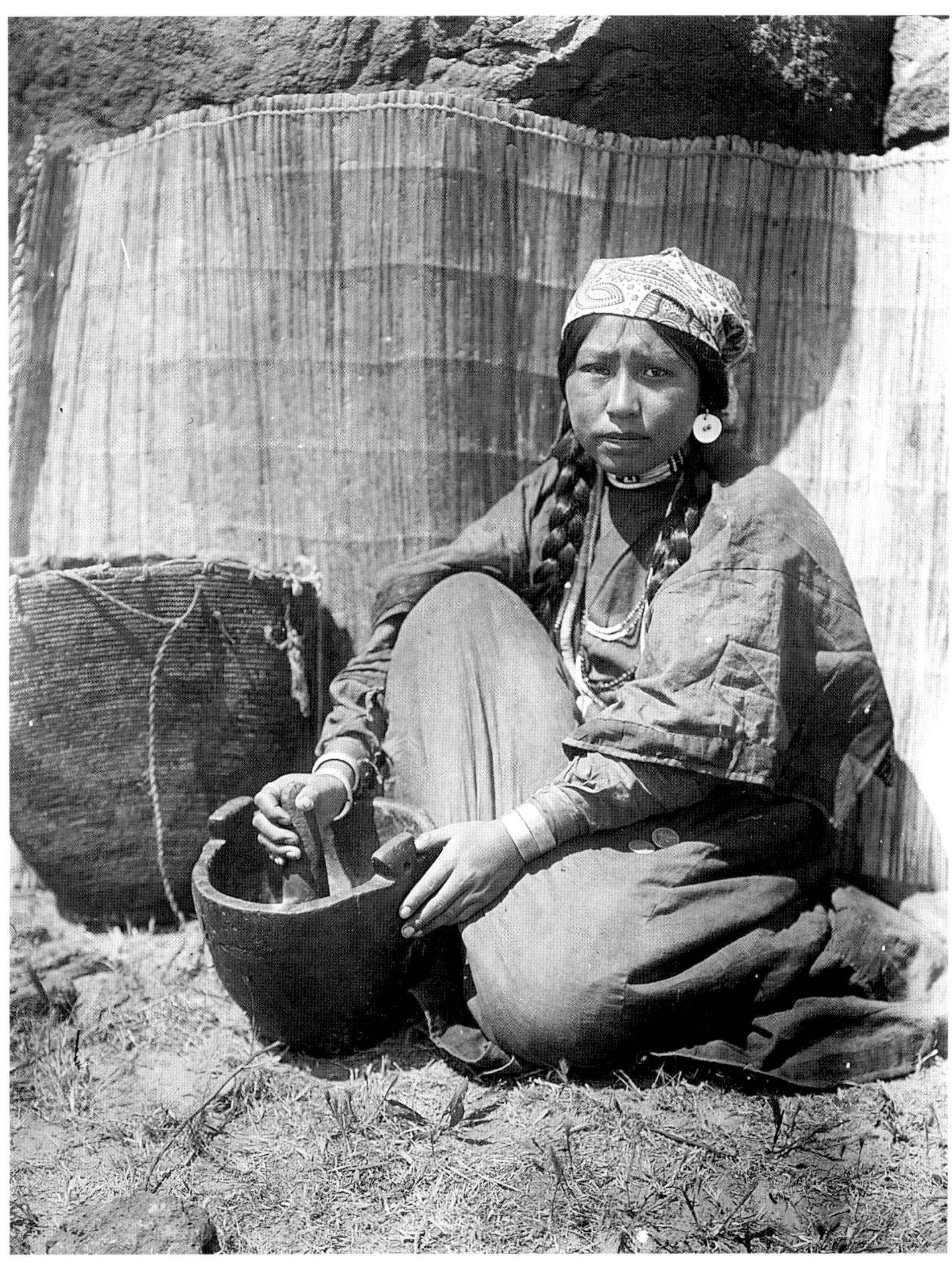

POUNDING FISH—WISHHAM, ©1909

While salmon was the mainstay of the Plateau people's diet, other fish—steelhead and other trout, sturgeon, eel—were also netted, speared, or trapped by the men. The surplus was processed by the women: filleted, sun-dried on racks, smoked on cedar fires, and pounded into a thick, powdery substance. Plateau women relied on their exceptional basketry skills to create both gathering and cooking containers. However, the wooden mortar and pestle shown in this photograph were also commonly used in traditional cooking in the Plateau region.

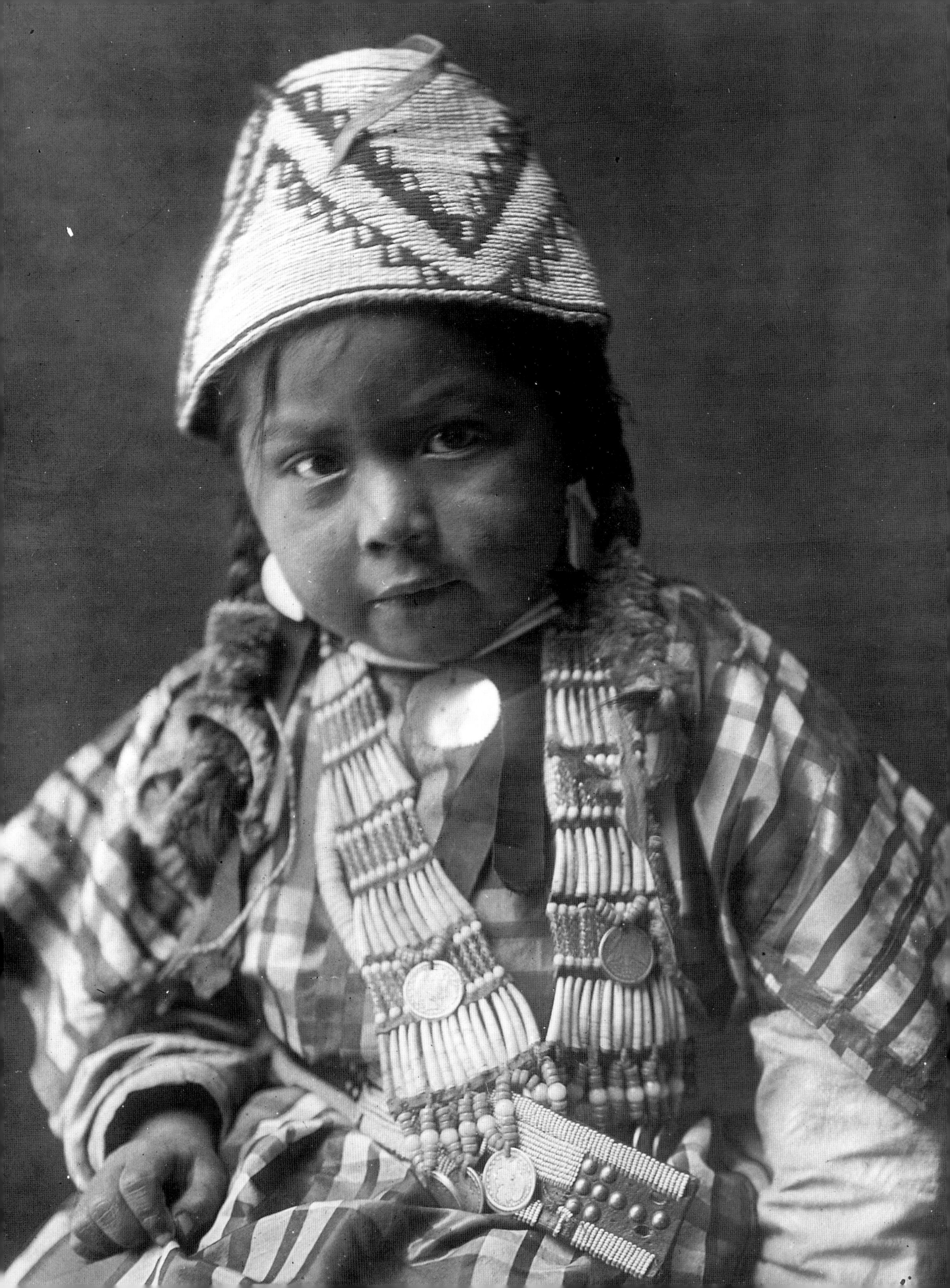

Wishham Child, ©1909 *(opposite)*

No doubt in anticipation of posing her child for Curtis's portrait, a Wishram mother dressed her daughter to indicate the family's wealth. The necklace is made of beads, shells, and dentalium, with foreign coins attached. (Native Americans did not mint metal currency.) The cloth for the girl's dress, cut in a traditional pattern, was acquired in trade. She also wears a tightly woven hat; these hats were at one time worn daily by Chinookan women but, by this period, were used only for special occasions.

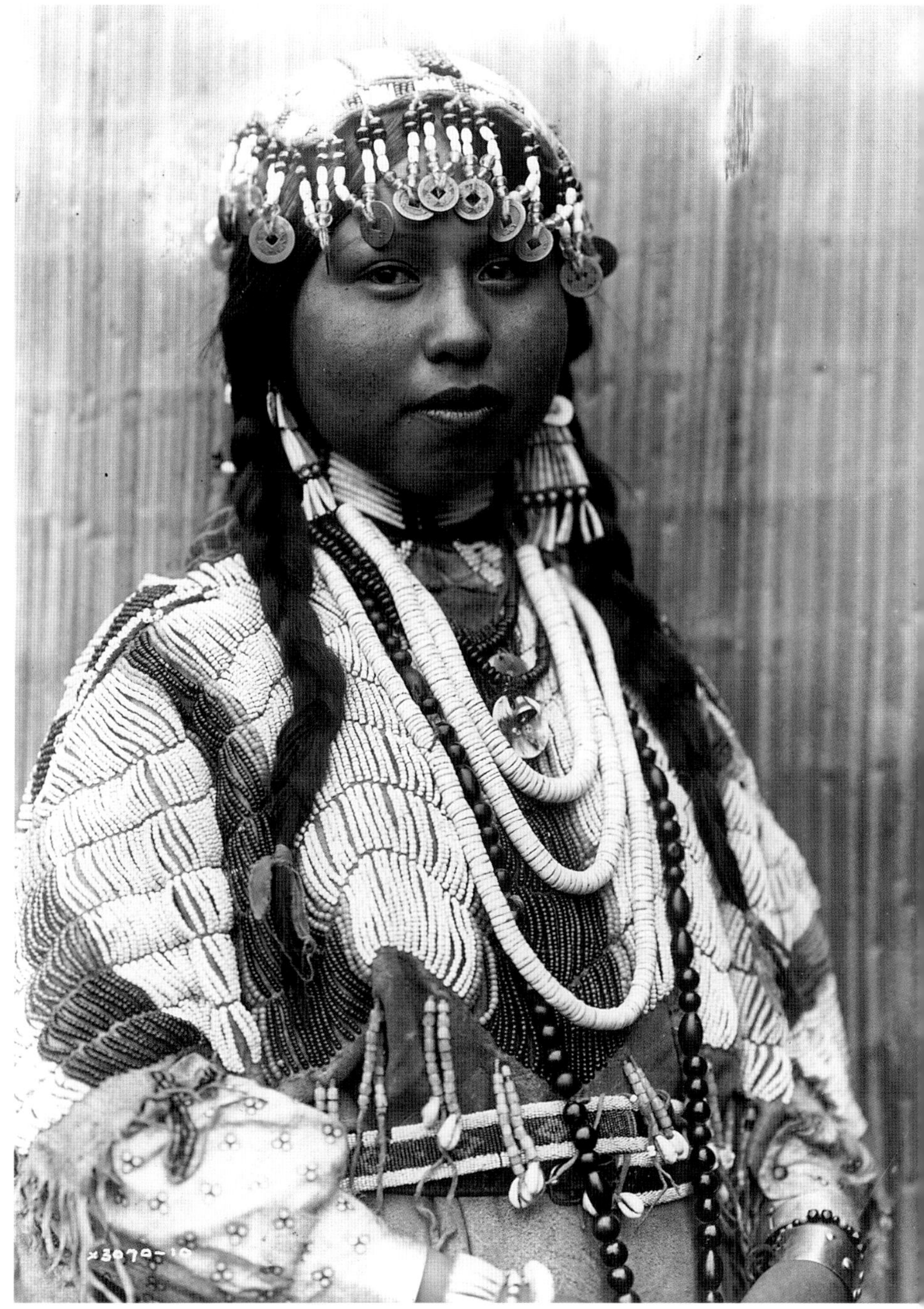

Wishham Bride, ©1910

The aesthetic accomplishments of her tribe are reflected in this Wishram bride's stunning wardrobe. The Wishram were influential in the salmon trade, and this bride's family was obviously one of great wealth. She wears a heavily beaded deerskin dress (possibly acquired in trade from a Plains tribe), shell bead necklaces (from a Northwest Coast tribe), dentalium earrings, and an ornate headdress that features, in addition to the intricate beadwork, some Chinese coins. Such headdresses were worn by Wishram girls at their marriage ceremonies. Preliminary negotiations began when a messenger from the suitor's family brought the girl's father an offer for her hand in marriage. When an agreement was reached, valuable gifts were formally presented by the bridegroom's family to the bride's family. This was followed by a number of feasts, and the marriage was validated by a series of gift exchanges between the two families.

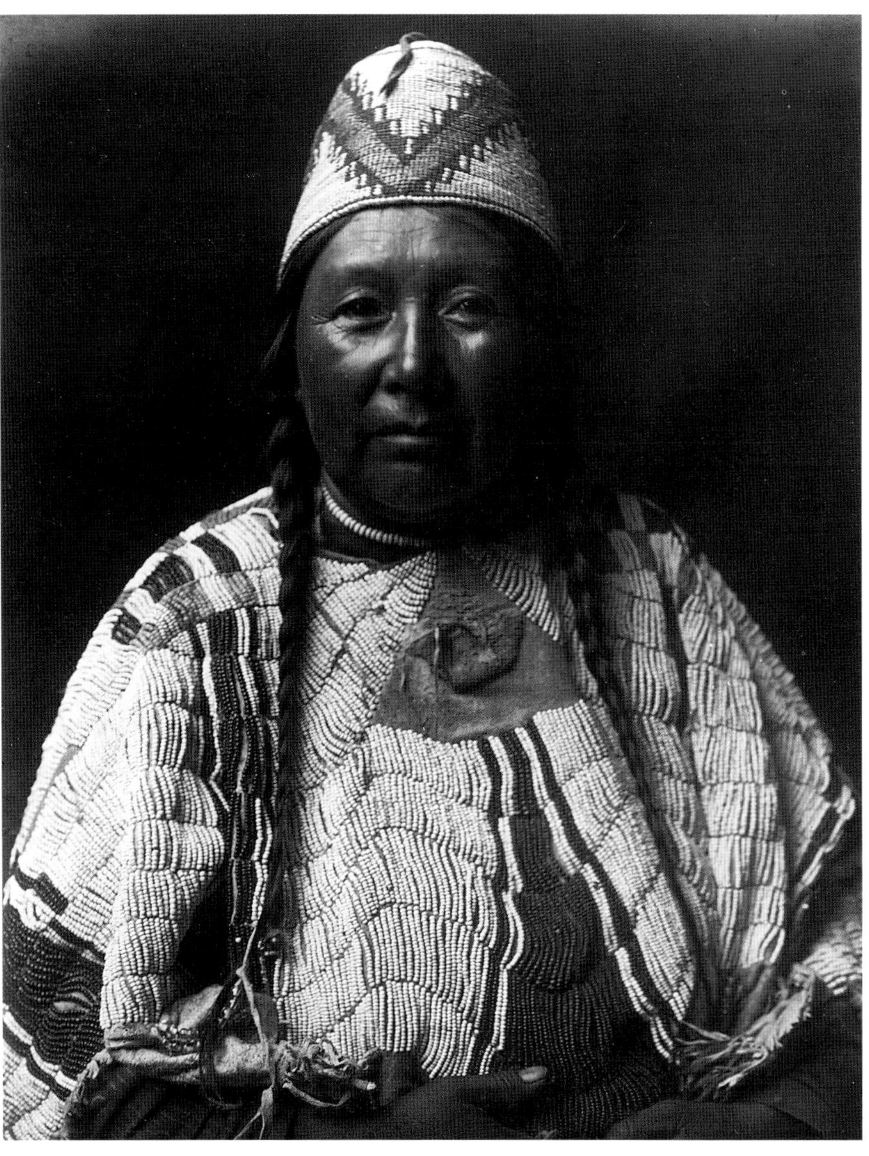

Wife of Mnaínak — Yakima, ©1910

Mnaínak was the son of a Yakima headman of the village called Skin located north of the Columbia River, Washington, near Celilo Falls. This summer fishing village was built near the foot of the falls and had many drying sheds, which were used to preserve the salmon catch. Traditionally, leaders were chosen for their wisdom and generosity, and leadership was often hereditary. Thus, according to Curtis, Mnaínak held great influence among the remnant of bands that constituted the Yakima in 1910. His wife wears a heavily beaded buckskin dress in this Curtis portrait, indicating her wealth.

When whites began to settle on their lands in the mid-1800s, the Yakima were instrumental in forming a union of various Plateau tribes for protection and to resist the taking of their lands. The Yakima War, involving many of the Columbia River tribes, began in 1855 after the discovery of gold caused a flood of prospectors. The war ended in 1858, and the following year the Yakima treaty of 1855 was ratified, leading to the formation of the Yakima Indian Agency. After the passage of the Dawes Severalty Act in 1887, some of the reservation's best land was sold by individuals to whom it had been allotted. In the 1970s, the Yakima Indian Reservation was about 1.5 million acres, but much of the irrigable land was leased to non-Indians.

DRYING PIAHÉ, YAKIMA, ©1909

The Yakima are a Sahaptin-speaking tribe who lived along a tributary of the Columbia River (the Yakima River) in southern Washington. When the salmon made their annual runs up the rivers in March and again in June, Yakima men netted, speared, or trapped the fish in weirs. According to Curtis, Yakima women gathered a wide variety of vegetable foods, including twenty-three kinds of roots, eighteen types of berries, as well as nuts and moss. Popular roots were carrots, camas, and bitterroot *(Lewisia rediviva)*, called *piahé*. This Yakima woman is processing piahé by peeling it and drying it in the sun. It was then pulverized, moistened, and pressed into cakes. When dry, the piahé cakes were strung on a thong for transportation. Piahé was often eaten boiled to a thin mush and mixed with salmon. Bitterroot's pink flower is now the state flower of Montana.

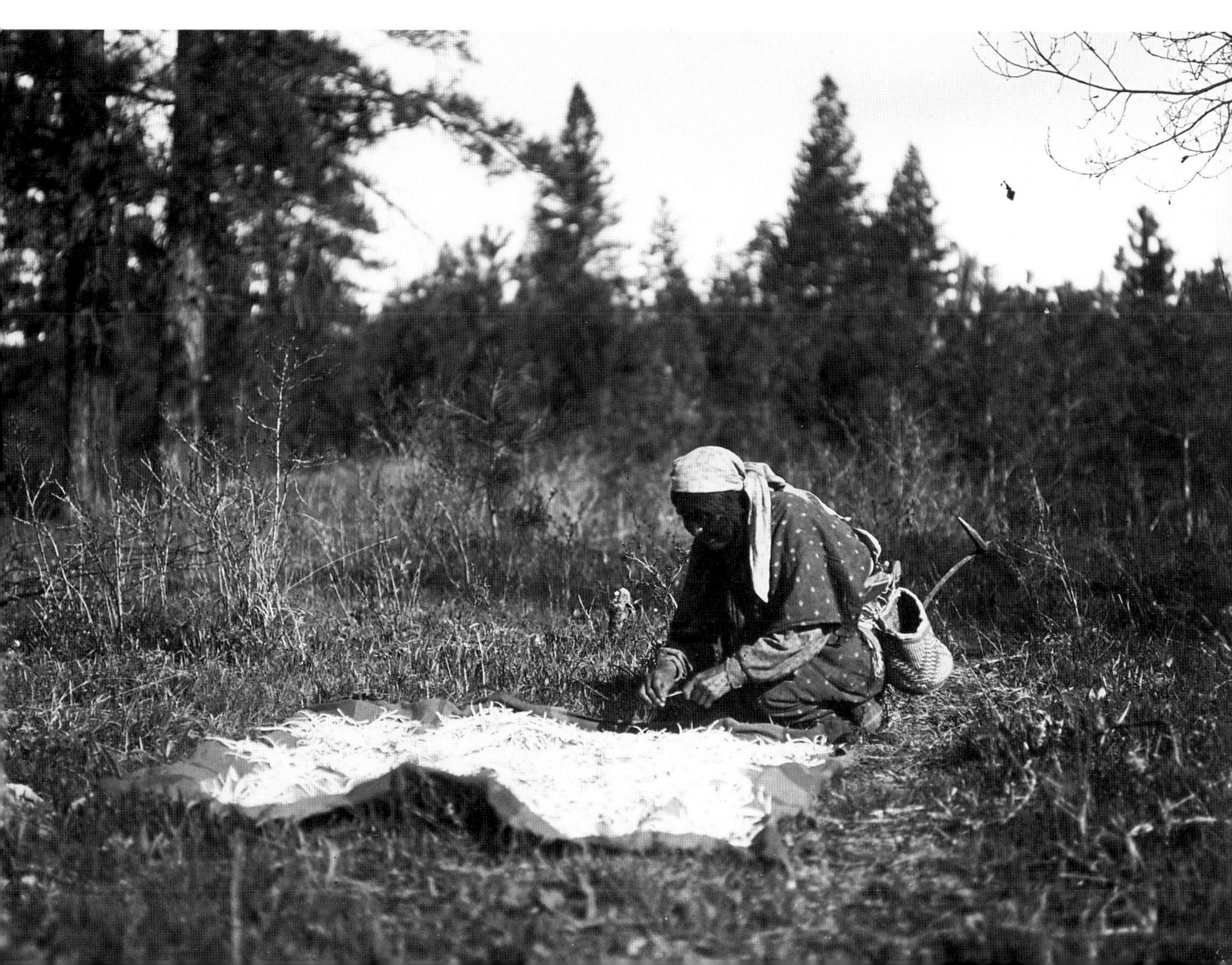

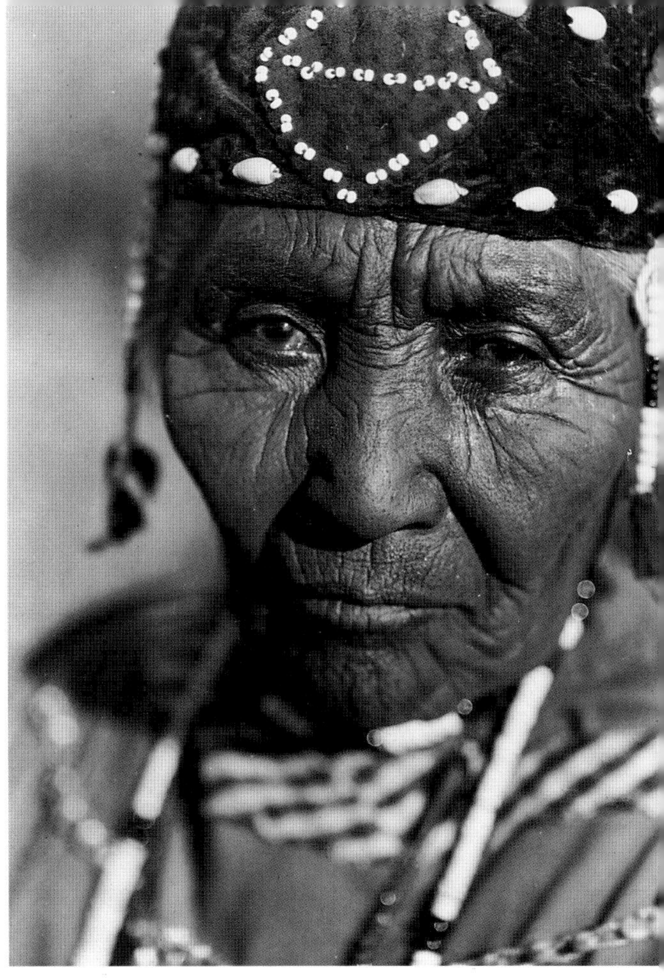

WIFE OF MODOC HENRY—KLAMATH, ©1923

The Klamath and Modoc speak dialects of a single language belonging to the Penutian phylum. They lived for centuries as neighbors along what is now the Oregon–California border. Anthropologist Theodore Stern wrote, "The Modoc diverged toward California and the Klamath toward the Plateau. . . . Despite their differences, the two peoples retained a substantial common base." Both the Modoc and Klamath fought fiercely to keep their lands—the Modoc were, in fact, among the last Native Americans to submit to "resettlement." This Klamath woman, married to a Modoc, wears a cloth cap decorated with shells and beads, a sign of affluence.

GRINDING WÓKAS—KLAMATH, ©1923

One of the food staples of the Klamath was *wókas,* the seedpod of the pond lily *(Nymphaea polysepala),* which could be found for miles around Upper Klamath Lake, Klamath Marsh, and the quiet tributaries of the Williamson and Sprague Rivers in southern Oregon. Although plentiful, wókas required an elaborate processing ritual before they could be eaten, with several bushels ultimately yielding only a few pounds of flour. The unripe seedpods of the wókas were gathered by canoe in August and September. After being stored in pits to decompose, the seeds were parched and hulled by Klamath women and then winnowed and stored for future use. By 1923, the Klamath were on a reservation near enough to the Klamath Lakes that, in all likelihood, Curtis did not have to re-create the traditional subsistence methods for the camera. They were still a self-supporting people, according to a government report, with little desire for outside assistance. In 1954, the Klamath reservation lands were "terminated" by the federal government—that is, the tribe's assets were liquidated and divided among individual tribal members. Although "termination" caused the loss of some of their lands, they successfully retained tribal identity, and in 1986 they regained federal recognition of tribal status.

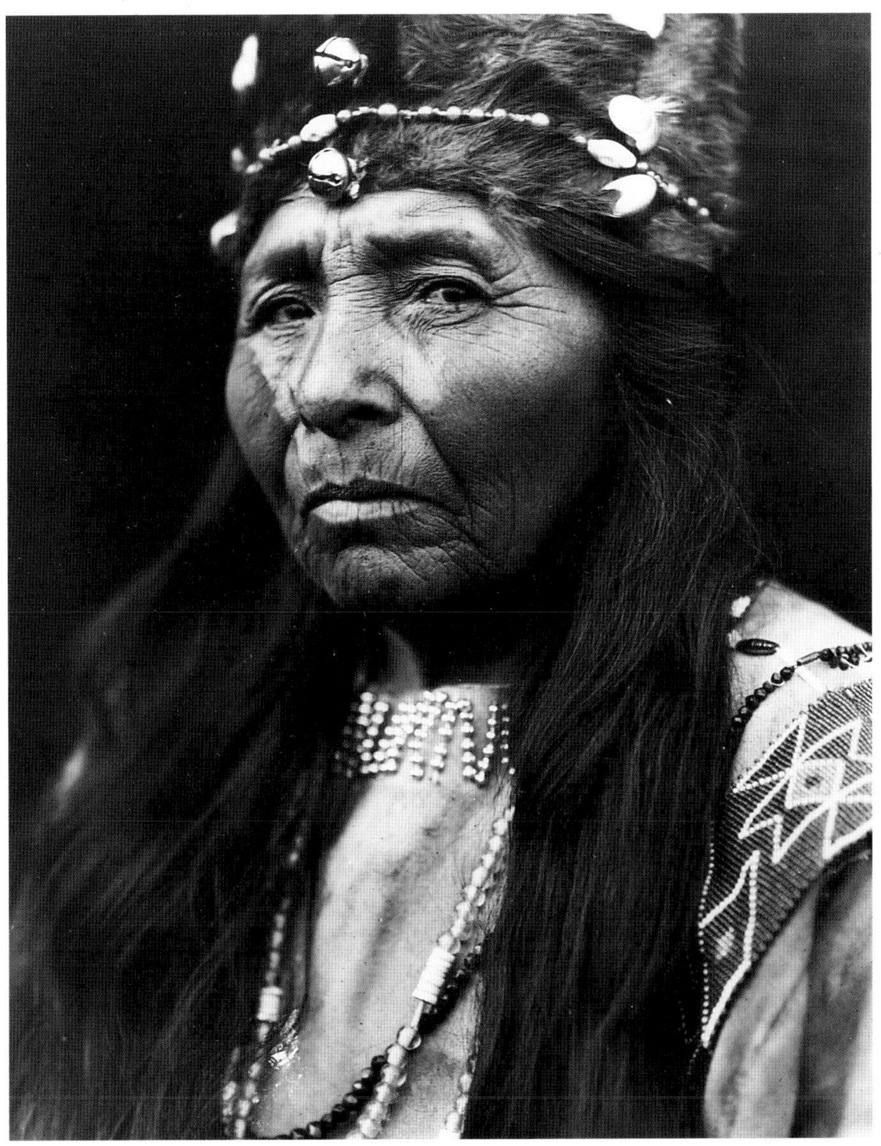

KLAMATH WOMAN, ©1923 Possessing one of the more memorable faces captured by Curtis, this Klamath woman combines a pride and a wariness of expression that speaks volumes about the Klamath people's continuing independence of lifestyle at that time, despite their confinement to a reservation. She is wearing a fur cap decorated with shells and beads—worn by wealthy individuals—and a beaded buckskin dress of Plains style.

The Northwest Coast

Curtis, a native of Seattle, began his study of Indians in his own backyard, with the Coast Salish peoples around Puget Sound. One of his earliest photographs was of "Princess" Angeline, daughter of Chief Siahl (or Sealth), after whom Seattle was named. Princess Angeline was a Suquamish, now recognized as part of the Southern Coast Salish. Speaking a Southern Lushootseed language, they were related to the Duwamish, Puyallup, and Nisqually. Another Southern Coast Salish group, the Skokomish, were speakers of Twana.

Curtis published his photographs and research on the Coast Salish peoples in 1913 as volume 9 of *The North American Indian*; it opens with his memorial to the project's principal patron, J. P. Morgan, who died before the volume was completed and less than halfway through the planned twenty-volume project.

Curtis spent considerable time with the Nootkan peoples on the western coast of Vancouver Island and the Kwakiutl tribes of the British Columbia coast, two branches of the Wakashan linguistic family. He devoted a portion of each field season from 1910 to 1914 to work among the Kwakiutl groups and collected so much data that he had to use a thinner paper to be able to include it in one standard-size volume.

Many of his photographs reflect cultures with highly structured social systems. The rich marine resources of the Northwest Coast made the Indians who fished and gathered them among the wealthiest in North America. They could collect and store enough in the summer to be able to concentrate on ceremony in the winter. Their permanent villages of plank houses faced beaches or streams, where they could easily beach their canoes.

Social alliances were validated by the potlatch, a public ceremonial and social event at which huge quantities of material wealth were distributed. Among the Kwakiutl, myth cycles and ceremonies were highly elaborate, and mythical beings were represented by dancers wearing carved masks often embellished with movable beaks or fins.

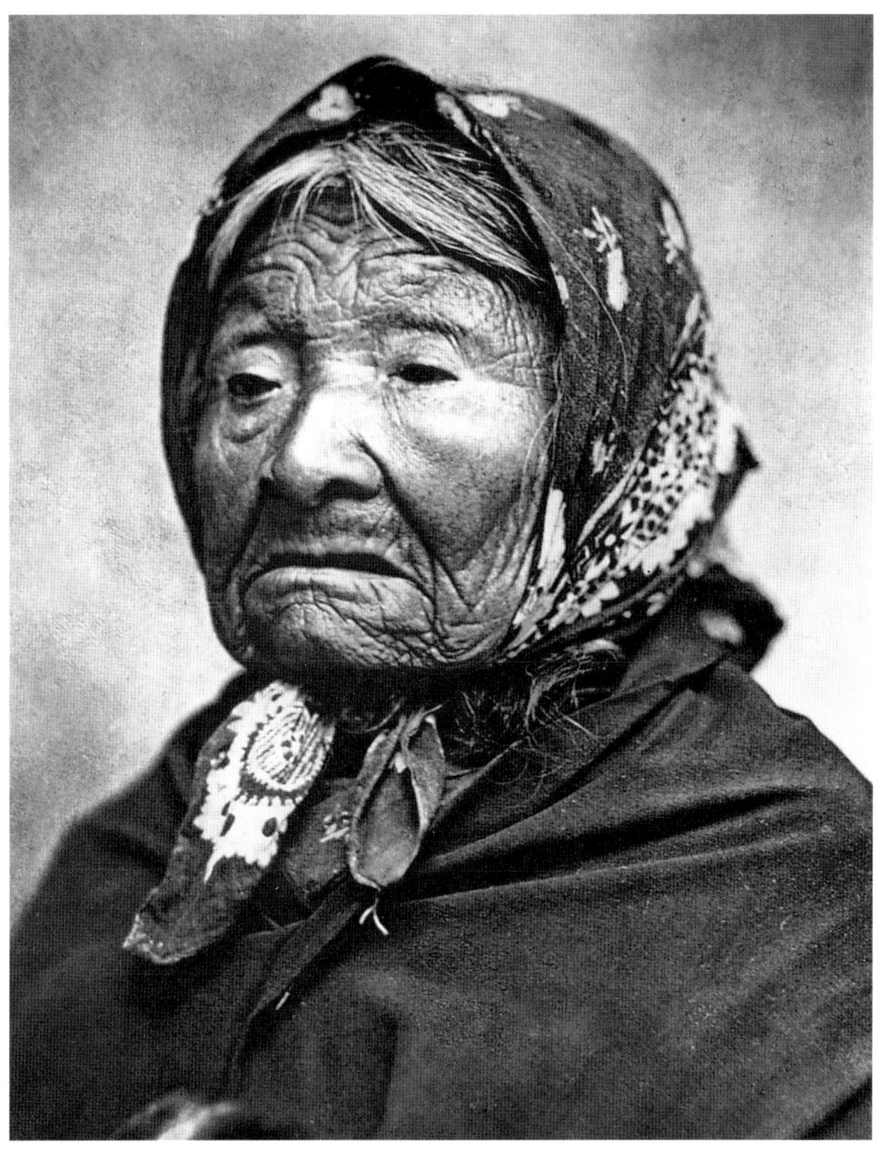

PRINCESS ANGELINE, ©1899

Princess Angeline was one of Curtis's first Native American subjects. A familiar figure on the streets of Seattle, Angeline was a daughter of Siahl, a Suquamish chief who sold the land on which the city stands and for whom the city was named. She lived in a shack along Seattle's waterfront, eking out a living by digging for clams. Over the years, she became one of the city's resident "characters," a reputation she may have cultivated in order to earn a modest income as a photography model. Curtis recalled years later, "I paid the princess a dollar for each picture I made." Besides earning Curtis's respect, Princess Angeline was responsible for his growing interest in all the Indians of the Puget Sound region. One of his shots of Angeline—digging clams out of the Puget Sound mudflats—won grand prize at the National Photographic Convention in 1896. This portrait of her is one of his best-known images. And "image" it was, published in a sepia soft-focus tone that soon became his nostalgic trademark—a remnant of his wedding and portrait photography style.

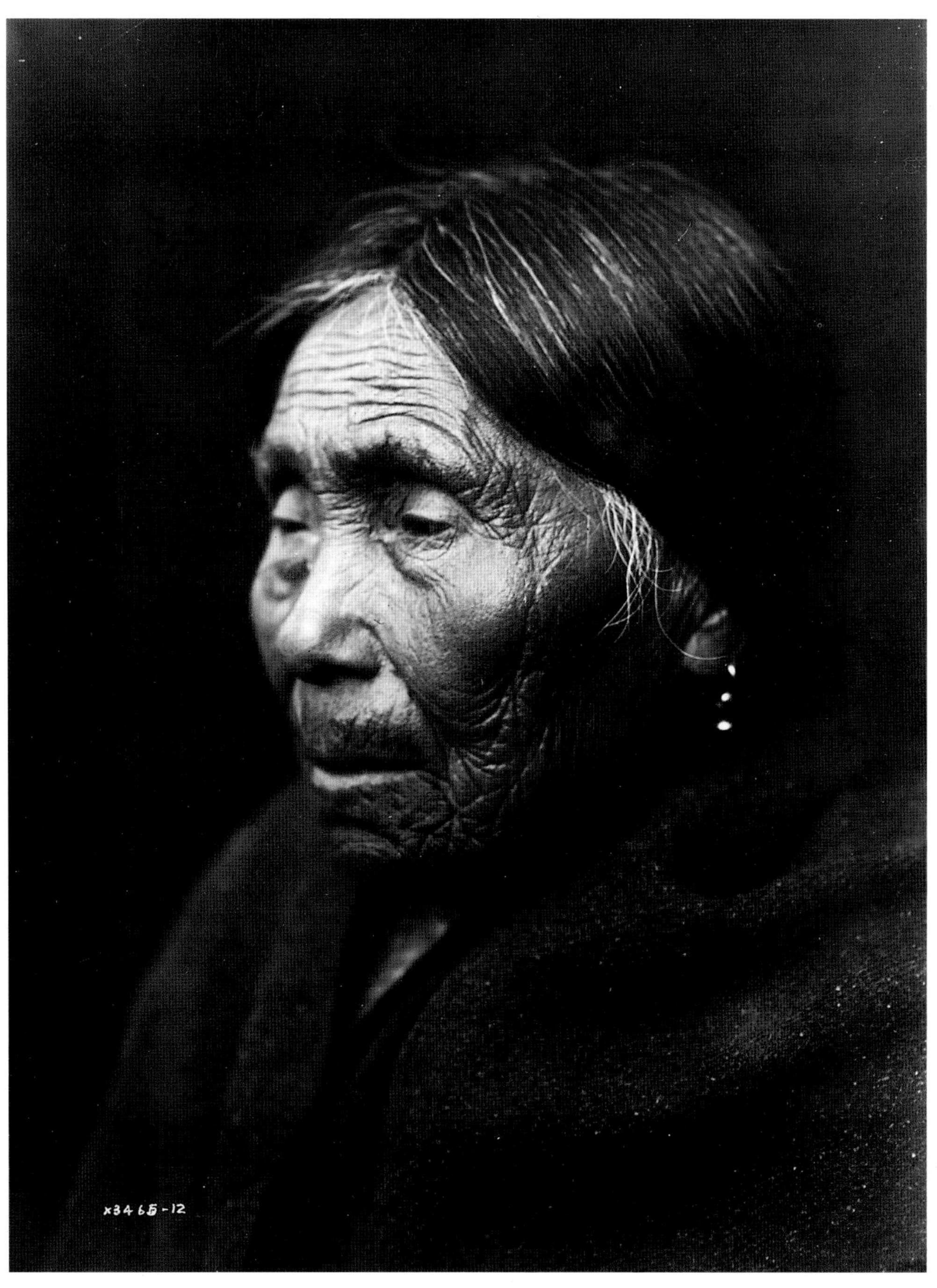

CHIMAKUM WOMAN, ©1912

In the case of the Chemakum (the spelling used today) tribe who lived on the northeastern corner of the Olympic Peninsula, in Washington, Curtis was able to realize his oft-stated goal of collecting and gathering vital information about native cultures that would otherwise "be lost for all time." As he wrote, perhaps with this dignified Chemakum woman in mind, "The passing of every old man or woman means the passing of some tradition, some knowledge of sacred rites possessed by no other." The Chemakum were part of the Chimakuan language family, which existed on the peninsula between Hood Canal and Port Townsend Bay. Chemakum men were excellent seal hunters and whalers, as were the neighboring Makah people. Chemakum women, in addition to their domestic duties, were responsible for gathering crabs, mussels, clams, seaweed, fern roots, camas bulbs, and assorted wild berries. However, by 1912, when Curtis photographed the Chemakum, the whale population had been hunted nearly to extinction and the 200 remaining Chemakum were being absorbed into other groups and disappearing as a distinct people. The Quileute people, living in coastal La Push and on the Lower Hoh River, are the only surviving people who speak the Chimakuan language.

The Tule Gatherer, ©1910

The Cowichan—the group to which this tule gatherer belonged—were Central Coast Salish peoples, a group that also included the Squamish, Clallam, Nooksak, and Halkomelem. Resources were plentiful, and these peoples traded and intermarried with one another. Tule, or cattail, is a tall and resilient reed that grows wild in the shallow waters of lakes and ponds and surrounding wetlands. Women gathered the tules in open boats, tying off bundles of the stalks, which were then transported back to the home base. The women wove the tule stalks into mats that could be used for a number of different purposes, including bedding, temporary rain coverings, roofing for their temporary summer shelters or walls of permanent winter houses, and padding for the bottom of their canoes. "If a family decided to move upstream for a time, or to visit the berry-patches or the root-digging grounds, or to sail to a distant bay for good fishing," wrote Curtis, "an indispensable part of their equipage was the great rolls of wide tule mats."

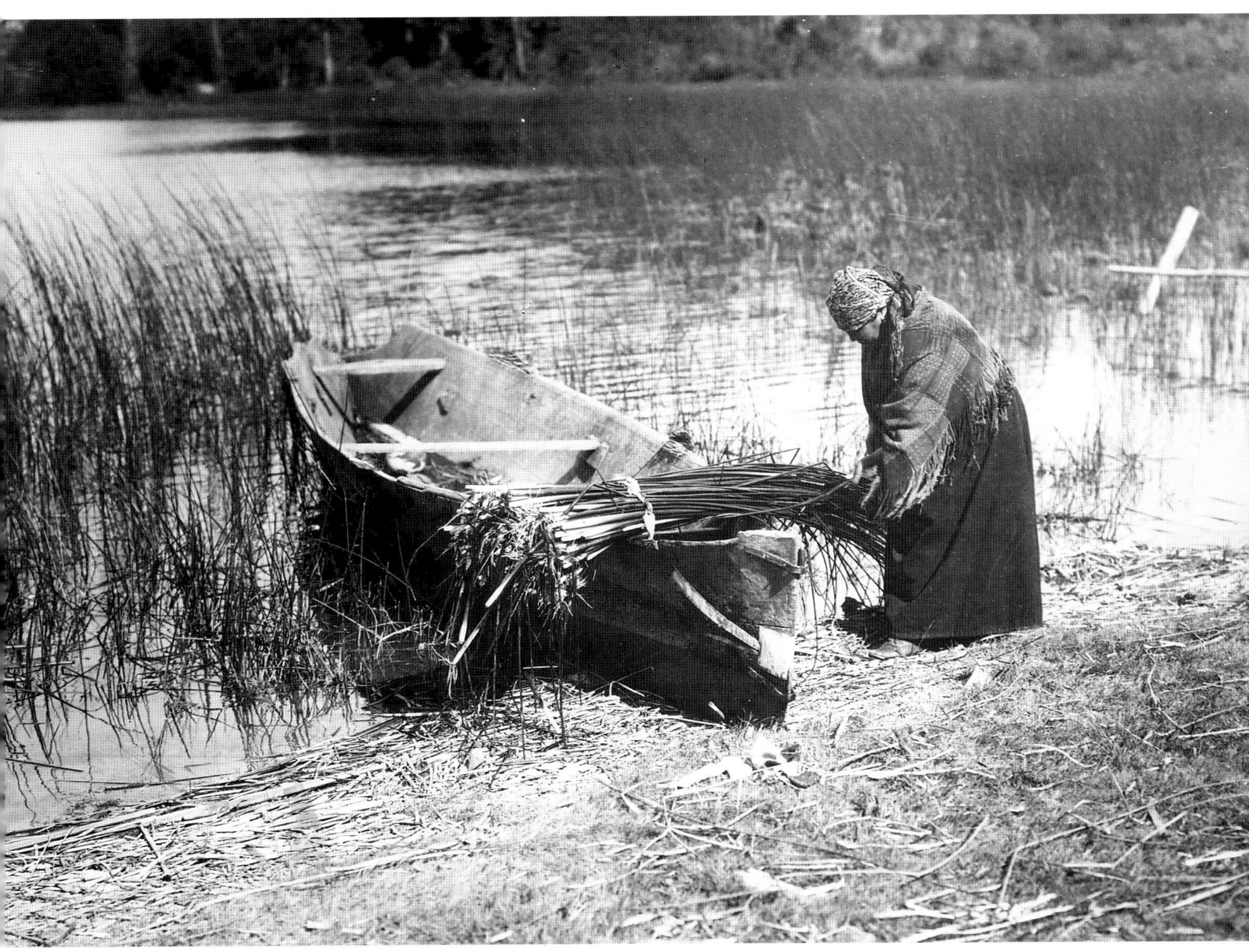

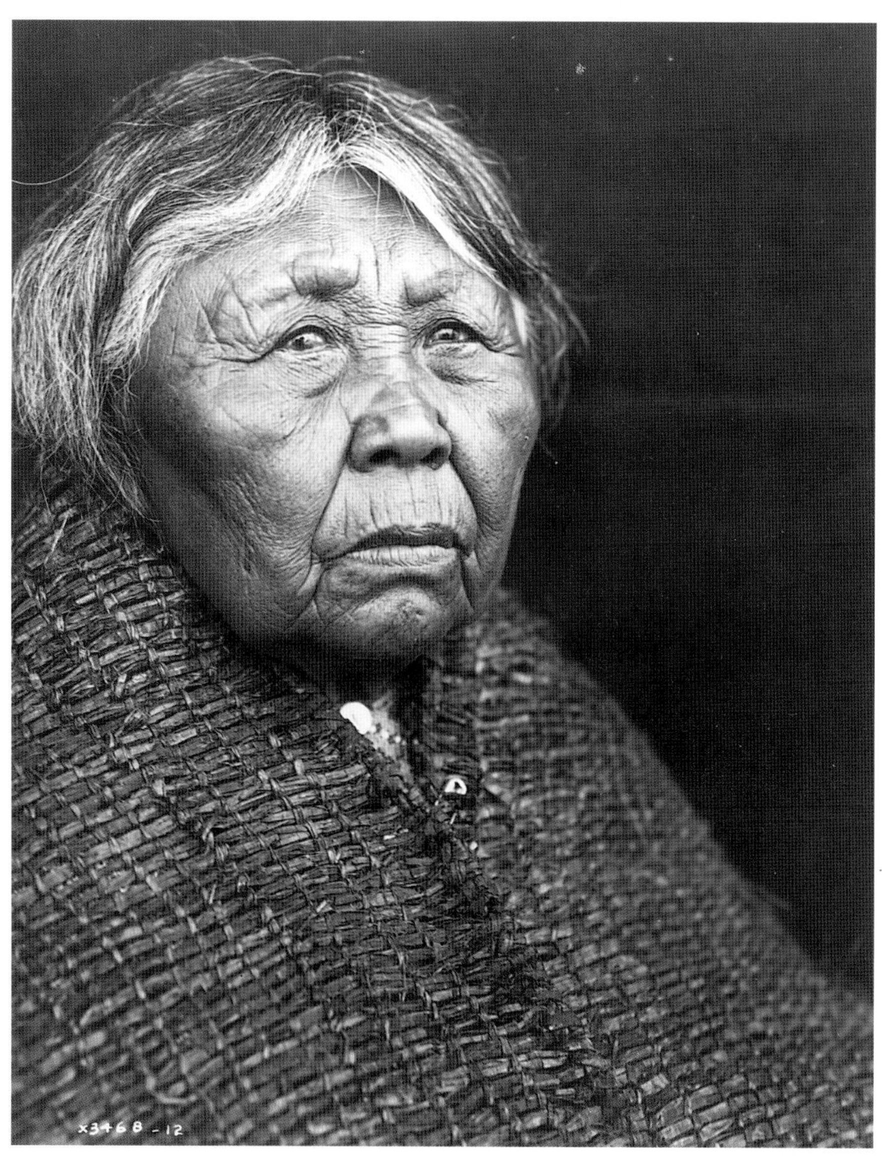

HLEÁSTŬNŬH—SKOKOMISH, ©1912

The Skokomish, or "big-river people," were the largest of the Twana speakers, Southern Coast Salish people occupying the Hood Canal drainage of western Washington State. They lived in permanent settlements along the Skokomish River in winter and moved out to hunting, fishing, and gathering camps in warmer weather. When the Twana were moved to the Skokomish Reservation at the mouth of the Skokomish River following the Treaty of Point No Point in 1855, they numbered about 300. The Skokomish lost much valuable land—including important cultural sites—in this century through purchase by non-Indians, damming, and other power projects. They have fought for compensation through claims and court cases. The tribe regained fishing rights in 1974 through the decision of *United States v. Washington*. As a result of this court decision, tribal members received much training in fishing management and administrative techniques. Traditional cultural resurgence has seen winter ceremonials and bone games bring many of the Southern Coast Salish together in recent years.

A Chief's Daughter —Skokomish, ©1912

Curtis posed this young woman with the indispensable attributes of her lifestyle: tule or cattail matting, both in rolls and erected for a summer shelter, baskets, and a sheaf of tule. The weaving of tule or cattail mats was done by the women. Curtis reported that "the women of the Skokomish band of Twana are especially skillful in weaving soft, flexible baskets." Made of the inner bark of the cedar, which was shredded and beaten until pliable, these baskets were used to collect vegetable foods and store them. Some of the coiled baskets were made watertight and used for cooking with hot stones. The Skokomish followed the Puget Sound catches, setting up temporary fishing encampments. Skokomish men fished using nets, weirs, and traps, while the women gathered shellfish and vegetable foods, cured and dried the catch, and tended the children.

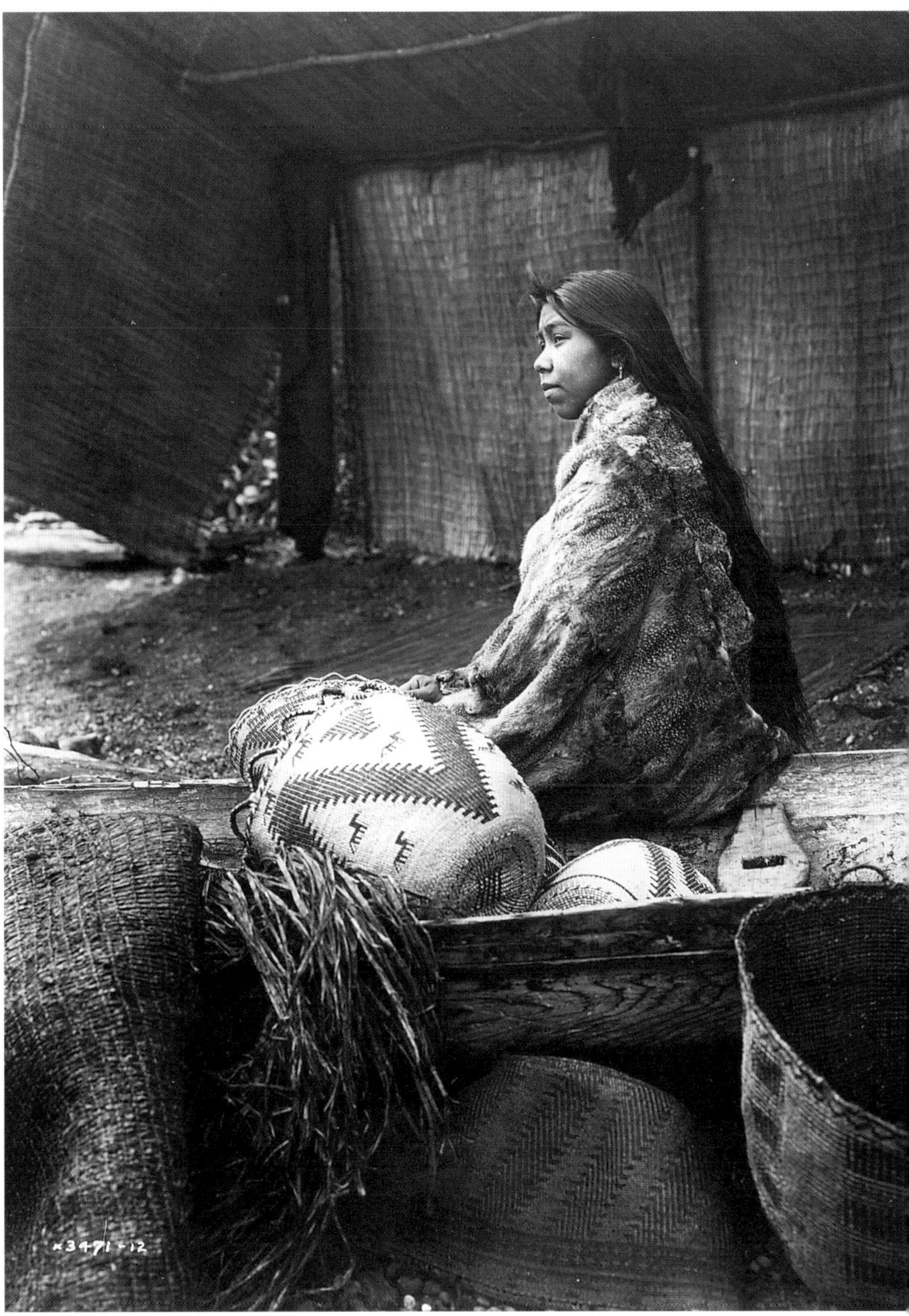

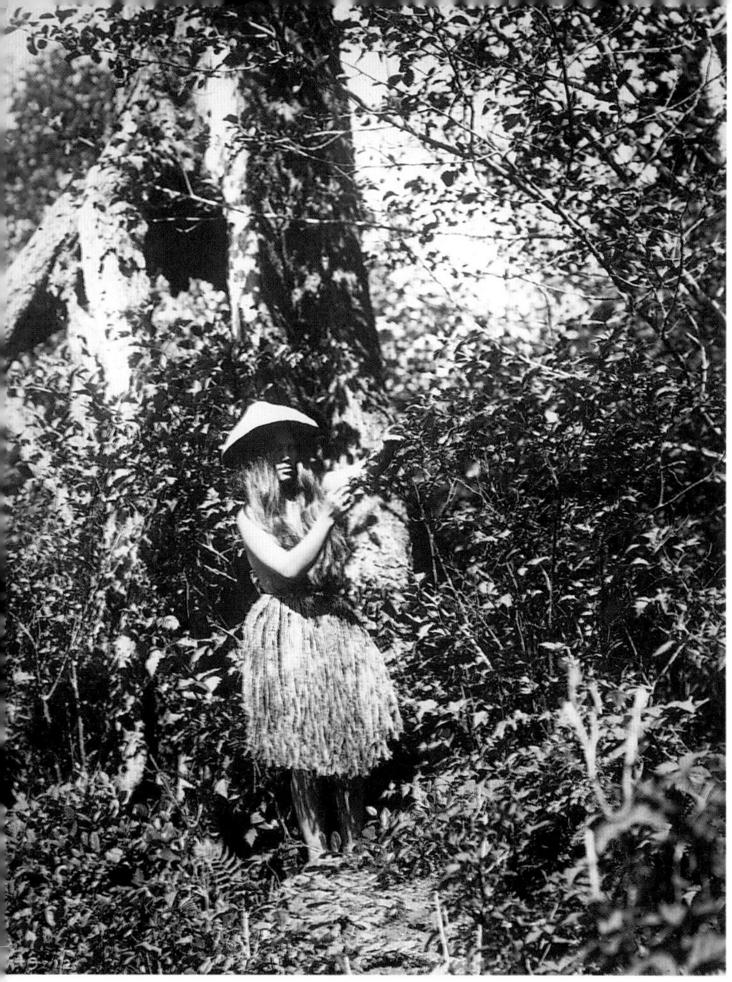

Quinault Berry Picker, ©1912

The coastal rain forests of Washington's Olympic Peninsula provided the Southwestern Coast Salish Quinault with a wide variety of plants and fish. Wild berries—including salmonberries, raspberries, thimbleberries, blackberries, huckleberries, elderberries, salalberries, and cranberries—were important in the Quinault diet, supplementing a seasonal bounty of salmon, rock cod, trout, and smelt. In addition to berry picking, responsibilities of Quinault women included the gathering of edible roots—camas, fern roots, clover roots, cow parsnip, wild celery—and fruits, such as crab apples. The women sun-dried or fire-dried those berries that were not eaten outright, which preserved them almost indefinitely as a food additive. This berry picker is wearing a knee-length skirt of cedar-bark and a basketry hat. Curtis, unable to cure himself of romantic "poses," was fond of photographs like this one, which suggested a natural, pre-modern state.

Lummi Type, ©1899 *(opposite)*

The Lummi, a Central Coast Salish people, lived north of Seattle, along Bellingham Bay and among the San Juan Islands, near enough to Curtis's home base to be among the first people he photographed for his North American Indian project. Descendants of the people who made their way to the Northwest Coast as early as 8,000 B.C., they lived by fishing, primarily for the much-prized sockeye salmon, as well as herring, halibut, and silver and humpback salmon. Lummi men trapped, raked, hooked, netted, and speared their catch from canoes and from land, and Lummi women dried and processed the catch. So centered were their lives around their skills in this regard that one contemporary Lummi said, "We never retire from fishing. We die from fishing."

Nor were the Lummi retiring in their battles. Before the arrival of white settlers, they were the most-feared warriors in the region, engaged in protracted territorial struggles with neighboring tribes, mostly over fishing rights. The vanquished groups were dealt with harshly, often exterminated or sold into slavery. The Lummi signed the Treaty of Point Elliott with the U.S. government in 1855, and a reservation was set aside at the mouth of the Nooksack River. Several unsuccessful attempts were made by both the state and the federal governments to turn the Lummi into farmers, but they burned their boats in protest and, many times this century, argued in court for their off-reservation reef net fishing rights. The Boldt Decision in 1979 *(United States v. Washington)* allocated 50 percent of the commercial harvest of salmon in western Washington to treaty Indians.

Lummi women were treated with great respect. One of the most important tales in Lummi mythology is "Salmon Woman and Her Children," which relates how Salmon Woman's powers brought sockeye salmon to the waters surrounding the San Juan Islands. Among the Lummi, there were three groups of people: worthy people, worthless people, and slaves. Judging from the regal gaze of this Lummi "type," she must have been considered a worthy person.

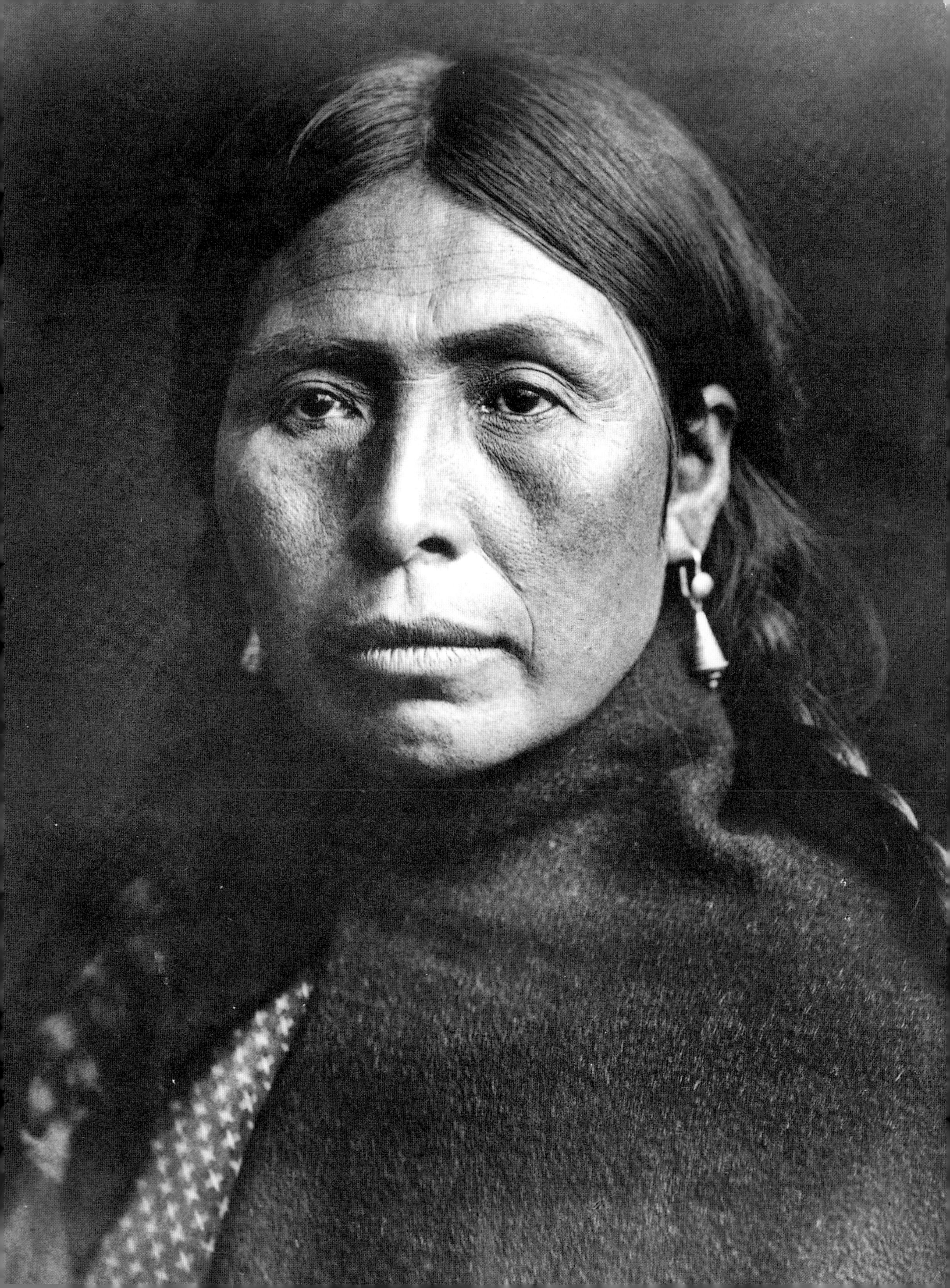

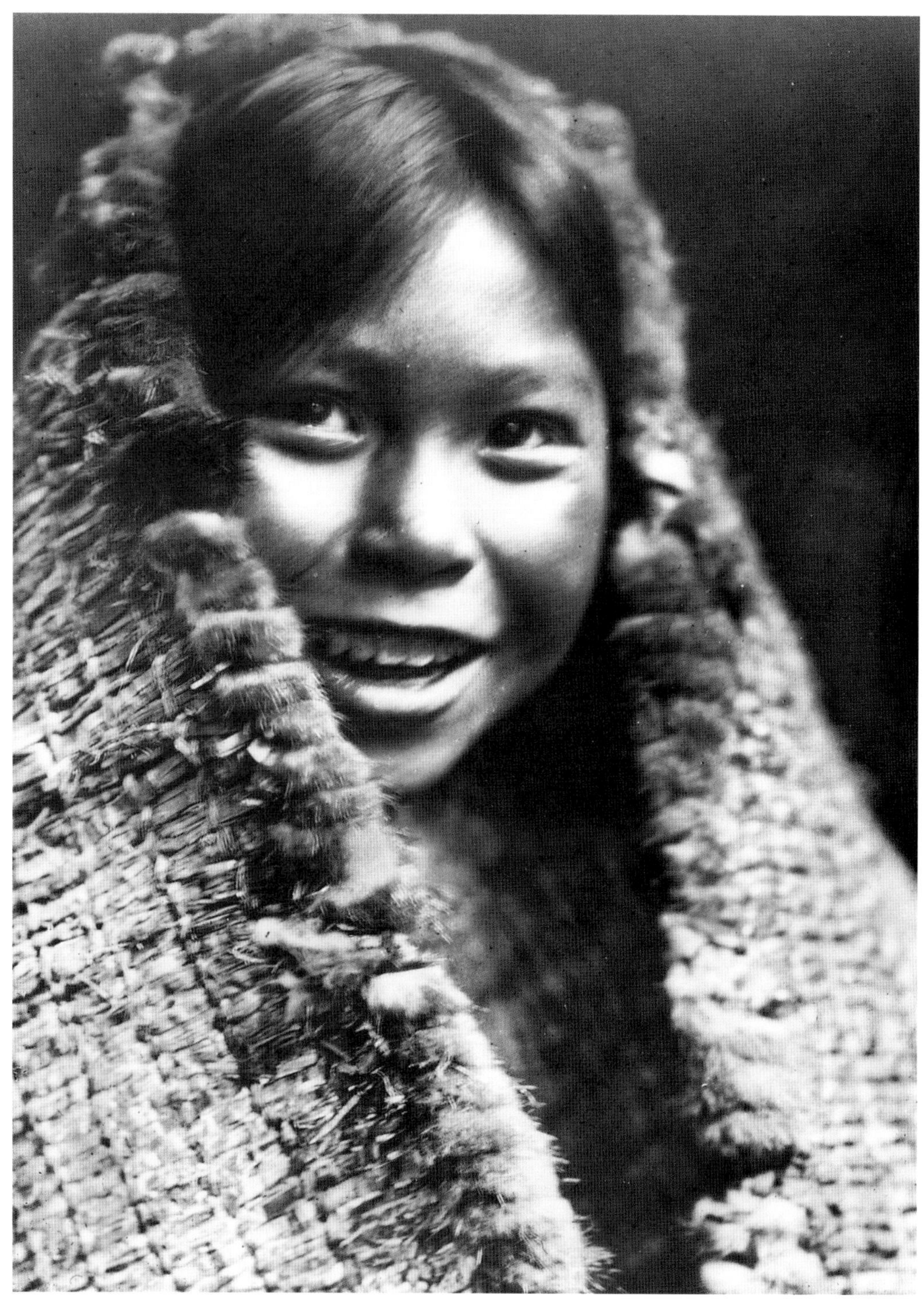

Clayoquot Girl, ©1915

In this study, Curtis shows an infectiously laughing Clayoquot girl wearing a double-matted cape of cedar bark, worn for protection against rain. Shredded cedar-bark robes, capes, and aprons were a regular part of the Nootkan wardrobe. Vancouver Island off the coast of British Columbia is the largest island off western North America (285 miles long, 80 miles wide) and was home to the Kwakiutl, Coast Salish, and Nootkan. The latter spoke Nootka and Nitinaht, of the Wakashan language family. One of the Central Nootkan groups was the Clayoquot, who lived on Clayoquot Sound on the southwest coast of the island. Like other Nootkan groups, the Clayoquot thrived on seasonal fishing and whaling runs and the wealth these catches brought through trade. One of the meteorological quirks of Vancouver Island is its rainfall, among the heaviest in North America.

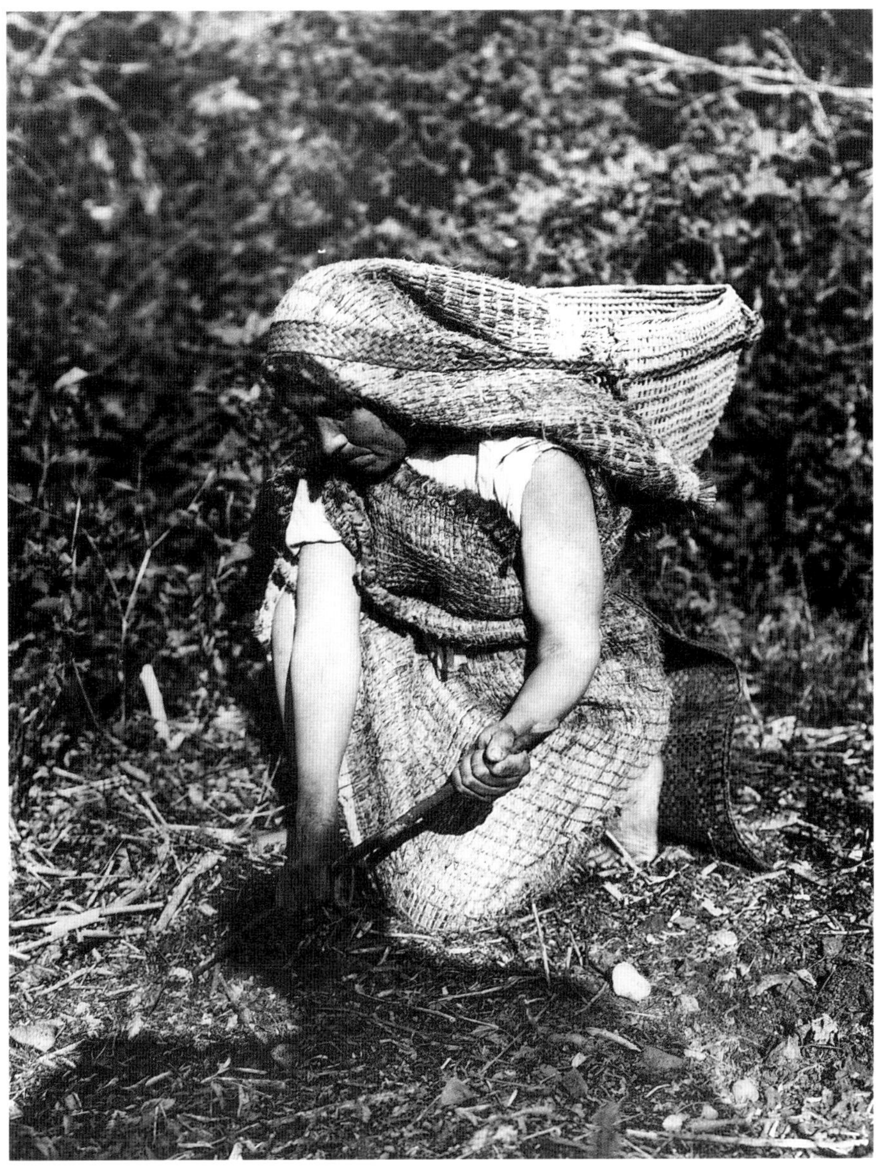

HESQUIAT ROOT DIGGER, ©1915

The Hesquiaht people—spelled Hesquiat by Curtis—were a small branch of the Central Nootkan who settled at Hesquiat Harbour on the west coast of Vancouver Island, north of the Clayoquot. Because the Nootkan—like the Makah, across the Strait of Juan de Fuca—were primarily fishers and whalers, vegetable foodstuffs were a seasonal and welcome addition to their diet. Like most Northwest Coast tribes, the Hesquiaht were well adapted to their lush and rich environment. This Hesquiaht woman, carrying a burden basket secured by a tumpline over her head, may have been digging for wild carrot, bitterroot, or camas (lily bulbs), depending on the season. In the spring, Hesquiaht women dug for silverweed roots, sword-fern rhizomes, cow parsnip, horsetail, and rice root bulbs, which were roasted for eating.

Gathering Seaweed, ©1915

It is not entirely clear whether these two Nootkan women are gathering seaweed—as Curtis's caption states—or shellfish. The woman on the left is wearing a cape and skirt of cedar bark, used for rain protection, and both women are carrying digging sticks. Marine invertebrates were important food resources in the spring, when heavy seas limited fishing and sea mammal hunting. The thick beds of seaweed provided a protected habitat for such desirable shellfish as mussels, clams, scallops, snails, and abalone, as well as sea urchins, which the women gathered—as did the men.

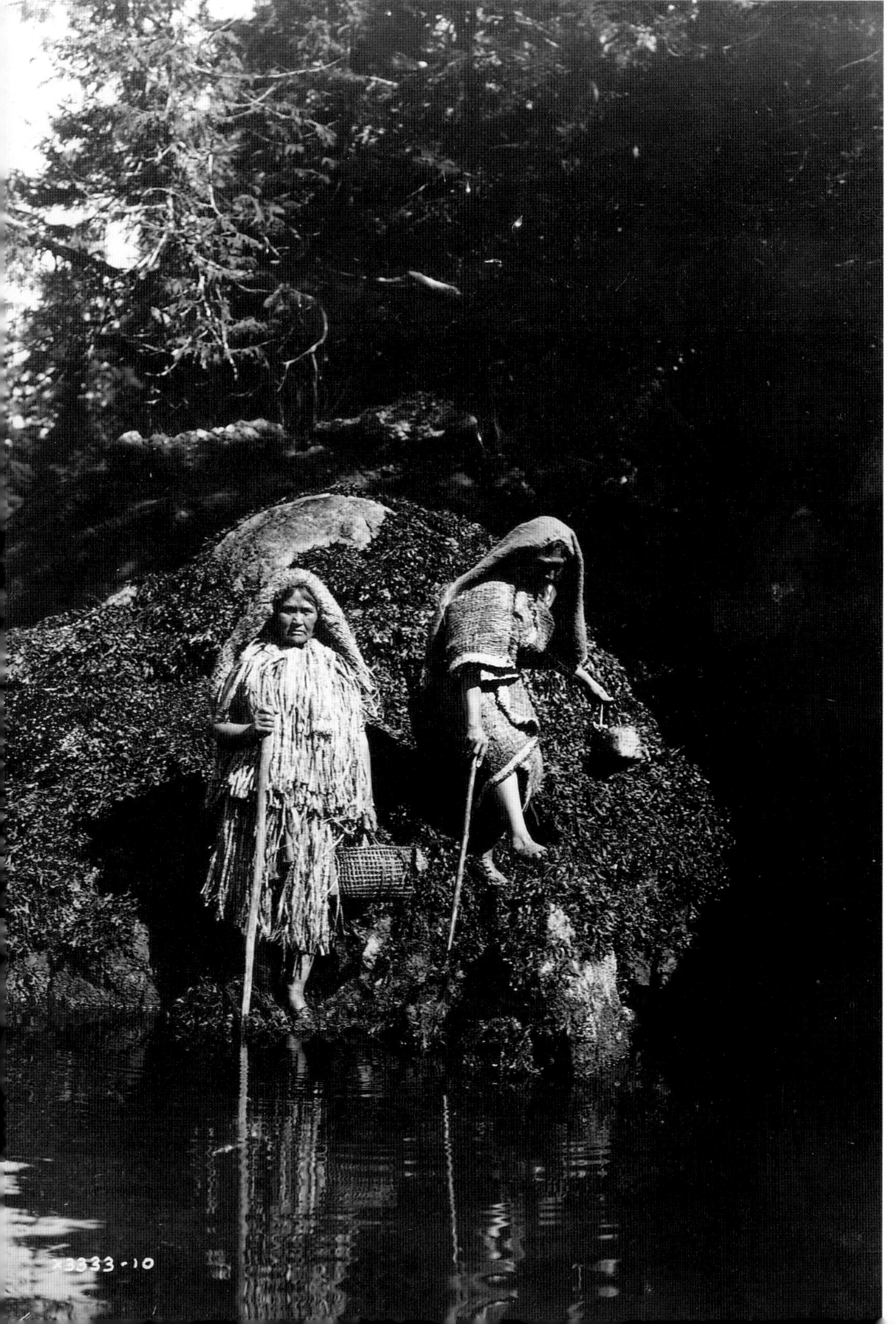

THE NAKOAKTOK (NAKWOKTAK) KWAKIUTL

Curtis received much cooperation from the Kwakiutl peoples, of which the Nakoaktok (currently spelled Nakwoktak) were one of about thirty groups living on northeast Vancouver Island and along the coast of British Columbia. His focused study allowed him to discern tribal organization, information that was lacking in some of his other field studies. The Kwakiutl placed enormous value on their genealogy, with each important family identified by a crest, often depicted in elaborate and unique wood carving, such as totem poles or house posts. They also built large, oceangoing canoes with elegant lines and carved prows.

Nakoaktok was a Kwakiutl village, formerly on Seymour Inlet, but located at Blunden Harbor when Curtis visited. As with all the Kwakiutl tribes, from the Gwasilla in the north to the Lekwiltok in the south, its hierarchical society consisted of nobility, commoners, and slaves.

A NAKOAKTOK CHIEF'S DAUGHTER, ©1914

According to Curtis, "when the head chief of the Nakoaktok holds a potlatch, his eldest daughter is thus enthroned, symbolically supported on the heads of her slaves." A Kwakiutl chief was descended from the supernatural ancestor of each *numaym,* or social division. Their oldest child—son or daughter—was heir to the position of chief. Elaborate ceremonies, called potlatches, were held to celebrate many important events in the tribe, including the return of a daughter to the house of her father after her marriage. Bridal dowries were often huge. Curtis reported that a Fort Rupert man paid 480 blankets ($240) and promised 520 more to marry a Nakoaktok woman of high rank. When he invited his wife's tribe to the Fort Rupert village, they gave him for distribution $1,100 worth of goods: 100 blankets, 40 hand-knitted sweaters, 40 shawls, a quantity of calico, 3 sloops, and 4 gold bracelets. One of her brothers, a gold and silver worker, promised additional goods worth $12,000: a copper (a shield-shaped plate of European copper usually decorated with a face form, which played a special role in the potlatch ceremony and was valued at double the value of the property distributed at the potlatch in which it had last changed hands—in this case the equivalent of 9,000 blankets), 500 button blankets, 500 pots and pans, 11 sloops, 50 sewing machines, 25 phonographs, 50 gold bracelets, 50 gold earrings, 700 silver bracelets, a quantity of silver finger rings and brooches, and many fathoms of beads. Another brother promised property worth about $2,200. The brothers vowed to pay this extraordinarily high marriage portion in order to ensure that their sister outdid a rival in wealth.

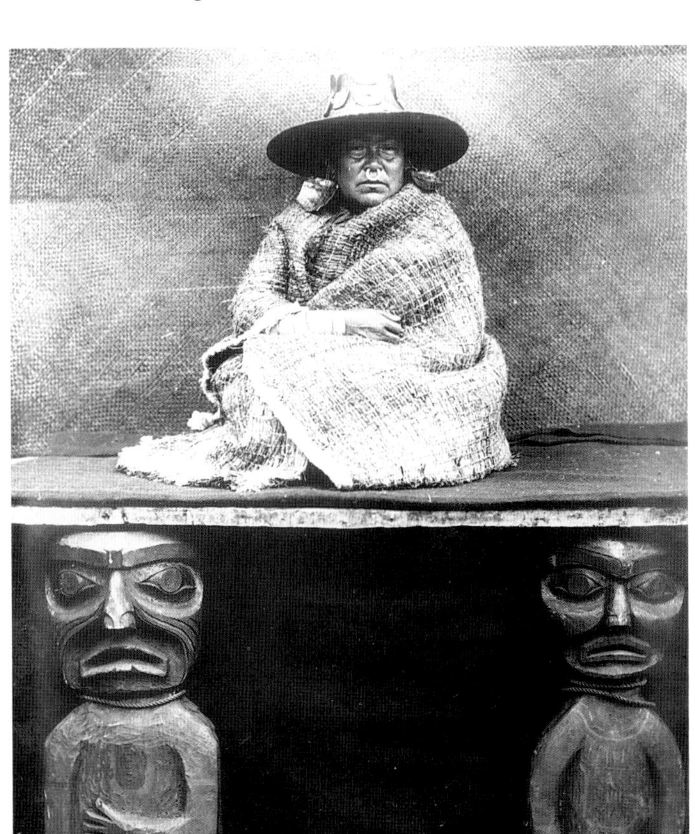

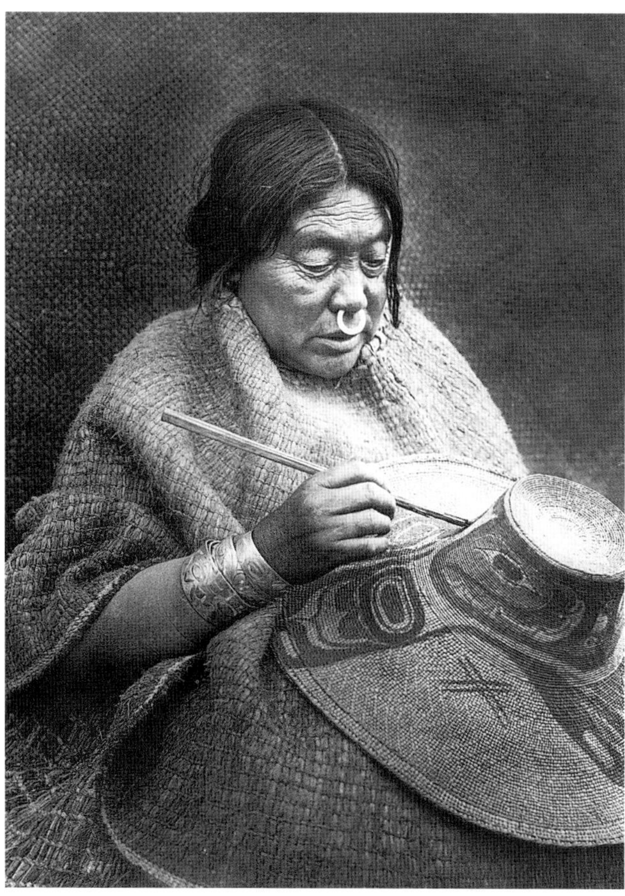

PAINTING A HAT—NAKOAKTOK, ©1914

Curtis photographed this woman, a chief's daughter, in several poses: he showed her seated on a ceremonial platform, gathering abalone, and preparing cedar bark. Here she is painting a hat with conventionalized figures of animals, possibly the wearer's ancestral crest. This form of waterproof hat, made of closely woven shreds of fibrous spruce roots, was similar to those of the Haida tribe. The painter, who is wearing a short, seamless, cedar-bark cape for protection against rain, is identified as a woman of rank and wealth by her abalone-shell nose ring and silver bracelets.

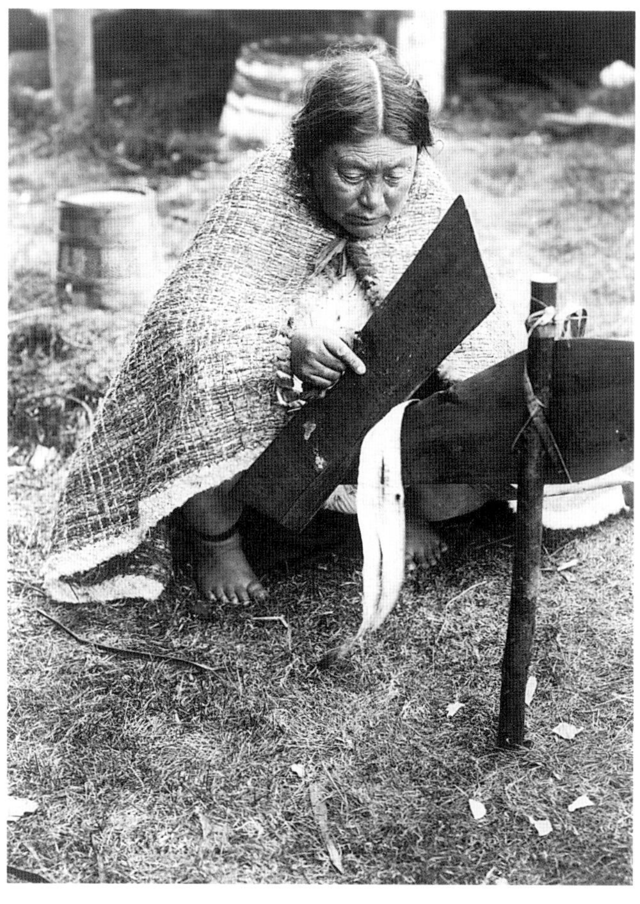

PREPARING CEDAR BARK—NAKOAKTOK, ©1914

The weaving of blankets, mats, and baskets from cedar bark was a very important technology. According to Curtis, women collected very long strips of yellow cedar bark in July and laid them in the shallows of a sheltered harbor until they sank. After wringing the water out, they beat the bark and worked it manually, tearing it into narrower strips, which became the warp; the weft was spun from mountain goat hair. They kept the bark strips flexible for weaving by storing them in water in wooden boxes until they were needed.

Gathering Abalones—Nakoaktok, ©1914

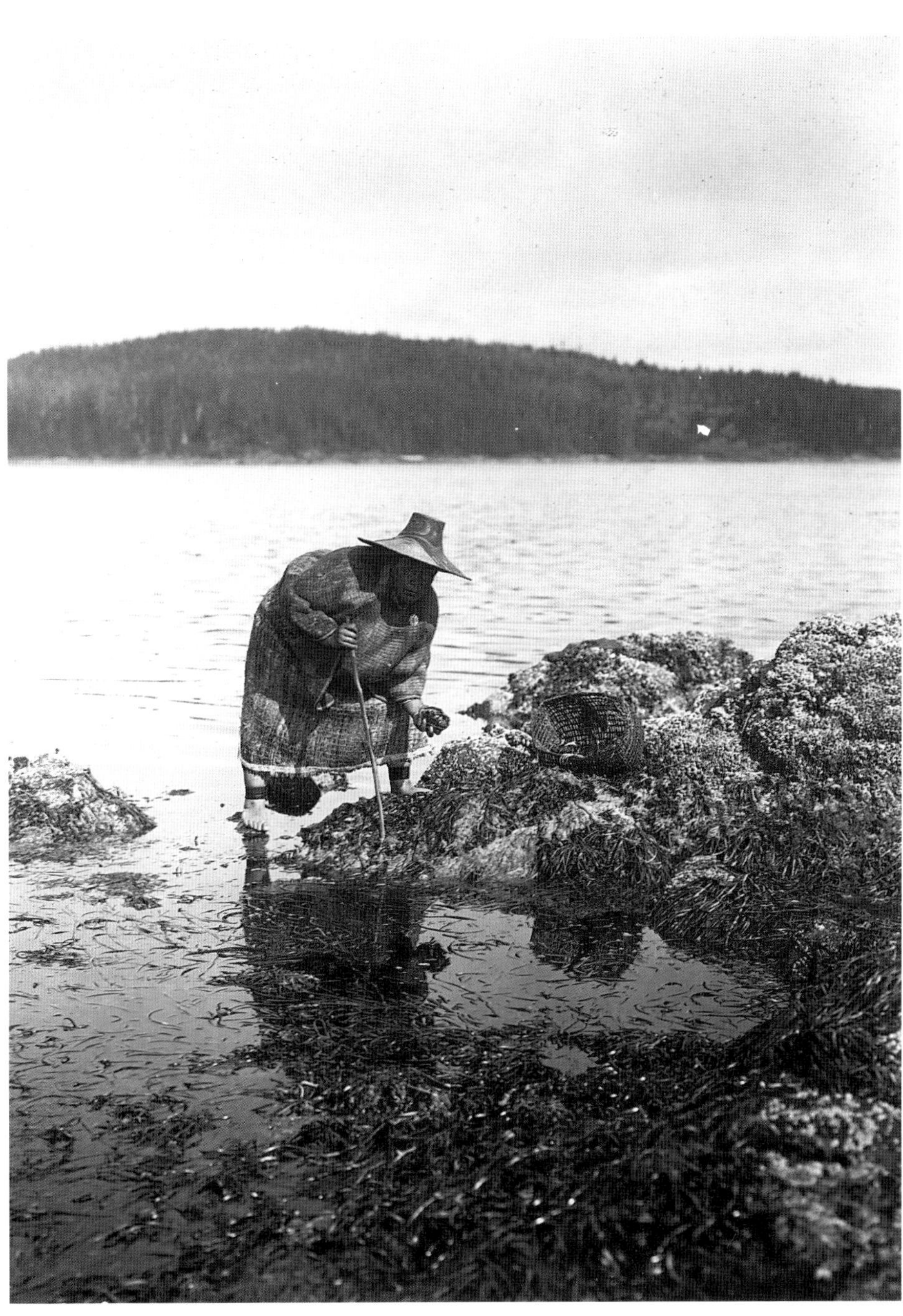

Because the supply of food in the Pacific Northwest waters was so rich, the Kwakiutl had no reason to turn their hands to agriculture. What plants, vegetables, and fruit they needed could be gathered from the lush coastal forests and valleys. Likewise, the ocean's largesse provided well. Kwakiutl men became stellar boat builders and fishers, and the women were responsible for combing among nearshore waters and low-tide mudflats for shellfish. Clams were most plentiful, but they could not compete in desirability with the abalone, a large mollusk found only on the West Coast of North America, ranging from four to ten inches in width. Abalone cling tenaciously to rocks in shallow waters and are often covered with—and further hidden by—other organisms. In order to wrest them from their perch, a Kwakiutl needed a "pry bar" like the pointed yew stick that this woman wielded. It required strength to extricate these large mollusks and to battle the sudden unpredictable waves that lashed the rocks, while great care was needed to avoid breaking the shell and killing the organism. Not only was the meat valued as a delicacy, but also the abalone shell was prized for ornamentation and as a sign of wealth. This "Nakoaktok" (or Southern Kwakiutl) woman was digging for abalone at low tide.

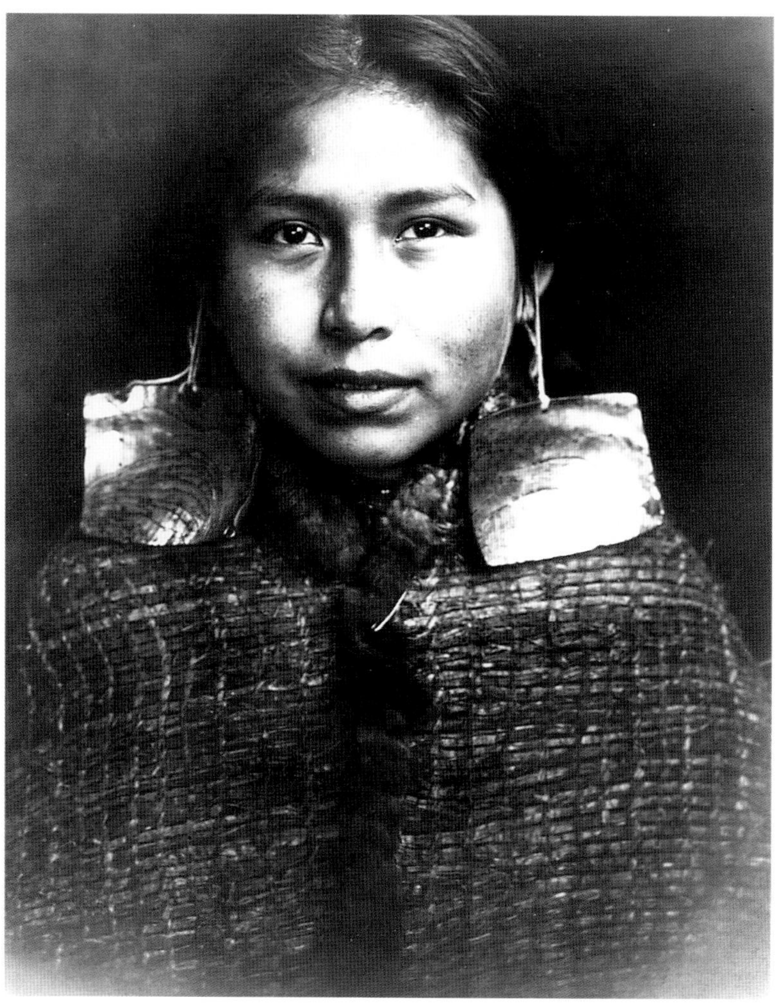

TSAWATENOK GIRL, ©1914

The Tsawatenok (now spelled Tsawatainuk) were distinguished by their complex religious rituals, dances, and secret societies. While known primarily for their artistic and prolific woodwork in masks, sculpture, and housefronts, the Tsawatainuk, like other Kwakiutl tribes, also used fibers and shells for personal ornamentation. The natural beauty of this Tsawatainuk girl was further enhanced with ear pendants made of abalone shell and a woven cape, possibly of cedar bark.

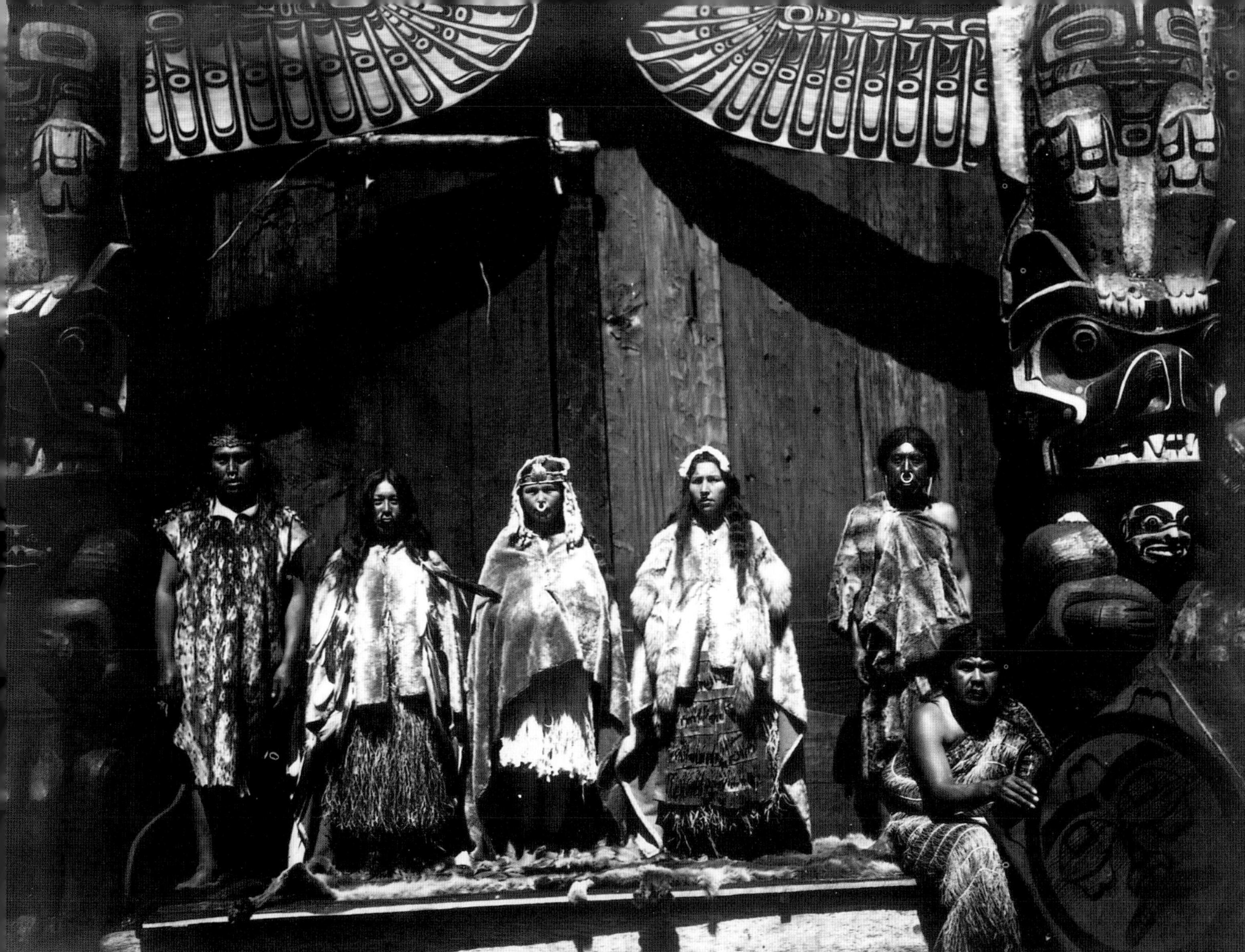

A BRIDAL GROUP, ©1914

Curtis spent a great deal of time among the Kwakiutl. In 1914, in fact, he made the Kwakiutl the subject of his only motion picture, *In the Land of the Headhunters.* That film, in turn, inspired Robert Flaherty to complete his masterful documentary *Nanook of the North.* Apparently, Curtis had so won the confidence of the Kwakiutl that he was allowed to photograph an actual wedding. According to his notes, the Kwakiutl bride stands in the middle, holding a carved wooden baton. On either side of her are two dancers hired for the occasion. Her father is at the far left, her new father-in-law at the far right, standing behind the man playing a box drum. Surrounding the participants is the visual evidence of the Kwakiutl's wood-carving skills and signs of their displayed wealth. Part of the wedding ritual is that the bridegroom's relatives carry a quantity of goods as dowry to the bride's home.

The Arctic

Curtis first saw the Pacific Eskimo on the Kenai and Alaska Peninsulas in 1899, when he was a photographer with the Harriman Expedition.

He returned to Alaska, with his daughter Beth, in the summer of 1927 and concentrated on the Eskimo people of Nunivak Island and those of the north shore of Kotzebue Sound—the Kotzebue, Noatak River people, Kobuk River people, and Selawik River people.

He was "exceptionally happy because they have been little affected by contact with civilization." He noted ecstatically in his diary while visiting the Inuit of Nunivak Island: "Think of it. At last, and for the first time in my thirty years of work I have found a place where no missionary has worked."

The carefully prescribed gender roles of the traditional Alaskan Eskimo (called Inuit by Curtis) allowed them to survive in the harsh environment of the Arctic. Because their duties were so different, Eskimo men and women were around each other for only limited periods of time. While the men were occupied for days on end with hunting seal, walrus, and whale and hauling the food back with the help of dog-driven sleds, the women cooked and cleaned, processed, and sewed skins. The Alaskan Eskimo also hunted birds and land animals, fished, and gathered whatever limited wood and vegetation could be found.

Although Curtis could stay to observe and photograph only the summer activities of the Eskimo due to his ill health at the time, he did collect myths and tales and as many details as possible of year-round daily life. This material became the twentieth, and last, volume of his great endeavor. He concluded his introduction to this volume as follows: "Great is the satisfaction the writer enjoys when he can at last say to all those whose faith has been unbounded, 'It is finished.'"

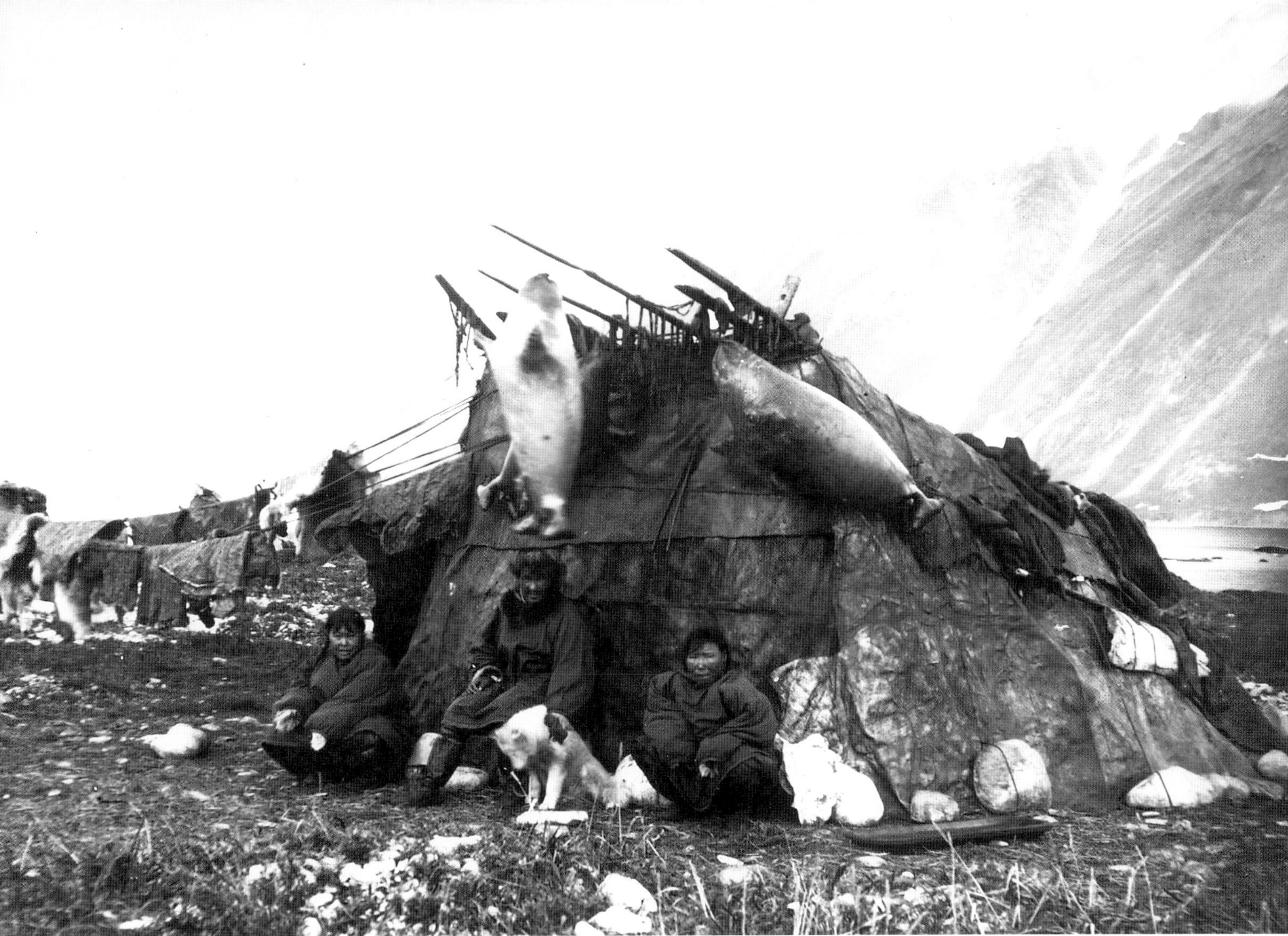

Inuit Hut and Family, ©1899

Curtis took this photograph of a Siberian Eskimo encampment at Plover Bay in 1899, while with the Harriman Expedition to Alaska. Inflated sealskins hang from the wooden poles of the tent frame. The inflated sealskins were used as floating devices, attached to a harpooned walrus or whale, to track the quarry and to prevent it from sinking. At this early point in his career, Curtis was less interested in the artistic element of his work or the aesthetics of his subject matter. His work on this fact-gathering mission was more scientific and documentary. Indeed, the rigors of Eskimo domestic life are fully captured in this early visual record.

The Nunivak

The Nunivak Island people still had a distinctive seal culture when Curtis visited them in the 1920s. Nunivak itself is a treeless island about fifty miles from east to west, lying about twenty-five miles from the mainland of the Kuskokwim and Yukon Rivers. It is characterized by tundra and low relief.

Villages varied in size. They included, in the nineteenth century, houses, storehouses, and a kashin*—the men's house. The men's house, which was the center of men's activity—where they made kayaks, weapons, and utensils; carved ivory; and took their sweatbaths—was no longer functional by Curtis's time.*

The 1890 census listed 702 inhabitants on the island. In 1940, the population numbered 218, and in 1980 the population was just 153.

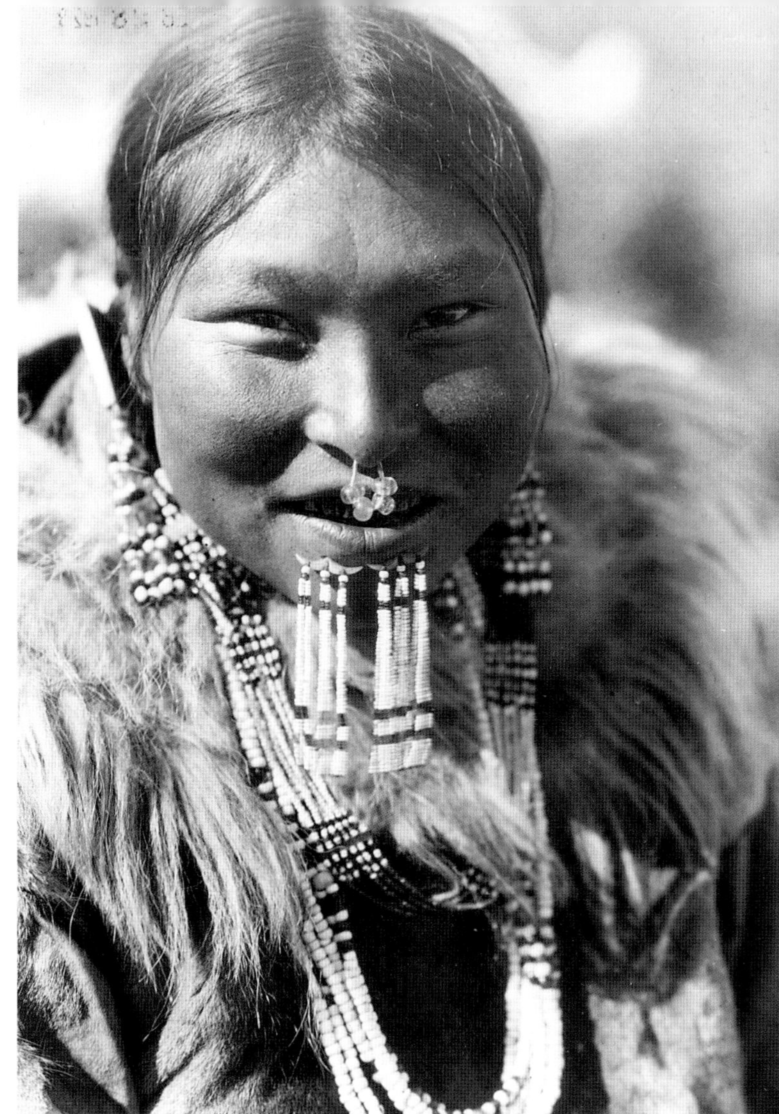

Kenówŭn—Nunivak, ©1928

In traditional culture, a Nunivak woman often decorated herself with facial adornment, including beaded nose rings, labrets, and earrings. This beaming Nunivak woman is wearing the long, elaborate earrings and labrets that were worn by women; men wore only the plainer labrets. The holes for labrets were punched through the flesh just below the lower lip around the age of puberty.

Marriages were usually arranged by heads of families. According to Curtis, the father of the future bride marked the couple's announcement by taking gifts to the men's house—where the men lived and worked together during the winter—to exchange for scarce, and therefore valuable, firewood. The marriage was recognized when he held a sweatbath for the men of the village in the men's house; the women brought food there for their husbands, and the bride placed food before the man who had chosen her. Because the communities were small, it was common for a man and a woman of greatly different ages to marry. A preferred marriage was between a young man of about twenty and a girl of about thirteen. The bride was expected to become a member of her husband's family.

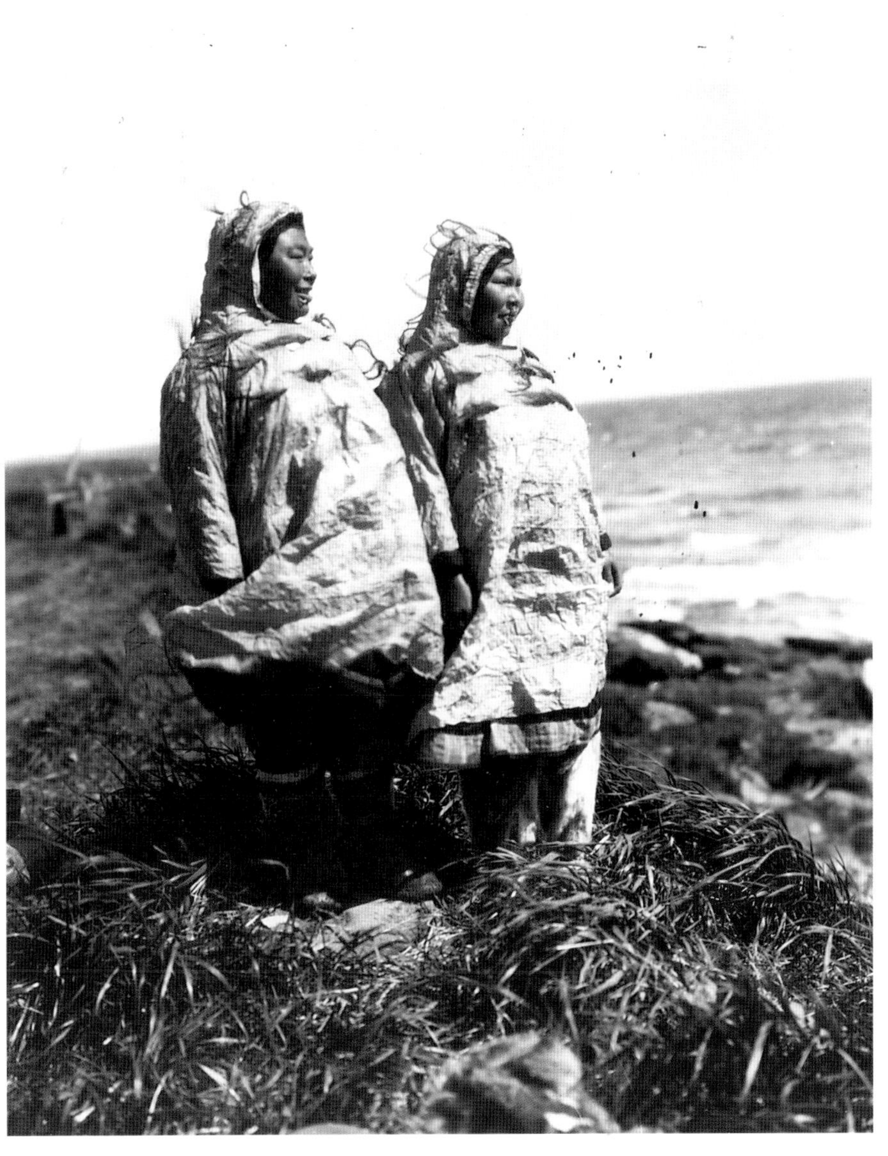

Waterproof Parkas —Nunivak, ©1928

Nunivak Island was besieged much of the year by ferocious weather and unprotected from the winds by any natural buffers. Curtis visited the island during the summer, when widespread thaw and seasonal rains combined to create a brief but persistent mosquito-infested dampness. Because of the change in climate, Nunivak switched from their winter bird-skin parkas to water-resistant seal-gut parkas. While these women may have been posed by Curtis to suggest fond and longing glances seaward to their husbands absent on hunting and fishing expeditions, their summer duties did not allow for lengthy daydreaming. Many aspects of domestic life were in their capable hands, as were the endless preparations for the fast-approaching winter. Women sewed all the clothing, as well as the skin covers of the kayaks, using sewing sinew shredded from fibers taken from the legs and backs of reindeer or caribou. They kept their needle cases, bodkins, thimbles, sinew twisters, and threaders in a special receptacle called a *tukiwih,* or "housewife."

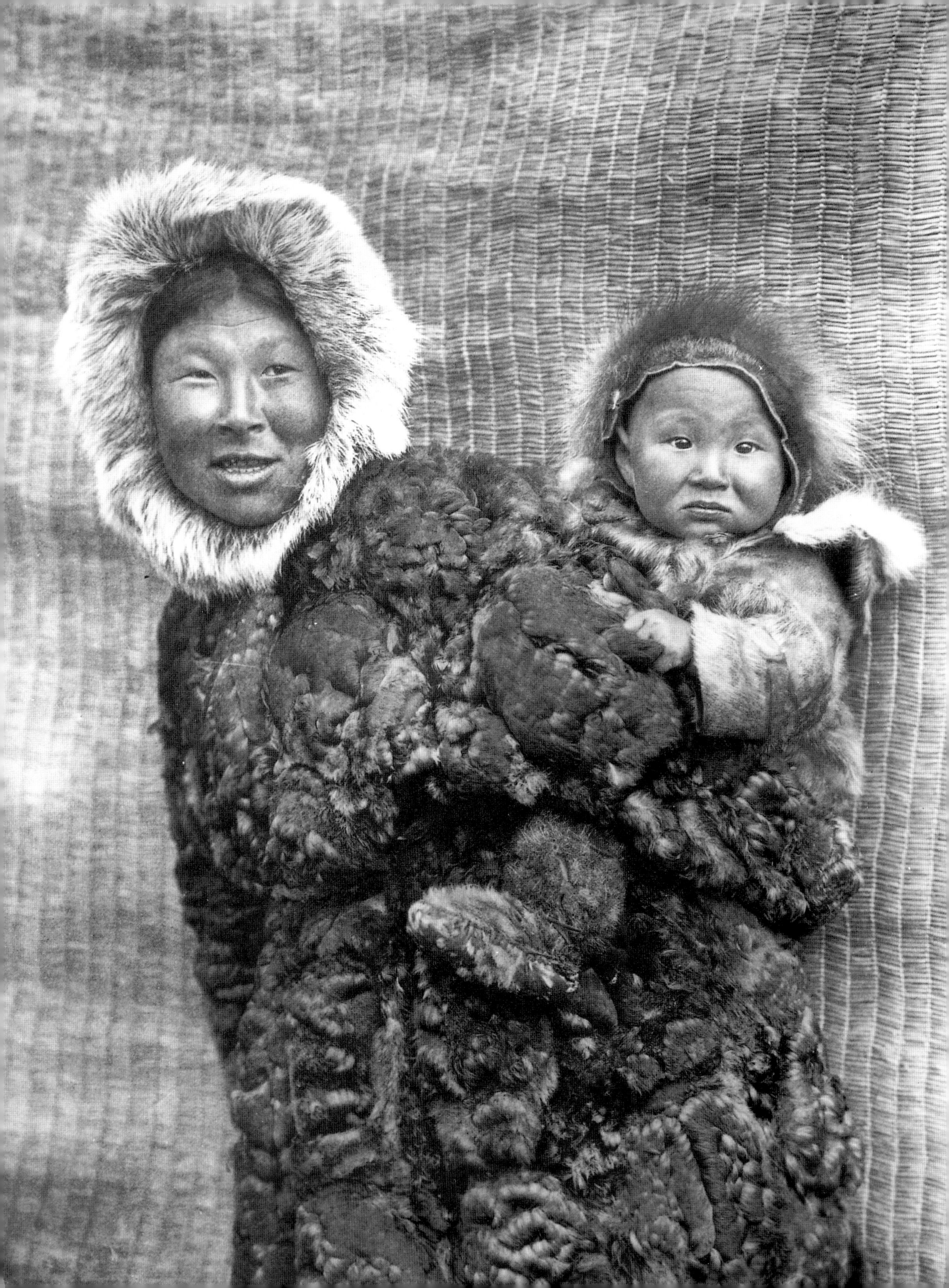

Woman and Child—Nunivak, ©1928 *(opposite)*

Because the division of labor demanded frequent separation of husbands and wives, Nunivak women were left in complete charge of early child-rearing. Children of both genders spent their entire infancies next to their mothers, carried in the ample parkas they sewed. Following a birth, the family was expected to avoid work and remain very quiet for three days, according to Curtis. The father took goods to the men's house to barter for wood, which he then offered for a sweatbath in celebration. The firstborn boy was given the father's name and the girl the mother's name, after which the parent was known as "Father of . . ." or "Mother of . . . ." Other children were given the names of relatives. If a couple died childless, their names were lost to their family.

Selawik Women, ©1928

The Arctic Circle runs right through the Selawik River basin in Alaska, along the southeastern shore of Kotzebue Sound. The summer sun allowed these Selawik (or Siilivingmiut) women a rare moment of quiet leisure. Their parkas were made from untanned skins sewn together with caribou sinew. The woman on the right is wearing an inner pullover parka with the hair on the inside, and the two women to the left appear to be wearing summer parkas made of ground squirrel skins, with decorative borders of caribou fur. The pointed hoods were spacious enough inside to be used for carrying infants and small children.

According to Curtis, the Selawik erected a special hut for a woman in labor. She remained there with her infant for three months if it was a firstborn and for two months for subsequent babies. Her return home was celebrated with a feast and a naming ceremony.

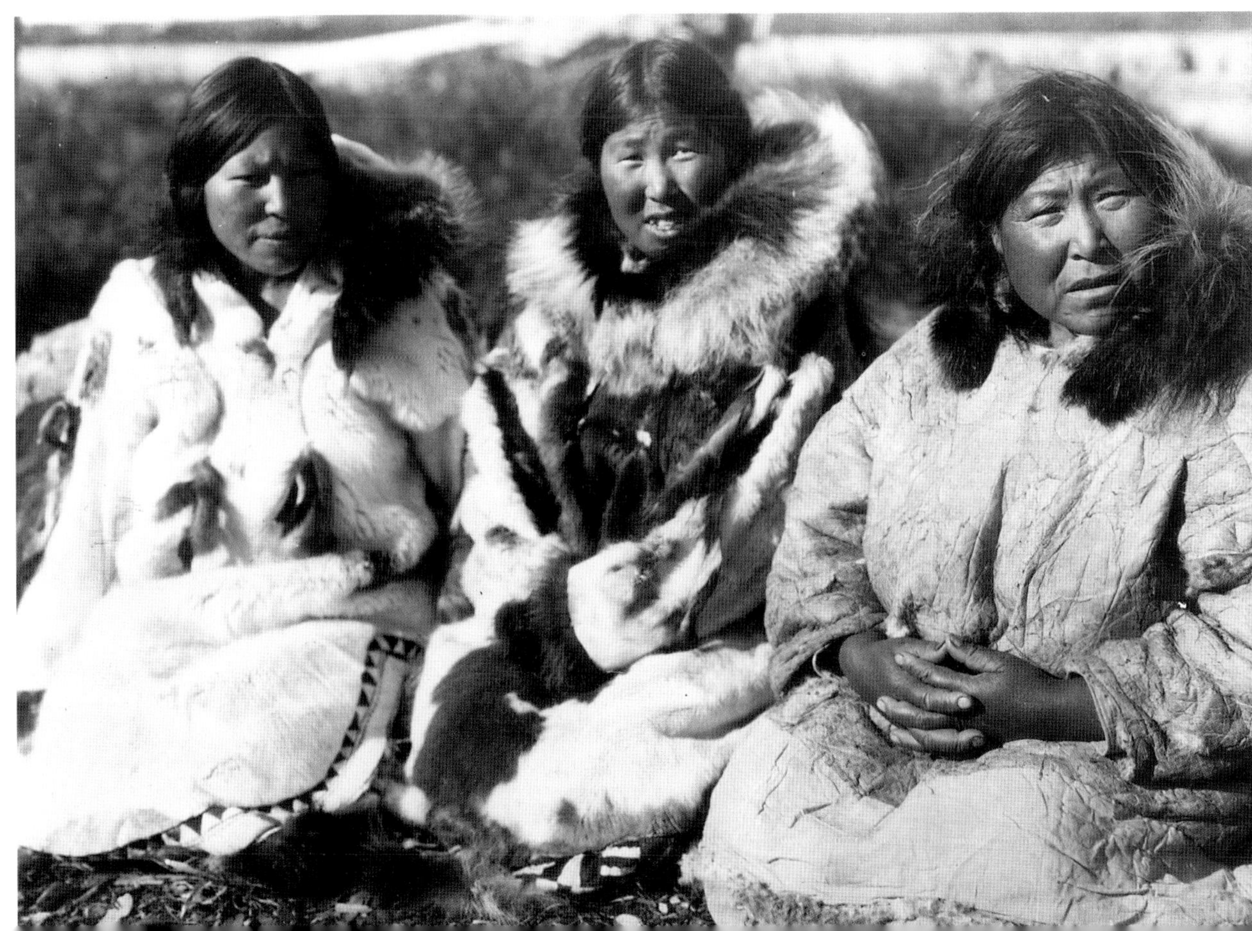

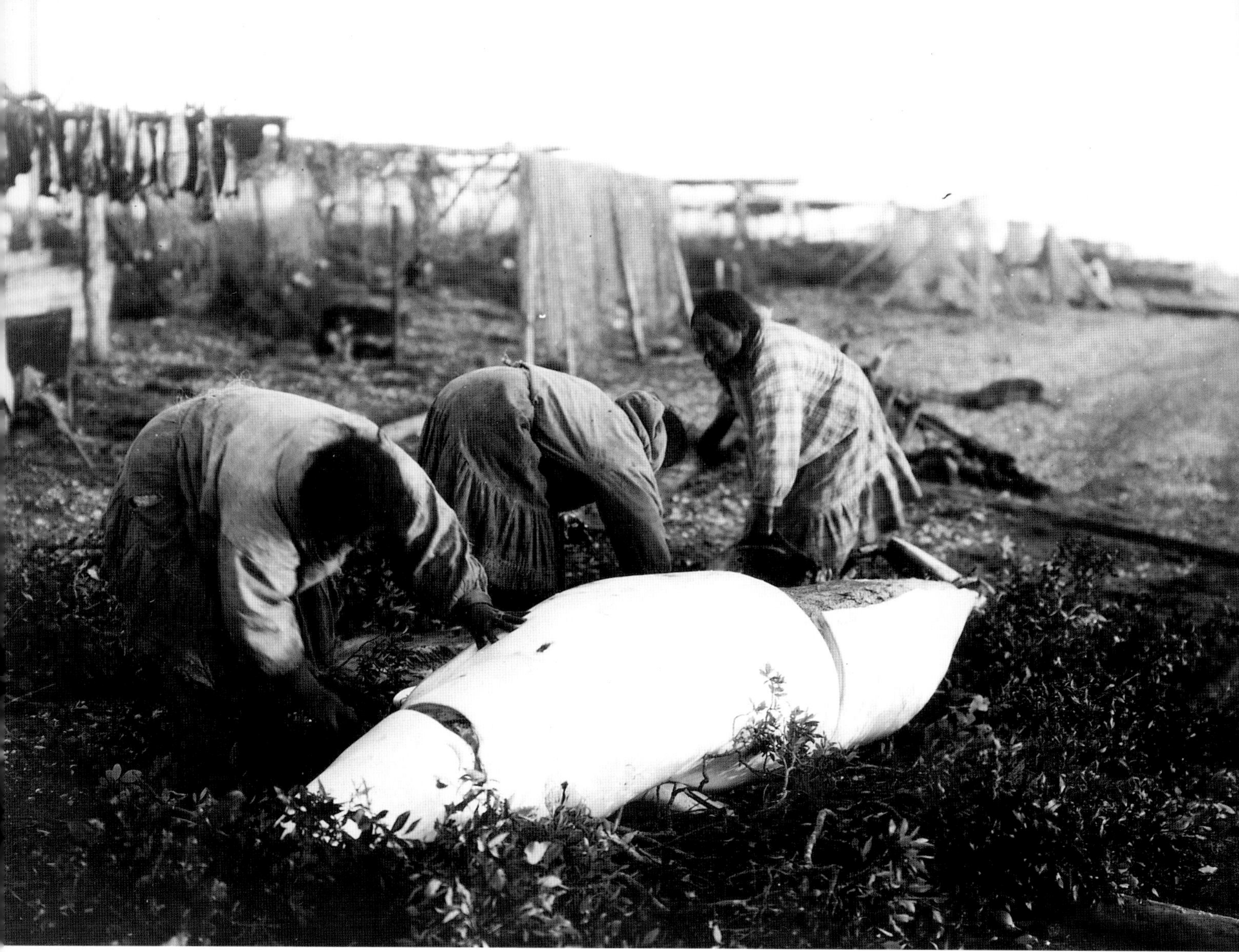

Cutting up a Beluga—Kotzebue, ©1928

Toward the end of his magnum opus, Curtis came upon these Eskimo women in Alaska's Kotzebue Sound—along the Arctic Circle, west of the Bering Strait—cutting up a beluga whale. The beluga was one of the prizes taken by the Eskimo men during a recent whale-hunting expedition in the waters of the Bering Sea. Curtis reported that no woman was allowed to touch a whale (or walrus or seal) until her husband had given permission, a ritual intended to assure the return of more belugas. However, once they were given the nod, the women were required to sever the head of the whale and place it in Kotzebue Sound so that the animal's spirit would return to the sea and enter the bodies of other belugas.

The women would process the beluga *muktuk,* or blubber, cutting it into long sections. Curtis reported that it was customary for all the people to sleep before the beluga meat was hung to dry for four days and four nights; during the drying the people danced. The dried meat was then boiled in salt water, drained, and stored in its own oil in sealskin containers. Kotzebue women also gathered a profusion of berries, greens, roots, mosses, and edible shrubs to be eaten fresh or stored for winter use. A favorite dish was a combination of berries, meat, fish, and oil, mixed with snow.

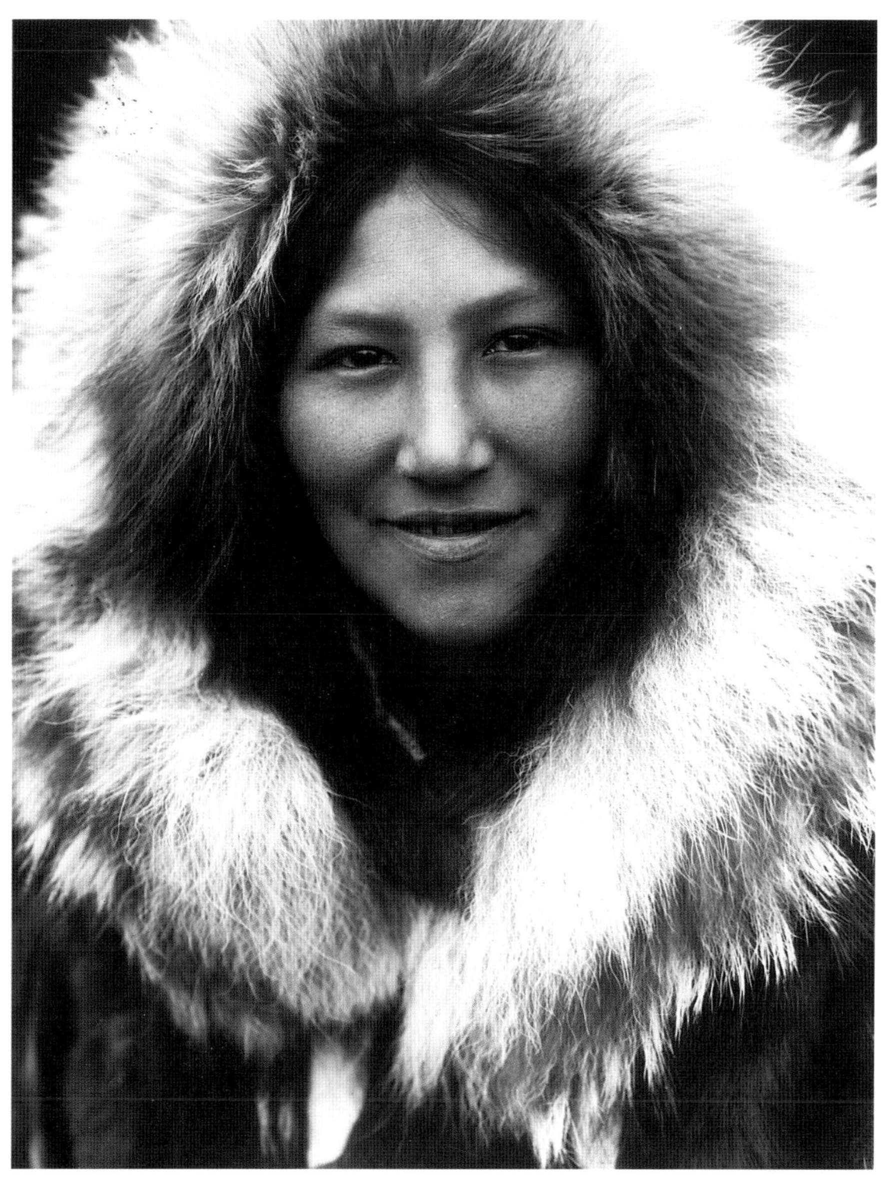

ÓLA—NOATAK, ©1928

Curtis gave us no personal details about this handsome young woman, who is wearing a summer parka probably made of ground squirrel skins trimmed around the hood with luxuriant fox or wolverine fur. Eskimo women made clothing from untanned skins, which they shaped and sewed together with caribou sinew. According to Curtis, the winter village of the Noatak people was situated "nearly a week's journey by skin boat up the swift, shallow Noatak River, which empties into the narrow strait connecting Hotham Inlet with Kotzebue Sound." The Noatak River people traveled downriver in their skin boats in late spring when the ice broke up and pitched tents at Sheshalik, where an annual fair lasting two to three weeks served as an important social event.

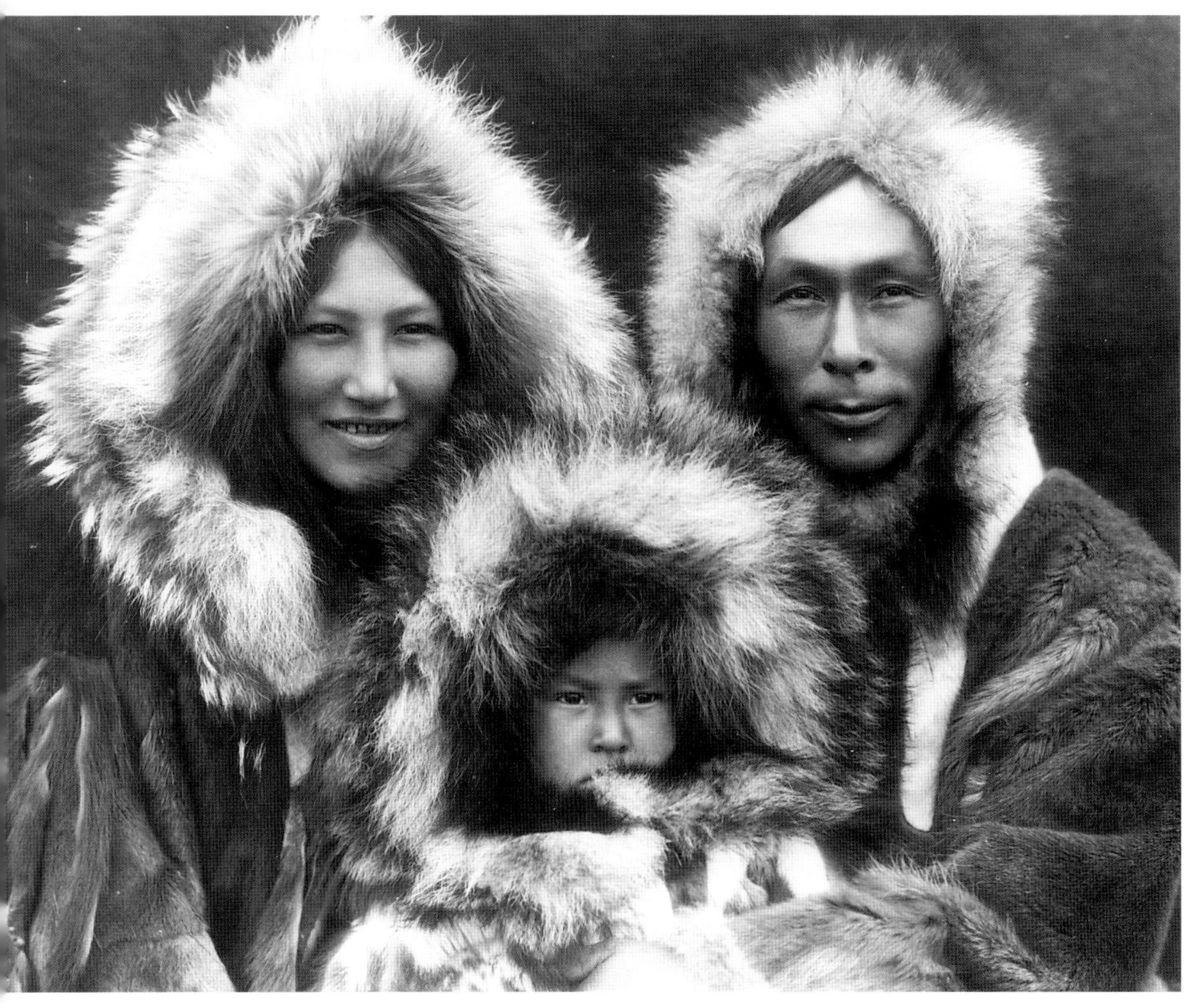

A Family Group—Noatak, ©1928

The extended local family group was the most important component of Eskimo social and political organization. The Noatak lived even farther north than the Selawik, along the northwestern coast of Kotzebue Sound, and were part of the group known today as the Kotzebue Sound Eskimo. Curtis restricted his travels in these far north locales to the summer months, but often he photographed his subjects in winter garments (as in this family portrait). Curtis was fortunate indeed to have caught a family group on this trip. Childhood, per se, was short. By about age ten, boys were accompanying their fathers on the summer hunt, and girls were in charge of tending to the infants and younger children and helping with domestic chores. Eskimo children were greatly valued, and it was rare for them to be punished or beaten.

Acknowledgments

The authors want to thank eight Native American women who generously offered their personal reactions to photographs Curtis took of the women of their tribes, contemporaries of their grandmothers and great-grandmothers. Nancy Ackerman, Val Crews, Wanda Frenchman, Carolyna Smiley-Marquez, Ann Strange Owl-Raben, Nico Strange Owl-Hunt, Lark Real Bird Paz, and Janelle Sixkiller shared not only their perceptions of the Curtis images, but also something of what it means to be a Native American woman today. We also are grateful to Lois Flury of Flury & Co., Seattle, who explained the place of Curtis's photographs of Native American women within the contemporary world of art.

At the Library of Congress, the authors want to thank Jennifer Brathovde, reference specialist in Native American photographs in the Prints and Photographs Division and an enrolled member of the Devil's Lake Sioux, who assisted us with our research and read various drafts of the text. Jennifer Manning and Roger Walke of the Library's Congressional Research Service made significant suggestions for the introductory text.

Joanna Cohan Scherer, anthropologist/illustrations researcher for the Smithsonian Institution's *Handbook of North American Indians* (1978–), read the entire text for accuracy and tone. She provided the authors with valuable guidance and additional information for the captions from the *Handbook*, a twenty-volume encyclopedia that is a comprehensive source on the history and anthropology of Native North Americans.

The following negative numbers can be used to order prints through the Library of Congress Photoduplication Service. To order call (202) 707-5640.

THE PLAINS AND THE SUBARCTIC

1. Piegan Woman, ©1911 LC-USZ62-115821
2. A Blackfoot Travois, ©1926 LC-USZ62-64891
3. Fleshing a Hide—Blackfoot, ©1926 LC-USZ62-111134
4. Cheyenne Girl, ©1905 LC-USZ62-83569
5. Wife of Old Crow—Cheyenne, ©1927 LC-USZ62-115823
6. Dog Woman—Cheyenne, ©1927 LC-USZ62-116529
7. Camp Gossips—Atsina, ©1908 LC-USZ62-66670
8. Winter—Apsaroke, ©1908 LC-USZ62-46970
9. Hide Scraping—Apsaroke, ©1908 LC-USZ62-46967
10. Crow Chief's Daughter, ©1910 LC-USZ62-106768
11. Slow Bull's Wife, ©1907 LC-USZ62-50160
12. Ogalala Girls, ©1907 LC-USZ62-106991
13. Drying Meat, ©1908 LC-USZ62-46993
14. Yellow Bone Woman, ©1908 LC-USZ62-101183
15. The Rush Gatherer—Arikara, ©1908 LC-USZ62-77211
16. Hidatsa Mother, ©1908 LC-USZ62-96195
17. Buffalo-Berry Gatherers—Mandan, ©1908 LC-USZ62-46987
18. Wichita Mortar, ©1927 LC-USZ62-115824
19. A Wichita Matron, ©1927 LC-USZ62-115822
20. A Cree Woman, ©1926 LC-USZ62-116528
21. Moss for the Baby-Bags—Cree, ©1926 LC-USZ62-106995

THE SOUTHWEST

1. Women at Campfire—Apache, ©1903 LC-USZ62-101172
2. At the Ford—Apache, ©1903 LC-USZ62-47851
3. Jicarilla Maiden, ©1904 LC-USZ62-90798
4. A Navajo Smile, ©1904 LC-USZ62-46943
5. The Blanket Weaver—Navajo, ©1904 LC-USZ62-9532
6. Hipáh with Arrow-Brush—Maricopa, ©1907 LC-USZ62-115805
7. Saguaro Fruit Gatherers—Maricopa, ©1907 LC-USZ62-111943
8. Gathering Hánamh, ©1907 LC-USZ62-111283
9. Pima Ki, ©1907 LC-USZ62-83600
10. Qahátika Girl, ©1907 LC-USZ62-83601
11. Mohave Potter, ©1907 LC-USZ62-93744
12. "Mohave" Girl and Papoose, ©1903 LC-USZ62-15204
13. At the Old Well of Acoma, ©1904 LC-USZ62-46879
14. Acoma Roadway, ©1904 LC-USZ62-69898
15. Grinding Meal, ©1907 LC-USZ62-94089
16. The Piki Maker, ©1906 LC-USZ62-115802
17. Hopi Bridal Costume, ©1900 LC-USZ62-41455
18. Watching the Dancers, ©1906 LC-USZ62-80169
19. The Potter Mixing Clay, ©1921 LC-USZ62-83583
20. Tablita Woman Dancer—San Ildefonso, ©1905 LC-USZ62-115816
21. Street Scene at San Juan, ©1925 LC-USZ62-56048
22. Winnowing Wheat, San Juan, ©1905 LC-USZ62-106259
23. The Potter—Santa Clara, ©1905 LC-USZ62-115803
24. Zuni Ornaments, ©1903 LC-USZ62-102041

CALIFORNIA AND THE GREAT BASIN

1. The Mush-Basket—Karok, ©1923 LC-USZ62-84563
2. A Yurok Widow, ©1923 LC-USZ62-115818
3. Woman's Primitive Dress—Tolowa, ©1923 LC-USZ62-113078
4. Hupa Female Shaman, ©1923 LC-USZ62-101261
5. Hupa Mother and Child, ©1923 LC-USZ62-110505
6. A Kato Woman, ©1924 LC-USZ62-107616
7. Achomawi Mother and Child, ©1923 LC-USZ62-110225
8. Achomawi Basket-Maker, ©1923 LC-USZ62-98674
9. The Burden-Basket—Coast Pomo, ©1924 LC-USZ62-116527
10. Gathering Seeds—Coast Pomo, ©1924 LC-USZ62-116525
11. Construction of a Tule Shelter—Lake Pomo, ©1924 LC-USZ62-98673
12. A Chukchansi Matron, ©1924 LC-USZ62-115813
13. Old Woman in Mourning—Yuki, ©1924 LC-USZ62-115809
14. A Desert Cahuilla Woman, ©1924 LC-USZ62-107207
15. Under the Palms—Cahuilla, ©1924 LC-USZ62-96453
16. The Harvester—Cahuilla, ©1924 LC-USZ62-96454
17. A "Serrano" Woman of Tejon, ©1924 LC-USZ62-115825
18. A Santa Ysabel Woman—Diegueño, ©1924 LC-USZ62-115820
19. Diegueño House at Campo, ©1924 LC-USZ62-98666
20. Datsolali, Washo Basket-Maker, ©1924 LC-USZ62-114784

THE PLATEAU

1. Nez Percé Matron, ©1910 LC-USZ62-113085
2. Holiday Trappings—Cayuse, ©1910 LC-USZ62-115021
3. Jerking Meat—Flathead, ©1910 LC-USZ62-113094
4. Flathead Mother, ©1910 LC-USZ62-115804
5. Kutenai Woman, ©1910 LC-USZ62-99612
6. Dusty Dress—Kalispel, ©1910 LC-USZ62-111294
7. Nespilim Girl, ©1905 LC-USZ62-116526
8. Preparing Salmon—Wishham, ©1909 LC-USZ62-111293
9. Pounding Fish—Wishham, ©1909 LC-USZ62-113089
10. Wishham Child, ©1909 LC-USZ62-105382
11. Wishham Bride, ©1910 LC-USZ62-105387
12. Wife of Mnainak—Yakima, ©1910 LC-USZ62-115806
13. Drying Piahé—Yakima, ©1909 LC-USZ62-99794
14. Wife of Modoc Henry—Klamath, ©1923 LC-USZ62-83961
15. Grinding Wókas—Klamath, ©1923 LC-USZ62-115814
16. Klamath Woman, ©1923 LC-USZ62-110506

NORTHWEST COAST

1. Princess Angeline, ©1899 LC-USZ62-83573
2. Chimakum Woman, ©1912 LC-USZ62-115808
3. The Tule Gatherer, ©1910 LC-USZ62-115020
4. Hleástunuh—Skokomish, ©1912 LC-USZ62-108466
5. A Chief's Daughter—Skokomish, ©1912 LC-USZ62-110504
6. Quinault Berry Picker, ©1912 LC-USZ62-105858
7. Lummi Type, ©1899 LC-USZ62-83575
8. Clayoquot Girl, ©1915 LC-USZ62-83576
9. Hesquiat Root Digger, ©1915 LC-USZ62-116530
10. Gathering Seaweed, ©1915 LC-USZ62-115812
11. A Nakoaktok Chief's Daughter, ©1914 LC-USZ62-59010
12. Painting a Hat—Nakoaktok, ©1914 LC-USZ62-52413
13. Preparing Cedar Bark—Nakoaktok, ©1914 LC-USZ62-106282
14. Gathering Abalones—Nakoaktok, ©1914 LC-USZ62-105860
15. Tsawatenok Girl, ©1914 LC-USZ62-108465
16. A Bridal Group, ©1914 LC-USZ62-52209

THE ARCTIC

1. Inuit Hut and Family, ©1899 LC-USZ62-101338
2. Kenówun—Nunivak, ©1928 LC-USZ62-74130
3. Waterproof Parkas—Nunivak, ©1928 LC-USZ62-88326
4. Woman and Child—Nunivak, ©1928 LC-USZ62-83592
5. Selawik Women, ©1928 LC-USZ62-89842
6. Cutting up a Beluga—Kotzebue, ©1928 LC-USZ62-115975
7. Óla—Noatak, ©1928 LC-USZ62-89841
8. A Family Group—Noatak, ©1928 LC-USZ62-89847